Pursue your dreams and you will realize them. All you need is one little spark to set off the giant potential lying latent within you. I sincerely hope that you will stumble across that little spark hidden somewhere in the following pages.

Shall Sinha

Other Books by Shall Sinha

- From Ordinary to Extraordinary
  100 Selected Essays

- 24 Heroic Journeys
  Pathways of Ordinary People to Extraordinary Achievements

Currently Under Production ....
- Roots of Motivation
  A Review of 500 Great Lives
- *YESUCAN*
  500 Great Lives in Brief

Words of Wisdom, Roots of Motivation and *YESUCAN* will soon be available on CD ROM.

Words of Wisdom
From 500 Great Lives

Researched and Compiled by
Shall Sinha, Ph. D.

Dedicated to Rotarians

I dedicate this book to the 1.2 million Rotarians in 155 countries throughout the world, who are donating a part of their life to fight major humanitarian problems such as hunger and illiteracy, to bring relief from natural calamities such as famine, earthquakes, floods and draughts, to preserve the planet earth from environmental pollution and damage, to foster peace through cultural exchange and better understanding among the various cultures, to promote better health through shared health programmes and health education, to promote better life through numerous community projects and to build a better future by focusing on the welfare of the new generation.

I will donate, to Rotary International, 20% of all revenue that I will receive from the sale of the copies of this book, *Words of Wisdom*, as a small token of my heartfelt appreciation of the Rotary motto: **Service above Self**.

Shall Sinha

SKS Publishing, 7 Medhurst Crescent, Sherwood Park, Alberta, Canada. T8A 3T5.
email address: sinhask@freenet.edmonton.ab.ca

Canadian Cataloguing in Publication Data:
Sinha, Shall, 1942 -
Words of Wisdom: Over 3600 Gems from 500 Great Lives
Includes Index on more than 1300 names and subjects
ISBN: 0-9694381-2-5

1. Motivation   2. Inspiration   3. Goals
4. Personal Development

Design: Danie Hardie
Page Production: Linda J. Hawk
Danie Hardie Creative Communications Ltd.
Edmonton, Alberta, Canada T6E 5V1

Printed in Canada

Foreword

About ten years ago I began a serious study of the stories of men and women who had started their life either under very ordinary circumstances or with some sort of a handicap such as colour, lack of education, gender, race, slavery, physical disability, broken family or extreme poverty, and had succeeded in achieving something truly remarkable during their lifetime. I deeply felt that their examples would motivate and inspire most of the people who knew about their hardships. I, therefore, undertook the challenge of bringing a brief but comprehensive story of those great lives, particularly for the benefit of the majority of us who lack either the patience or the time to read voluminous details. On the basis of the obstacles that those extraordinary men and women had to overcome, I selected 500 of them and set down to summarize their life story in 1200 to 1400 words, which in my estimate would require less than 5 minutes for an average person to read. This work will soon be released under the title *YESUCAN*. Every time that I read one of those stories, I asked myself, "Wouldn't it be exciting if we could meet those extraordinary people, chat for a few minutes and seek a few words of advice?" Since many of those great men and women are no longer alive, and it is not easy to solicit a quick word of wisdom from the ones who are still alive, I felt that the second best blessing would be to research and compile some of the advice that they have already given to some others sometimes during their life. Since I was not interested in a passing-comment, a rebuff, a humorous quote or some heavy philosophy, I focused my research on some down to earth, nuts and bolts advice, which I call **Words of Wisdom**.

I have searched through more than two thousand books in order to distill over 3600 Words of Wisdom that I have included in this book. Since we are all individuals, with our own particular interests, it is impossible to organize these Words of Wisdom in an order that would satisfy everyone's need and interest. Therefore, I have simply grouped them under the name of the person (who advocated those words of wisdom) and then compiled the groups in alphabetical order. Within each group, I have presented the Words of Wisdom in a random order. I ask you to imagine that you are taking a walk through the woods in which case you do not look for anything particular but expect to stumble upon, or notice, something quite fascinating to you. I ask you also to keep in mind the era in which the particular person lived. For this purpose I have noted down the life span of the person beneath his or her name in the book. For example, Abraham Lincoln (1809 - 1865) lived during a time when it took seven days to travel from Chicago to Washington, D.C. and there was no electricity. Lincoln had to address audiences of up to two thousand people in open areas without the aid of a microphone! Those days it took almost six months to travel from New York to Los Angeles! By having some idea of the facilities available to the person, you can have a better understanding of the difficulties that he or she had to overcome and thereby realize the sincerity of their Words of Wisdom.

You can read this book in several ways. You can just open any page and read a few pieces and if they do not strike your chord, you can randomly move to some other page and keep doing that for a few minutes. If you still do not find anything interesting then you may not be in the right frame of mind to receive any Word of Wisdom at that particular moment. Do not despair. Just close the book and go to some other activity. You may come back later.

You can also choose a subject from the Index and search through the pages where you will find some relevant Words of Wisdom. If you wish to receive a few Words of Wisdom from a particular person (from among the 500), you can do so either by searching that person's name alphabetically in the book or using the Index at the end of the book.

It is quite possible that you disagree with a few pieces. Some of them may not make sense to you, probably because you cannot see the same picture that that person had seen. There is no use arguing or beating your head against a rock, to try to make the right meaning. Just skip those pieces.

As far as possible, I have tried my best to use exact quotes. Since some of the books that I searched were published by British publishers while some others by Americans, I have accepted both the British and the American English spellings.

I sincerely hope that you will find this book not only enjoyable but also very valuable.

Shall Sinha

The 500 Great Lives

1 Hank Aaron
2 Alfred Adler
3 Louis Agassiz
4 Louisa May Alcott
5 Grover Alexander
6 Muhammad Ali
7 Dick Allen
8 Steve Allen
9 Roald Amundsen
10 Marian Anderson
11 Julie Andrews
12 Roy Chapman Andrews
13 Susan B. Anthony
14 Elizabeth Arden
15 Louis Armstrong
16 Mary Kay Ash
17 Arthur Ashe
18 Isaac Asimov
19 Chet Atkins
20 J. J. Audubon
21 Liberty H. Bailey
22 James Baldwin
23 Lucille Ball
24 Honoré de Balzac
25 Roger Bannister
26 Tom Barnardo
27 James Miranda Barry
28 Ethel Barrymore
29 Lionel Barrymore
30 Bela Bartok
31 Henry Ward Beecher
32 Ludwig van Beethoven
33 Harry Belafonté

34 Alexander Graham Bell
35 Hugh Bennett
36 Jack Benny
37 Irving Berlin
38 Hector Berlioz
39 Sarah Bernhardt
40 Yogi Berra
41 Mary Mcleod Bethune
42 Frank Bettger
43 Ernest Bevin
44 Elizabeth Blackwell
45 William Booth
46 Margaret Bourke-White
47 Tom Bradley
48 Louis Braille
49 Marlon Brando
50 Laura Bridgman
51 Joyce Brothers
52 Jim Brown
53 Larry Brown
54 Mordecai Brown
55 Elizabeth Barrett Browning
56 Paul "Bear" Bryant
57 William Cullen Bryant
58 Art Buchwald
59 Ole Bull
60 John Bunyan
61 Luther Burbank
62 George Burns
63 John Burroughs
64 Richard F. Burton
65 Leo Buscaglia

66 Richard E. Byrd
67 Michael Caine
68 Mary Calderone
69 Erskine Caldwell
70 Maria Callas
71 Roy Campanella
72 Glen Campbell
73 Charles Camsell
74 Chester Carlson
75 Thomas Carlyle
76 Dale Carnegie
77 Wallace H. Carothers
78 Rachel Carson
79 Henri Cartier-Bresson
80 Enrico Caruso
81 Johnny Cash
82 Mary Cassatt
83 Carrie Chapman Catt
84 Miguel de Cervantes
85 Marc Chagall
86 Wilt Chamberlain
87 Coco Chanel
88 Charlie Chaplin
89 Cesar Chavez
90 Anton Chekhov
91 Maurice Chevalier
92 Agatha Christie
93 Walter Chrysler
94 Georges Clemenceau
95 Roberto Clemente
96 Ty Cobb
97 Jaqueline Cochran
98 Gabrielle Colette
99 Christopher Columbus

100 Nadia Comanecki
101 Maureen Connolly
102 Joseph Conrad
103 Calvin Coolidge
104 Gary Cooper
105 James F. Cooper
106 Peter Cooper
107 Nicolaus Copernicus
108 Ezra Cornell
109 Bill Cosby
110 Norman Cousins
111 Jacques Cousteau
112 Prudence Crandall
113 Joan Crawford
114 Bing Crosby
115 Glen Cunningham
116 Louis Daguerre
117 Salvador Dali
118 Alighieri Dante
119 Charles Darwin
120 Bette Davis
121 Sammy Davis Jr.
122 Dorothy Day
123 Eugene Debs
124 Mary Decker
125 Lee De Forest
126 Agnes de Mille
127 Daniel Defoe
128 Demosthenes
129 Jack Dempsey
130 Charles Dickens
131 Emily Dickinson
132 Marlene Dietrich
133 Phyllis Diller
134 Joe DiMaggio
135 Walt Disney
136 Benjamin Disraeli
137 Dorothea Dix
138 Phil Donahue

139 Frederick Douglass
140 Theodore Dreiser
141 Isadora Duncan
142 Jimmy Durante
143 Amelia Earhart
144 Mary Baker Eddy
145 Thomas Edison
146 Dwight Eisenhower
147 Lee Elder
148 George Eliot
149 Duke Ellington
150 Ralph Waldo
    Emerson
151 Julius Erving
152 Jean Fabre
153 Michael Faraday
154 James Farley
155 David Farragut
156 Frederico Fellini
157 Cyrus Field
158 Marshall Field
159 W. C. Fields
160 Bobby Fischer
161 F. Scott Fitzerald
162 Henry Fonda
163 Henry Ford
164 George Foreman
165 Benjamin Franklin
166 Joe Frazier
167 Robert Frost
168 Elizabeth Fry
169 Robert Fulton
170 Clark Gable
171 Galileo
172 M. K. Gandhi
173 Greta Garbo
174 E. Stanley Gardner
175 James Garfield
176 Judy Garland

177 James Garner
178 William Lloyd
    Garrison
179 Paul Gauguin
180 Lou Gehrig
181 Bob Geldof
182 Gratien Gelinas
183 Edward Gibbon
184 Althea Gibson
185 Lillian Gilbreth
186 Joe Girard
187 Stephen Girard
188 Lillian Gish
189 Jackie Gleason
190 Robert Goddard
191 Samuel Gompers
192 Evonne Goolagong
193 Berry Gordy
194 Maxim Gorky
195 Billy Graham
196 Martha Graham
197 U. S. Grant
198 Pete Gray
199 Horace Greeley
200 Wilfred Grenfell
201 Wayne Gretzky
202 D. W. Griffith
203 The Grimké Sisters
204 Johann Gutenberg
205 Janet Guthrie
206 Alice Hamilton
207 Scott Hamilton
208 George Handel
209 Lorraine Hansberry
210 Rick Hansen
211 Thomas Hardy
212 William Harvey
213 Nathaniel
    Hawthorne

214 Franz Haydn
215 William Herschel
216 Milton S. Hershey
217 Thor Heyerdahl
218 James Jerome Hill
219 Napoleon Hill
220 Rowland Hill
221 Conrad Hilton
222 E. Cora Hind
223 Alfred Hitchcock
224 Ho Chi Minh
225 Dustin Hoffman
226 Ben Hogan
227 Robert Hooke
228 Herbert Hoover
229 Bob Hope
230 Elias Howe
231 Gordie Howe
232 Rock Hudson
233 Alexander von
    Humboldt
234 H. L. Hunt
235 Zora Hurston
236 Aldous Huxley
237 Lee Iacocca
238 Henrik Ibsen
239 Washington Irving
240 Andrew Jackson
241 William James
242 Edward Jenner
243 Joan of Arc
244 Steven Jobs
245 Earvin Johnson
246 Howard Johnson
247 Pauline Johnson
248 Tom Jones
249 James Joyce
250 Franz Kafka
251 Karen Kain

252 Wassily Kandinsky
253 Paul Kane
254 Yousuf Karsh
255 Legson Kayira
256 Kip Keino
257 Helen Keller
258 John F. Kennedy
259 Elizabeth Kenny
260 Johannes Kepler
261 Andre Kertesz
262 Charles Kettering
263 Jean Claude Killy
264 Billie Jean King
265 Mary Kingsley
266 Kris Kristofferson
267 Ray Kroc
268 Frederick Laker
269 Ann Landers
270 Allen Lane
271 Fritz Lang
272 Dorothy Lange
273 Niki Lauda
274 Le Corbusier
275 Stephen Leacock
276 Louis B. Leakey
277 Antony van
    Leeuwenhoek
278 Ron LeFlore
279 Lotte Lehmann
280 Jack Lemmon
281 Suzanne Lenglen
282 Leonardo da Vinci
283 R. G. LeTourneau
284 Jerry Lewis
285 John L. Lewis
286 Abraham Lincoln
287 Charles Lindberg
288 Art Linkletter
289 Carl Linnaeus

290 David Livingstone
291 Vince Lombardi
292 Sophia Loren
293 Greg Louganis
294 Joe Louis
295 Henry Luce
296 Loretta Lynn
297 Mary Lyon
298 Mary McCarthy
299 Nellie McClung
300 Cyrus McCormick
301 Willie McCovey
302 Carson McCullers
303 William McKinley
304 Steve McQueen
305 Edouard Manet
306 Horace Mann
307 Alice Marble
308 Rocky Marciano
309 Orison S. Marden
310 J. W. Marriott
311 Thurgood Marshall
312 Dean Martin
313 Harriet Martineau
314 Bob Mathias
315 Henry Matissé
316 Mathew Maury
317 William W. Mayo
318 Margaret Mead
319 Ved Mehta
320 Golda Meir
321 Lise Meitner
322 Hermann Melville
323 Gregor Mendel
324 Dmitry Mendeleyev
325 Michelangelo
326 Arthur Miller
327 John Milton
328 Jack Miner

329 Comte de Mirabeau
330 Joan Miró
331 Robert Mitchum
332 Marilyn Monroe
333 Maria Montessori
334 Lucy Montgomery
335 Henry Moore
336 Marianne Moore
337 Akio Morita
338 Grandma Moses
339 Daniel Patrick Moynihan
340 John Muir
341 Emily Murphy
342 Anne Murray
343 Ralph Nader
344 Martina Navratilova
345 Willie Nelson
346 Isaac Newton
347 Vaslav Nijinsky
348 Alfred Nobel
349 Christopher Nolan
350 Rudolf Nureyev
351 Diana Nyad
352 Lawrence Olivier
353 Frederick Olmsted
354 Kitty O'Neil
355 Bobby Orr
356 William Osler
357 Nikolaus Otto
358 Robert Owen
359 Jesse Owens
360 Ignace Paderewski
361 Leroy Satchel Paige
362 Emmeline Pankhurst
363 Francis Parkman
364 Gordon Parks
365 Rosa Parks
366 Dolly Parton

367 Louis Pasteur
368 George S. Patton
369 Norman Vincent Peale
370 Pelé
371 Wilder Penfield
372 J. C. Penny
373 Pablo Picasso
374 Mary Pickford
375 Gifford Pinchot
376 Samuel Plimsoll
377 Jim Plunkett
378 Edgar Allan Poe
379 Sidney Poitier
380 Alexander Pope
381 Beatrix Potter
382 John Wesley Powell
383 William Hickling Prescott
384 Elvis Presley
385 Marcel Proust
386 Joseph Pulitzer
387 Raffi
388 Robert Redford
389 Pierre Renoir
390 Bob Richards
391 Branch Rickey
392 Sally Ride
393 Jacob Riis
394 Paul Robeson
395 Jackie Robinson
396 Sugar Ray Robinson
397 John D. Rockefeller
398 Jerome I. Rodale
399 Washington Roebling
400 Will Rogers
401 Franklin D. Roosevelt
402 Diana Ross

403 Jean Jacques Rousseau
404 Helena Rubinstein
405 Wilma Rudolf
406 Bayard Rustin
407 Babe Ruth
408 Jonas Salk
409 George Sand
410 Carl Sandburg
411 Harland Sanders
412 Margaret Sanger
413 David Sarnoff
414 Robert Schuller
415 Charles Schulz
416 Richard Sears
417 Lord Shaftsbury
418 William Shakespeare
419 Dmitri Shostakovich
420 Igor Sikorsky
421 Red Skelton
422 B. F. Skinner
423 Benjamin Spock
424 Sylvester Stallone
425 Henry R. Stanley
426 Elizabeth Cady Stanton
427 Ellsworth M. Statler
428 Danielle Steel
429 Viljhalmur Stefansson
430 Edward Steichen
431 Gertrude Stein
432 Gloria Steinem
433 Charles Steinmetz
434 George Stephenson
435 Robert Louis Stevenson
436 W. Clement Stone
437 Harriet Beecher Stowe

438 Johan A. Strindberg
439 Anne Sullivan
440 Ed Sullivan
441 David Suzuki
442 Valentina Tereshkova
443 Nikola Tesla
444 Margaret Thatcher
445 Isiah Thomas
446 Lowell Thomas
447 Tom Thomson
448 Henry David Thoreau
449 Jim Thorpe
450 James Thurber
451 John Tolkien
452 Leo Tolstoy
453 Lee Trevino
454 Edward L. Trudeau
455 Harry Truman
456 Sojourner Truth
457 Harriet Tubman
458 Gene Tunney
459 Ron Turcotte
460 Ted Turner
461 Mark Twain
462 Vincent van Gogh
463 Cornelius Van Horne
464 Cornelius Vanderbilt
465 Giusseppe Verdi
466 Jules Verne
467 Voltaire
468 Richard Wagner
469 Lillian Wald
470 Alfred Wallace
471 Andy Warhol
472 Booker T. Washington
473 George Washington
474 Tom J. Watson, Sr.

475 James Watt
476 John Wayne
477 Daniel Webster
478 Noah Webster
479 Thurlow Weed
480 Johnny Weissmuller
481 Lawrence Welk
482 George Westinghouse
483 James Whistler
484 Gilbert White
485 Walt Whitman
486 Eli Whitney
487 Emma Willard
488 Frances Willard
489 Tennessee Williams
490 Kemmons Wilson
491 Oprah Winfrey
492 Stevie Wonder
493 Grant Wood
494 F. W. Woolworth
495 Christopher Wren
496 Orville/Wilbur Wright
497 Richard Wright
498 Chuck Yeager
499 Cy Young
500 Babe Zaharias

Words of Wisdom

1

- Hank Aaron
The All Time Champion Home Run Hitter
Born in 1934

1 I think what separates the superstars from the average ballplayer is the fact that he concentrates just a little bit longer.

2 I did not want to let failure stand in the way of doing what I wanted to do. I have seen a lot of athletes who were as gifted as I was, but they could not concentrate and would accept failure a lot quicker. I concentrated on what I had to do and I was not going to accept failure.

3 The main secret of my success was that I was never late for practice and I always came to spring training in shape. I believe in baseball rules.

4 I need to depend on someone who is bigger, stronger and wiser than I am. I don't do it on my own. God is my strength. He gave me a good body and some talent and the freedom to develop it. He helps me when things go wrong. He forgives me when I fall on my face. He lights my way.

5 If it was going to be a night game, I would take a nap about one o'clock, and for some reason, I would always remember if I had to face a particular pitcher, and I could see him in my sleep pitching to me. When I woke up, I was ready to go to the ballpark.

2

- Alfred Adler
The Founder of the School of Individual Psychology
1870 - 1937

1 It is easier to fight for one's principles than to live up to them.

2 The true meaning of life is not power and domination but making contribution to the community.

3 Man knows much more than he understands.

4 There can be but a single goal of education: education to courage.

5 I am convinced that a person's behaviour springs from his ideas. How we interpret the great and important facts of existence depends upon our style of life.

6 Exaggerated sensitiveness is an expression of the feeling of inferiority.

7 If we make ourselves smile we actually feel like smiling.

8 The feeling of inferiority rules the mental life and can be clearly recognized in the sense of incompleteness, and in the uninterrupted struggle both of individuals and of humanity.

9 It is the individual who is not interested in his fellow men who has the greatest difficulties in life and provides the greatest injury to others. It is from among such individuals that all human failures spring.

10 We can be cured of depression in only 14 days, if every day we will try to think of how we can be helpful to others.

11 To be a human being means the possession of a feeling of inferiority that is constantly pressing on towards its own conquest.

3

1 If I could live by a brook which had plenty of gudgeons, I should ask nothing better than to spend my life there.

2 I cannot afford to waste my time making money.

3 To have a smattering of something is one of the great fallacies of our time. A teacher ought to know some one thing well.

4 Train pupils to be observers. Ramble with them and let them see the objects. Provide them with specimens; let them hold the specimens.

5 To understand the relations of different branches of knowledge, read their history.

6 A laboratory of natural history is a sanctuary, in which nothing improper should be exhibited. I would tolerate improprieties in a church sooner than in a scientific laboratory.

7 I want to prepare those who shall attend and observe for themselves.

8 There should be a little museum in every school-room.

4

1 Life is my college. May I graduate well, and earn some honours.

2 The World lies fair about us, and a friendly sky above;
Our lives are full of sunshine, our homes are full of love;
Few cares and sorrows sadden the beauty of our day;
We gather simple pleasures like daisies by the way.

3 I am glad a task to me is given
To labour at day by day;
For it brings me health, and strength and hope,
And I cheerfully learn to say, -
Head, you think; heart, you may feel;
But hand, you shall work always!

4 A philosopher is like a man up in a balloon; he is safe as long as three women hold the ropes on the ground.

5 Far away there in the sunshine are my highest aspirations. I may not reach them, but I can look up and see their beauty, believe in them and try to follow where they lead.

5
- Grover Alexander
An Incredible Comeback Player in Baseball History
1887 - 1950

1 Baseball is my life.

2 I was never the worrying kind. I always knew how to pitch. I wouldn't have pitched these many years in the major leagues if I did worry.

3 As a man grows old, he begins to look back rather than forward.

6
-Muhammad Ali
The Greatest Boxer of All Time
Born in 1942

1 I may have been the best fighter, but I was also the poorest. I owned one T-shirt, two pairs of pants, several pairs of shoes with holes in them. My jackets were torn and patched and hardly a day went by when my pants did not split somewhere. And although I had won nearly all my fights, and was on the verge of turning professional, I had never been able to afford first-class mouth piece to protect my teeth. I had to wait until other fighters finished so I could borrow their headgear, or their trunks or bandages. I wanted my own training gloves, my own gear.

2 The woman is the fiber of the nation. She is the producer of life. A nation is only as good as its women.

3 Friendship is the hardest thing in the world to explain. It's not something you learn in school. But if you haven't learned the meaning of friendship, you really haven't learned anything.

4 No one knows what to say in the loser's room.

5 Everybody is negotiable.

6 Pleasure is not happiness. It has no more importance than a shadow following a man.

7 What keeps me going is goals.

8 If they can make penicillin out of moldy bread, they can sure make something out of you.

7
- Dick Allen
Baseball Superstar Despite Vision Problem
Born in 1942

1 Philadelphia taught me that people can be the cruelest things in the world. I find even horses are a lot better than most people.

2 I'm no angel, and I have taken up a nip here and there, but not to excess. Truthfully, at times I've taken a couple of belts before I've gone on the field, to calm down. I expect to be booed, not stoned.

3 We were poor, but being poor made us close.

8

- **Steve Allen**

The Creator and First Host of the Tonight Show
Born in 1921

1 We often do not recognize our greatest opportunities.

2 I have never met anyone over the age of 10 who wasn't a critic of television. What is true of television is true of life and the universe itself - part of it is magically wonderful and part of it is dreadful.

3 When you walk into a meat market you don't spend anxious moments at the door wondering what you will say to the butcher. When you meet friends you don't waste time planning in advance how you are going to address them. Obviously the ability to communicate is something most of us share. The trick, of course, is in being relaxed enough to speak on the air as easily as you do in the living room.

4 Audiences laugh more readily at an ad-libbed quip, even though it might not be as funny as a prepared and polished joke.

5 Nothing is quite as funny as the unintended humour of reality.

9

- **Roald Amundsen**

The First Person to Reach the South Pole
1872 - 1928

1 There is no quicker way to break men down under strain than to allow them to live haphazardly.

2 An ordered existence engenders confidence. The calm and unhurried way of doing things seems to symbolize the ability of intelligence to overcome the inimical forces of nature.

3 There is no man or woman so humble that he or she cannot work for the good of the fatherland. In that, we are all equal. The goal is the same; the means must vary according to talent, destiny and a view of life.

4 It's not in mortals to command success, but we will deserve it.

5 The power of the unknown over the human spirit drove men to Polar regions. As ideas have cleared with ages, so has this power extended its might, and driven man willy-nilly onwards along the path of progress. It drives us into Nature's hidden powers and secrets, down to the immeasurably little world of the microscope, and out into the unprobed expanses of the Universe. It gives us no peace until we know this planet on which we live, from the greatest depth of the ocean to the highest layers of the atmosphere. This power runs like a strand through the whole history of Polar exploration. In spite of all declarations of possible profit in one way or another, it was that which, in our hearts, has always driven us back there again, despite all setbacks and suffering.

10

1 Understanding is the basis of all peace.

2 The longer one lives, the more one realizes that there is no particular thing one can do alone.

3 If someone is holding you down in the gutter, at least part of him must be in the same gutter.

4 I have a great belief in the future of my people and my country.

5 I don't feel that I opened a door. I think that those who came after me deserve a great deal of credit for what they have achieved. I don't feel that I am responsible for any of it, because if they did not have it in them, they would not be able to get it out.

11

1 Listen, I am only just beginning to feel as if I have anything under my belt at all. And I mean that.

2 I seem to have been very blessed with an unusual number of very fortunate incidents that have helped me along the way. And then the rest had to be up to me.

3 Once you are on a pedestal many start throwing rocks at you to knock you off.

4 Trends change rapidly. Every time I think I know where it's at, it's usually somewhere else. You can only try to do what pleases you.

5 You need a family. You can't take the audience home with you. You can't depend on the loyalty of fans who, after all is said and done, are just faceless people one seldom sees. Very few stars have their fans for ever. But a child is for ever; that bond and relationship is timeless and doesn't depend on your looks, age or popularity at the moment.

12

1 A man's home in a civilized country is one of the most dangerous places in the world to live in.

2 I don't believe in hardship. Eat well, dress well, sleep well whenever possible, is a pretty good rule. If a bit of hardship does come along, why you're ready to take it in your stride and laugh while it's going on.

3 Go on the biggest and most exciting hunt of all - the search for the bones of our ancestors. It will give you more thrills and more satisfaction than any other job I know and I speak from a lifetime of adventure.

13

1 Cautious, careful people, always casting to preserve their reputation and social standing, never can bring about a reform. Those who are really in earnest, must be willing to be anything or nothing in the world's estimation and publicly and privately, in season and out, avow their sympathy with despised and persecuted ideas and their advocates, and bear the consequences.

2 I have never lost faith, not for a moment in 50 years.

3 Very few people are capable of seeing that the cause of nine-tenths of all the misfortunes which come to women, and to men also, lies in the subjection of women, and therefore the important thing is to lay the ax at the root.

4 I am able to endure the strain of daily traveling and lecturing at over three score and ten mainly because I have always worked and loved work. As machinery in motion lasts longer than idle, so a body and soul in active exercise escapes the corroding rust of physical and mental laziness, which prematurely cuts off the life of so many women.

5 I am used to defeat every time and know how to pick up and push on for another attack.

6 A race capable of enslaving any other race or class is incapable of justice to themselves.

14

1 You must spend money in order to make money.

2 If you live long enough, you find you have either worn out your enemies or outlived them.

3 When things get tough, that's the time to stick your little chin out.

4 A little new blood perks up the old arteries.

5 Get your facts right. Keep it short, keep it sweet and keep it to the point. You can write a book about what you don't know but you have really got to know your subject to put it in one sentence.

6 Women invented management, and we originated group control. Government itself is simply a magnified copy of household law and order, for which our great grandmothers furnished the pattern. The word *economics* means home regulation.

7 Beauty and optimism go hand in hand.

8 Treat a horse like a woman and a woman like a horse, and they will both win for you.

15

1 Music is the surest way of communicating among all people.

2 When you play jazz, you don't lie. You play from the heart.

3 I don't need words; it's all in the phrasing.

4 If you don't look out for your chops and pipes, you can't blow the horn and sing. Anything that will get in the way doing that, out it goes. That trumpet comes first, before everything, even my wife. Got to be that way. I love Lucille, man, but she understands about me and my music.

16

1 Whatever I start out to do, I make it a point to learn everything I can about that. I knew nothing about the cosmetics business. I had no prior knowledge of that when I started this company, but today I think I rank up there with Estée or anybody else as far as cosmetics are concerned.

2 I write little thank-you notes. I am very, very detail oriented. Every single letter that comes in here must be answered as quickly as possible.

3 There are two things people want more than sex and money......recognition and praise.

4 Men are more motivated by money. For women recognition comes first, self-fulfillment second and pride third.

5 Whatever it is that I am doing, I am very much into and have to get it done. If I start doing something at one in the morning, until I finish it, I can't quit.

6 I try to get everybody to get up at 5 o'clock in the morning and do all those things that women particularly don't like to do, like bookkeeping and writing notes and doing newsletter and things that are important in our business. To do all those things before the family gets up, before all of the intrusions begin.

7 Our P&L statement does not stand for *Profit and Loss*, it stands for *People and Love*.

8 Praise people to success.

9 Work is often the best antidote to grief.

10 Give yourself something to work toward - constantly.

11 Success must be a shared experience.

12 God first, family second and career third.

13 Credit is what decays America. Pay as you go, yearn it and earn it.

14 I truly believe that whatever you send into the lives of others, comes back into your own.

17

- Arthur Ashe
The First Black Male to Win the Wimbledon Championship
1943 - 1993

1 Regardless of how you feel, you always try to look like a winner. Even if you are behind, a sustained look of control and confidence can give you a mental edge that results in victory.

2 You are not going to believe this, but living with AIDS is not the greatest burden I've had in my life; being black is.

3 You have got to be intense when it counts. If you try to be intense 24-hours a day, you aren't going to last very long.

4 You are born with certain abilities, be they physical or mental or a combination. Not all of us are gifted in equal shares in these departments, and I guess I was just blessed with physical ability, and the mental ability to go with it. But there is no doubt that you have to be persistent and determined to succeed.

5 If you are talented, and if you have correct training and teaching, it's going to show, no matter what the breaks are.

6 Tennis is a metaphor for life. Many aspects of the game can be translated into life experiences. The traits needed for success in tennis are useful in other circumstances. The ultimate connection between tennis and life is in the *doing* - not in the *winning*.

18

- Isaac Asimov
The Most Prolific Writer of Science Fiction
1920 - 1992

1 The essence of life for me is finding something you enjoy doing that gives meaning to life, and then being in a situation where you can do it.

2 The lucky break doesn't help you much if you don't take advantage of it. I honestly think that everybody has lucky breaks now and then, so that only what counts is taking advantage.

3 I have never called myself a genius. If other people want to call me that, that's their problem. I myself shoot for other more meaningful and more significant goals - like being the best science-fiction writer/ science writer/ public speaker in the world. That's good enough for me.

4 Know your ending, or the river of your story may finally sink into the desert sands and never reach the sea.

5 I don't worry much about small details. I am not a perfectionist. I sometimes describe myself as an imperfectionist.

6 What I resent most in my life is having to give time to other people.

7 There is no one future; human beings make the future out of a vast array of possibilities. I prefer to consider the future in terms of the ideal, wherein all people act sanely and with judgment and decency.

8 It is unlikely that science and technology in their great sweeps will outstrip science fiction in many small and unexpected ways; however, there will

undoubtedly continue to be surprises that no science fiction writer or scientist, for that matter, has thought of. It is these surprises that are the excitement and glory of the human intellectual adventure.

9 There is a single light of science, and to brighten it anywhere is to brighten it everywhere.

10 Violence is the last refuge of the incompetent.

11 God loves all men, but is enchanted by none.

19

- Chet Atkins
An Extraordinary Instrumentalist
Born in 1924

1 I am a little square, but it helps to be that way.

2 Ever since I was a little boy, I wanted to be a famous guitar player. I did not want to be a movie star. I did not want to host a game show. I did not want to act. I just wanted to be a famous guitar player. And I did that.

3 As you get older, it's so tough to keep mediocrity from creeping in. You get so you perform and you are predictable and people know what you are going to do before you do it. That's what you have to fight as you get to be successful. You make money; you go home and watch TV. You don't have to go downstairs and practice anymore.

4 Nobody ever makes it the same way. I made it by being a fiddle player. They needed a fiddle player and I got the job. Then they heard me playing the guitar a few nights later and gave me a job as a guitar player. You got to be in the right place at the right time.

5 You got to know your instrument. You leave it in the case for three days and it doesn't know you any more. You can't play it. You don't know the positions. It's easy if you just strum chords, but if you play solos, it's very, very difficult.

6 The cat that comes up with something different is the cat that doesn't know any better.

20

- John J. Audubon
The Most Remarkable Painter of American Birds
1785 - 1851

1 Birds of all kinds are full of courage. Have you not seen the little Robin chase a cat? An Eagle will keep a man away from the nest. A cock will attack even a Lion.

2 Every bird speaks to me, every tree nods gently to me.

3 One of the most powerful attractions to be considered is the love of offspring - so deeply rooted in Nature as to be a rule, with almost no exceptions, among birds and quadrupeds.

4 The virtue of hospitality, although agreeable to the stranger, is not always duly appreciated.

5 There is a huge difference in the knowledge of things acquired by personal observation and those of hearsay.

6 Students of nature spend little time over introduction of persons likely to take an interest in their pursuits.

21

- Liberty H. Bailey
An Extraordinary Horticulturist
1858 - 1954

1 Accept conditions as they exist. Neither reject creature comforts and amenities nor let money be your primary consideration. Never lose sight of aspirations and keep as a chief aim the artistic expression of life.

22

- James Baldwin
A Highly Acclaimed Black American Writer
1924 - 1987

1 Most contemporary theater is designed to corroborate your fantasies and make you walk out whistling. I don't want to make you whistle at my stuff. I want you to be sitting on the edge of your chair waiting for the nurses to carry you out.

2 The only thing worse than being Black in America is being White.

3 A ghetto can be improved in one way only - out of existence.

4 People can cry much easier than they can change.

5 The world is before you, and you need not take it or leave it since it was already here when you came in.

23

- Lucille Ball
A Highly Popular Comedienne of 1950s and 60s
1911 - 1989

1 Nothing is going to be perfect. But I want it to be the best it can be and I want to see the people who are getting paid well because they are supposed to know what they are doing, doing it. You can still try for perfection even though you know you will never achieve it.

2 Divorce is defeat; it's an adult failure.

3 I like people who love their work, love their families, love life; people who, fundamentally, love themselves. Nothing is more important than being able to stand up on your feet.

4 Learn the art of taking care of yourself and remember that there is a very fine distinction between being selfish and taking care of yourself. If you take care of yourself, others won't have to.

5 I learn from my mistakes. I don't admire people who beat their heads against the same mistakes over and over again. I don't like people who flounder too long. I don't admire these everyday martyrs, the pitiful drunken masses, the hysterical

floundering women, the Beats shouting "The world owes me a living" - all these people who cling to you, who need your help. You help them up to a point, but after a while you wish they'd go cry on somebody else's shoulder.

6 Life takes guts.

7 I am happy that I have brought laughter because I have been shown by many the value of it in so many lives, in so many ways.

8 In the television series business you have to know when to get off.

9 I hate failure and our divorce was a number one failure in my eyes. It was the worst period of my life. Neither Desi nor I have been the same since, physically or mentally.

24 - Honoré de Balzac
One of the Greatest Writers of France
1799 - 1850

1 Necessity is often the spur to genius.

2 Modesty is the conscience of the body.

3 Hatred is the vice of narrow souls; they feed it with all their littleness, and make it the pretext of base tyrannies.

4 Cruelty and fear shake hands together.

5 Life cannot go on without much forgetting.

6 Once I find a new idea, I treat it like a valuable treasure - like the humble egg from which a brilliant cook concocts a hundred different dishes.

7 One is never criminal in obeying the law of Nature.

8 The sublime comes from the heart, and has nothing to do with the mind.

9 It is not enough to be an upright man; we must be seen to be one. Society does not exist on moral ideas only.

10 There are no little events with the heart. It magnifies everything. It places on the same scales the fall of an Empire and the dropping of a woman's glove; and almost always the glove weighs more than the Empire.

11 Irony is the essence of the character of Providence.

25 - Roger Bannister
The Man Who Broke the 4-Minute Mile Barrier
Born in 1929

1 Each of us has to find his own activity. It may be mountain climbing, running or sailing, or it may be something quite different. The important thing is that we should perform rather than watch others. By absorption in the pursuit we forget ourselves, and it fills the void between the child and the man.

2 Life must be lived forwards, even if sometimes it only makes sense as we look back.

3 If there is ever a time when the real core of a person is revealed, it is in

childhood. Perhaps we all have some concept of our own *specialness* and purpose at a very early age, but we never dare to admit it.

4 There is no harm in having ideals. If we aim at a star, we may occasionally reach a height normally beyond us. We are sometimes wrong to criticize ambition, if we can shelve it when the right moment comes, and not become embittered because of failure to reach the target.

26

- Tom Barnardo
A Pioneer Builder of Homes for Destitute Children
1845 - 1905

1 I am very hopeful that through God's goodness a bright future is before the big rough lads of our great cities, which may turn myriad of lives into useful careers.

2 To be a life-giving force and center of usefulness, the lake must have its outlets as well as its tributaries.

27

- James Miranda Barry
The Woman Doctor Disguised as a Man
1795 - 1865

1 Good orders must be preserved but no cruelty nor deprivation of food must be ever resorted to. Persons with poor hygiene must be considered not as convicts but as unfortunate. The strictest attention must be paid to personal cleanliness.

28

- Ethel Barrymore
The Reigning Queen of the Stage for Half of a Century
1879 - 1959

1 An actress to be a success must have the face of Venus, the brains of Minerva, the grace of Terpsichore, the memory of Macaulay, the figure of Juno and the hide of rhinoceros.

2 You grow up the day you have your first laugh at yourself.

3 You must learn day by day, year by year, to broaden your horizon. The more things you love, the more you are interested in, the more you enjoy, the more you are indignant about - the more you have left when anything happens.

4 We who play, who entertain for a few years, what can we leave that will last.

5 An artist, a theatrical artist, must be a human being first and an artist second. When you applaud, it is not only our art but our life, for we are what we have been, not only on the stage, but off it.

6 Thinking, thinking, thinking - that is what acting is all about. It is the only thing in acting. The thought running through the person's mind is what the actor has to capture. You pounce on that thought; you reach out and grasp it and never let it go.

29

1 A famous name is often a handicap.

2 The artist's life is the most glorious in the world - with one slight exception - you don't eat.

3 I have been up and down all my life. Lots of people said I was through, but I never thought much about it. I was always too darn busy to worry about my troubles.

30

1 The highest form of folk-influenced music is that in which the folk atmosphere has been completely assimilated.

2 The composer has a right to use musical material from all sources. What he judges suitable for his purpose becomes, through the very use, his mental property. The questions of origin can only be interesting from the point of view of musical documentation.

3 I would recommend to anyone the attempt to achieve a state of spiritual indifference in which it is possible to view the affairs of the world with complete indifference and with the utmost tranquillity. Of course, it is difficult, extremely difficult - in fact the most difficult thing there is - to attain this state, but success in this is the greatest victory man can ever hope to win: over other people, over himself and over all things.

4 Emotion plays a far more prominent role than one would imagine. All my music has depended on instinct and emotion.

31

1 Never ask a question if you can find the answer yourself. But never hesitate to ask if you can't find it. Remember always, you have a tongue in your mind.

2 If a man can have only one kind of sense, let him have common sense. If he has that and uncommon sense too, he is not far from genius.

3 A man without mirth is like a wagon without springs. He is jolted disagreeably by every pebble in the road.

4 Good humour makes all things tolerable.

5 A tool is but the extension of a man's hand, and a machine is but a complex tool. And he that invents a machine augments the power of a man and the well-being of mankind.

6 I do not like these cold, precise, perfect people, who, in order not to speak wrong, never speak at all, and in order not to do wrong, never do anything.

7 Education is the knowledge of how to use the whole of one's self.

8 It is not work that kills men; it is worry. Work is healthy; you can hardly put more on a man than he can bear. But worry is rust upon the blade. It is not movement that destroys the machinery, but friction.

9 Defeat is a school in which truth always grows strong.

10 There is no such thing as white lies; a lie is as black as a coal pit, and twice as foul.

11 Every charitable act is a stepping stone toward heaven.

12 Compassion will cure more sins than condemnation.

13 There is one thing that will be hard, but that is to be the root of all success and enjoyment. That is the habit of boning down to things which you don't like. In all your afterlife, your success will depend upon your ability to do things which you do not particularly like to do. Duty must become your watchword, and not *pleasure* or *liking*.

14 It is sometimes of God's mercy that men in the eager pursuit of worldly aggrandizement are baffled; for they are very like a train going down an inclined plane - putting on the break is not pleasant, but it keeps the car on the track and from ruin.

15 It is defeat that turns bone to flint, and gristle to muscle, and makes men invincible, and formed those heroic natures that are now in ascendancy in the world. Do not then be afraid of defeat. You are never so near to victory as when defeated in a good cause.

16 It is a trial that proves one thing weak and another strong. A house built on the sand is in fair weather just as good as if built on a rock. A cobweb is as good as the mightiest cable when there is no strain upon it.

17 We are always in the forge, or in the anvil; by trials God is shaping us for higher things.

18 Victories that are easy are cheap. Those only are worth having which come as the result of hard fighting.

19 The soul without imagination is what an observatory would be without a telescope.

20 It is not well for a man to pray for cream and to live on skim-milk.

21 In the ordinary business of life, industry can do anything which genius can do, and very many things which it cannot.

22 He who is false to present duty breaks a thread in the loom, and will find the flaw when he may have forgotten its cause.

23 An impure man is every good man's enemy.

24 True obedience is true liberty.

25 Love cannot endure indifference. It needs to be wanted. Like a lamp, it needs to be fed out of the oil of another's heart, or its flame burns low.

26 Flowers are the sweetest things that God ever made, and forgot to put a soul into.

27 There is a dew in one flower and not in another, because one opens its cup and takes it in, while the other closes itself, and the dewdrops run off. God rains his goodness and mercy as widespread as the dew, and if we lack them, it is because we will not open our hearts to receive them.

28 What the heart has once owned and had, it shall never lose.

29 God pardons like a mother, who kisses the offense into everlasting forgiveness.

30 A man's character is the reality of himself. His reputation is the opinion others have formed of him. Character is in him; reputation is from other people - that is the substance, this is the shadow.

31 Heaven will be inherited by every man who has heaven in his soul.

32 Doctrine is nothing but the skin of truth set up and stuffed.

33 The first five years in the life of a church determines the history of that church and gives to it its position and genius.

34 Weeds change to flowers. The moment a plant inspires intelligent emotion in us, it ceases to be a weed and becomes a flower.

35 It is the heart that makes a man rich. He is rich according to what he is, not according to what he has.

36 There never was a person who did anything worth doing that did not receive more than he gave.

37 Troubles are often the tools by which God fashions us for better things.

38 Love is the river of life in this world.

39 A man's true state of power and riches is to be in himself.

40 Hold yourself responsible for a higher standard than anybody else expects of you. Never excuse yourself.

41 An acorn is not an oak tree when it is sprouted. It must go through long summers and fierce winters; it has to endure all that frost and snow and side-striking winds can bring before it is a full-grown oak. These are rough teachers, but rugged school-masters make rugged pupils. So, a man is not a man when he is created; he is only begun. His manhood must come with years.

32

- Ludwig van Beethoven
The Greatest Composer of All Time
1770 - 1827

---

1 I will take fate by the throat. My infirmity shall not get me down.

2 To me the highest thing, after God, is my honour.

3 The barriers are not erected which can say to aspiring talents and industry, "Thus far and no farther."

33

1 I would like to be recognized for using my platform to enhance the human commitment.

2 I am not a great singer; I am an interpreter of songs - more of an actor and a performer - and lucky enough to have a voice that would be accepted musically.

3 In the future I will be doing exactly what I am doing now and have been doing for 20 years, only better and I will still be trying to use my life wisely.

4 I like to feel that each new song I record represents growth.

5 There has never been progress without conflict.

6 If Justice with her smile can't enforce right, then Justice with her sword must do it.

34

1 Don't stay forever on the public road, going only where others have gone. Leave the beaten path occasionally and dive into the woods. You will be certain to find something you have never seen before. It will be a little thing but do not ignore it. Follow it up, explore around it; one discovery will lead to another and before you know it, you will have something really worth thinking about.

2 To take night from me is to rob me of life.

3 I often feel like hiding myself away in a corner out of sight.

4 "Mr. Watson, come here, I want you."   (the first telephone conversation in history)

5 Concentrate all your thoughts upon the work at hand. The sun's rays do not burn until brought to a focus.

6 The most successful men in the end are those whose success is the result of steady accretion. It is the man who carefully advances step by step, with his mind becoming wider and wider - and progressively better able to grasp any theme or situation - persevering in what he knows to be practical and concentrating his thought upon it, who is bound to succeed in the greatest degree.

7 What this power is I cannot say; all I know is that it exists and it becomes available only when a man is in that state of mind in which he knows exactly what he wants and is fully determined not to quit until he finds it.

8 A man, as a general rule, owes very little to what he is born with - a man is what he makes of himself.

35

1 There is no sense or economy in ruining farms in your eagerness for gold and diamonds.

2 Don't talk so much of your difficulties. For a change, let me hear just one thing that you think might possibly be practicable

3 The crucial problem of our generation is to safeguard, maintain, develop, increase and wisely use for the common benefit of mankind the natural resources of the earth.

4 The catastrophe that threatens civilization results from man's failure to live in harmony with the principles that govern his environment. Man has abused the earth which is his principal source of wealth; and the earth therefore dispassionately makes his existence even more precarious and threatens him with extinction. Until he brings himself to live in harmony with nature there is no hope for peace or plenty or progress.

36

1 It's how you start that counts. Once you get rolling, and get the attention of the audience, it's not important how you finish. You will be a hit. You can always get off the stage. It's what you do when you get that counts.

2 At heart we are all as prudent and parsimonious as the imaginary *Jack Benny*. Most of us would be as stingy as *me* if we had the courage. We're ashamed to show how much we value every nickel and dime of the money that we've had to work for, scrounge for, suffer for. The stingiest people I've known have been wealthy persons who inherited their wealth. They know they are filthy rich. They don't have to impress strangers by throwing their money around with reckless abandon. I've seen multimillionaires study a restaurant bill. They add up every item. They confirm the total. Then they compute the penny 15 per cent of the sum and leave that for the tip. The same tycoon might buy a painting for $150,000. - but he would not think he was buying recklessly because in his mind the painting is worth $200,000.

3 Begging letters are written by professional moochers who con enough suckers to get by.

37

1 You can't write a song out of thin air. You have to know and feel you are writing about.

2 There is an element of truth in every idea that lasts long enough to be called corny.

3 You can't sell patriotism, unless the people feel patriotic. For that matter, you can't sell people anything they don't want.

4 I am a songwriter, like dozens and dozens of others, and as long as I'm able, whether the songs are good or bad, I'll continue to write them; because song writing is not just a business or a hobby with me. It's everything.

5 You don't have to be different to be good. And if you are good, you are different.

6 It takes a very rare person to retire gracefully, especially if he has been a success.

7 I am a man without hobby, therefore, if I rest, I get restless. I have to keep writing songs because that's the only thing I know to do.

8 To be good at anything you must like to show off what you do.

9 It is nice to hear compliments about the many standards I have written over the years, but I can also hear that little bird chirp, "So what have you done lately?"

38
- Hector de Berlioz
One of the Most Important Figures of the Romantic Era
1803 - 1869

1 The heart that truly loved, never forgets.

2 If the recurrence of an aptitude for music in certain artistic families can be explained quite simply by the influence of example and upbringing, by the fact that it is relatively easy for children to follow in their father's footsteps, and even by natural inclination transmitting itself, like physical appearance, from one generation to the next, how is one to explain the extraordinary fantasies that visit so many young people quite out of the blue?

3 A ship's captain demeaned before his crew does not forgive the pilot who consigned him to the role of onlooker and tactlessly reduced him to the rank of lieutenant; he heartily curses his foolhardiness in venturing into latitudes where the rocks and shoals were unknown to him and vows in future to sail only in well-ploughed waters.

39
- Sarah Bernhardt
The Most Popular Stage Performer of Her Time
1844 - 1923

1 My theory of life is represented by the word *will*.

2 Life is short, even for those who live for a long time, and we must live for the few who know and appreciate us, who judge and absolve us, and for whom we have the same affection and indulgence.

3 We ought to hate very rarely, as it is too fatiguing.

4 We should remain indifferent a great deal, forgive often and never forget.

5 What is best is always best.

6 All things are possible.

7 No woman need be as old as her years, but only so old as she thinks herself.

8 I accept being maimed but I refuse to remain powerless. Work is my life.

40

1 It is hard to get started and much harder to finish.

2 People feel the way they want to feel.

3 The game isn't over till it's over.

4 You can observe a lot by watching.

5 You gotta believe.

41

1 Be a Daniel. Take the vow of courage. But let the weapons of determination be coupled with the armour of justice and forgiveness.

2 If civilization is to survive, we have to learn to live together and work together - all kinds of people, all over the world.

3 I am my mother's daughter, and the drums of Africa still beat in my heart. They will not let me rest, never as long as there is a single Negro boy or girl without the chance that every human being deserves - the chance to prove his worth.

4 Our enemies must be forgiven. Our aim must be to create a world of fellowship and justice where no man's colour or religion is held against him. Our children must never lose their zeal for building a better world.

5 My love, my heart, my very life's blood flows at Bethune-Cockman College.

6 With faith you can make it.

7 Here is my legacy: I leave you LOVE; I leave you HOPE; I leave you THIRST FOR EDUCATION; I leave you FAITH; I leave you RACIAL DIGNITY; I leave you DESIRE TO LIVE HARMONIOUSLY WITH YOUR FELLOW MEN; I leave you, finally, A RESPONSIBILITY TO OUR YOUNG PEOPLE.

42

1 One of the greatest satisfactions in life comes from getting things done and knowing you have done them to the best of your ability. If you are having trouble getting yourself organized, if you want to increase your ability to think and do the things in the order of their importance, set aside one day as Self-organization day, or a definite period each week. The whole secret of freedom from anxiety over not having enough time lies not in working more hours, but in the proper planning of the hours.

2 Nobody will remember the times you struck out in the early innings if you hit a home run with bases full in the ninth.

3 Selling is the easiest job in the world if you work it hard - but the hardest job in the world if you try to work it easy.

4 Irrespective of what your age is, it is later than you think. If you are not already 40, it won't be long before you will be and once you pass 40, time goes very fast.

5 Enthusiasm is by far the biggest single factor in successful selling. If you are enthusiastic, your listener is very likely to become enthusiastic, even though you may present your ideas poorly. Without enthusiasm, your sales talk is about as dead as last year's turkey.

6 To become enthusiastic, act enthusiastic.

7 The best way of overcoming fear and developing courage and self-confidence is by speaking before groups.

8 You must keep records. Without records you have no way of knowing what you are doing wrong.

9 The most important secret of salesmanship is to find out what the other fellow wants, and then to help him to find the best way to get it.

43

- Ernest Bevin
The Dominant British Trade Union Leader of 1920s and 30s
1881 - 1951

1 You must keep everything tidy.

2 The power to negotiate is the most valuable thing that one can have.

3 I have been a driver of horses, and I have learned that there are two ways of getting a horse to go; one is to feed him, harness him well and comfortably, and you do not need a whip; the other is to starve him and use a whip. I prefer the first method.

4 Nothing exists except through the producer; that is where wealth comes from.

5 Some of the greatest geniuses and people of great managerial capacity have sprung from the ranks of the working people.

44

- Elizabeth Blackwell
The First Woman American Doctor
1821 - 1910

1 Public opinion should be made, not followed.

2 I work chiefly in principles.

3 I love freedom. I act upon it and I require it for others.

4 We must be watchmen, guardians of the life and health of our generation, so that stronger and more able generations may come after.

5 Each soul must answer to its Maker, so I work on in joyful faith.

6 It is only when we have learned to recognize that God's law for the human body is as sacred - nay, is one with - God's law for the human soul that we shall begin to understand the religion of the heart.

7 Prevention is better than cure.

8 Wasting time is much more sinful than wasting money.

45

- William Booth
The Founder of the Salvation Army
1829 - 1912

1 A man may be down, but he is never out.

2 You cannot make a man clean simply by cleaning his shirt.

3 The first vital step in saving the outcasts consists in making them feel that some decent human being cares enough for them to take an interest in the question whether they are to rise or sink.

4 While women weep, as they do now, I will fight; while children go hungry, as they do now, I will fight; while men go to prison, in and out, in and out, as they do now, I will fight; I will fight to the very end.

5 When sky falls, we shall catch Larks.

6 Go for souls, and go for the worst.

46

- Margaret Bourke-White
One of the World's Foremost Photojournalists
1906 - 1971

1 My life and my career was not an accident. It was thoroughly thought out.

2 I would not want to change any of my life.

3 I have been particularly fortunate. Even my two broken marriages and the illness have been important to my own growth and development. They brought me closer to other human beings in a way I cannot put into words.

4 Only by his action can a man make himself (his life) whole. You are responsible for what you have done and the people whom you have influenced. In the end it is only the work that counts.

5 In the beginning I did not know that I had any special ability. I did not know in which direction I was headed except that it was upward. I did not know what exactly my goal was. I did not see a fixed goal but I knew that I was progressing and that I would succeed.

6 It is harder for a woman to begin, but once she gets started she has an easier time because her accomplishments attract more attention than a man's would.

47

- Tom Bradley
The First Black Mayor of Los Angeles
Born in 1917

1 There was a time when I could not afford to buy socks and my shoes often had holes in them. I'd put cardboard in the bottom of the shoes, but the cardboard would wear out and my socks would come out flapping through the hole. I determined that when I get a job I was never going to be without an ample supply of socks. They became a symbol of my poverty. When I was in the police department I can remember every sale that was held in downtown Los Angeles and I always managed to stop by and stock up on socks; it was like a security blanket. Then one day I noticed I had about two hundred pairs.

2 I treasure more than anything else I know that bond of trust which has been established over forty-seven years of my service to the people of this city, and I want nothing to tarnish it, nothing to question it, nobody to doubt it.

3 Anybody who tries to analyze me in a simplistic way will miss the boat. I'm a very complex man in my reactions, in my emotions, and in the way I do things.

4 I get a good feeling of satisfaction out of having an impact on somebody's life.

48

- Louis Braille
The Inventor of the Braille System
1809 - 1852

1 The blind are the loneliest people in the world. Only books can free them.

2 Access to communication in the widest sense is access to knowledge. We do not need pity, nor do we need to be reminded that we are vulnerable. We must be treated as equal - and communication is the way we can bring this about.

3 Our methods of printing require a great deal of space on paper. It is necessary, therefore, to compress thought into the fewest possible words.

4 What the blind so passionately desire and expect from us is that we draw them into the great family circle of mankind where they will be but one link in the same human chain, ordinary men and women.

49

- Marlon Brando
One of the World's Most Celebrated Screen Personalities
Born in 1924

1 I am not an actor. I am a human being - hopefully a concerned and somewhat intelligent one - who occasionally acts.

2 If you want something from an audience, you give blood to their fantasies. It's the *ultimate* hustle.

3 Shaw said that thinking was the greatest of all human endeavors, but I would say that feeling is - allowing yourself to feel things, to feel love or wrath, hatred, rage.

4 There is a big bugaboo about acting; it doesn't make sense to me. Everybody is an actor; you spend your whole day acting. Everybody has suffered through moments where you're thinking and feeling one thing and not showing it. That's acting.

5 When one stops thinking to find out who one is, one has reached the end of the rope. I have spent my whole life trying to know myself. If one is interested, as I am, in the history and conduct of mankind, one should begin with the material nearest to hand - oneself. That's what Socrates and other philosophers did. But of course, it's a challenge. Man is, isn't he, afraid when face to face with himself. I am.

50

- Laura Bridgman
The First Blind-Deaf-Mute to Learn to Communicate
1829 - 1889

1 When I do not sit still you tell me that I am restless. Why can I not say I am strongless when I do not feel strong?

2 Just because a person is blind it does not mean that he cannot think.

51

- Joyce Brothers
A Brilliant Psychologist, Columnist and Talk Show Host
Born in 1928

1 The person who truly knows what he wants out of life, and who is willing to work for it, will achieve that goal.

2 We make our own fortune.

3 Happiness is a byproduct, never a goal. The person who sets out to seek happiness, never finds it.

4 Money is a delusion. It can also be a snare - a trap that will prevent you from reaching your most cherished goals.

5 On their subconscious level most mature individuals know exactly what they want out of life. The challenge lies in bringing that knowledge up to the conscious level.

6 Almost every goal you set for yourself involves learning. The ability to learn, what you need to know in a hurry, is the basic tool for getting what you want. Learn how to absorb vital information faster than the next person.

7 If you are convinced that you have a high need to know, if you honestly believe that this knowledge is going to help you get what you want, you will absorb it easily. If you approach the material in a spirit of dutiful drudgery, you will never master it properly.

8 You will learn more and faster if you settle down to work in the same room, at the same desk, at the same time, every time you study.

9 Don't allow tension to build up. Stretch and relax frequently. You burn no more than 3 or 4 calories an hour, because of the thinking involved in your studies. You don't need extra snacks. Eating interferes with your concentration.

10 Mental activity thrives in a chilly atmosphere; 60 to 65 degrees Fahrenheit is most conducive to learning.

11 The more you know, the more your knowledge interferes with what you want to learn and the more you learn, the more it interferes with what you already know.

12 The more similar material you are trying to learn at one time, the more it interferes with your learning. Any activity you engage in, after learning something, will interfere with retention. The best thing to do, if you want to remember what you have just learned, is to go to bed when you finish.

13 There is not much use climbing the ladder just part way. People who succeed in business have the single minded devotion to their goal, that is best described as total commitment. They have the ability and desire to work to top capacity.

14 If you know what it is you want out of life, all sorts of opportunities open up. Many of them open up because of inertia, other people's inertia. Everyone is basically lazy. Understand this basic weakness and resolve not to give in.

15 Think of yourself as someone who enjoys challenge, someone who knows how to get ahead, and indeed you will get ahead.

16 Concentrate on one small part of one subject and become the world's greatest authority on it. The quality of uniqueness is the key. Acquire a cluster of skills that no one else has.

17 Men and women who are confident of their abilities are more likely to succeed. Make yourself believe that you will succeed.

18 Credit buying is much like being drunk. The buzz happens immediately and it gives you a lift. The hangover comes the day after.

19 Familiarity, truly cultivated, can breed love.

20 The best of all possible marriages is a seesaw in which first one, then the other partner is dominant.

21 The best proof of love is trust.

22 Change is seductive and frightening, in equal proportions.

23 Women tend to handle change far better than men do. Men really detest change.

24 Change is growth, both intellectual and emotional. People who are open to change enjoy life far more than those who are bogged down in a static status quo.

25 A positive attitude cannot turn back the chronological clock, but it can turn back the body clock and give you more strength, more energy, better health and possibly add years to your life. A negative attitude can hasten the onset of illness, weakness and other debilities.

26 Success is a state of mind. If you want success, start thinking of yourself as a success.

27 The person interested in success has to learn to view failure as a healthy, inevitable part of the process of getting to the top.

28 The power person achieves and increases his power by getting people to do what he wants them to do by making them want to do it.

29 Work to be a power person through learning how to learn and gaining the attributes of those in power.

30 People who have power have a strong sense of commitment, a unique pace to meet their own level of energy and concentration, and the skills of manipulating other people.

31 A person must get in touch with needs and figure out how to fill them.

52

- Jimmy Brown
The Foremost Football Running Back of 1950s and 60s
Born in 1936

1 An athlete can be pretty good at everything, but not excellent at everything. I chose to lock in on running the football and catching the football. Maybe my blocking suffered in the process.

2 Great running is an art so intensely personal, no two men do it quite alike. When a cat makes a beautiful run, it's poetry and jazz. That's why no coach can make a great runner. Great runners are works of God.

3 Money only has the value of how you use it. If you use a million dollars wrongly, it would not have the value of $100,000.

4 When people die, they don't call for some money or for some things. They call for somebody.

5 Everyone should watch their personal appearance. When you don't look good, you don't feel good.

6 I like to think and run like a half back and prefer speed and shiftiness to straight-ahead power.

53

- Larry Brown
A Remarkable Football Runner of 1970s
Born in 1947

1 Nothing has ever come easy for me.

2 In football I found myself on the bottom every place I went - in high school, at Dodge City and at Kansas State. Coaches were always looking down at me and saying I was too small or too inexperienced. I always had to fight my way up from the last team.

3 When I turned professional, nobody wanted to take chance on me. The scouting reports said I was small, that I had a hearing problem, that I had a wrist operation, and that I was inexperienced as a runner and a pass receiver. The only pluses were my blocking ability and my aggressiveness. I wasn't afraid to hit anybody. Most scouts had predicted that I could possibly make a taxi squad.

4 If anybody could have foreseen all the punishments I have taken and the injuries I have suffered as pro, I don't think they would have believed I could endure them and keep playing. They probably would not have wasted even an eighth-round draft choice on me.

54

1 I was often booed by the fans of the opposing team, especially when we were on the road. On many occasions I needed police escort to get to the ground, but by focusing on my pitching, almost like a lunatic, I was able to absorb the pressure like a sponge.

55

1 Books are men of higher stature, and the only men that speak aloud for future times to hear.

2 A man in armour is his armour's slave.

3 A poor man served by thee shall make thee rich;
A sick man helped by thee shall make thee strong;
Thou shalt be served thyself by every sense
Of service which thou rendered.

4 Earth's crammed with heaven
And every common bush afire with God.

56

1 I am a poor coach of great players. I am a good coach, I think, of that ordinary guy. The walls of my office are loaded with championship pictures of people who did not have the ability to win, but did not know it.

2 Coaching for me is fun. It is my hobby. You can laugh at this, but I honestly get a thrill going out to practice. The only *working* about coaching is the things you have to do that's not coaching.

3 The great players are going to play, but the ones who are going to win for you are the ones who are not great but don't know it.

57

1 Eloquence is the poetry of prose.

2 Truth, crushed to earth, shall rise again;
The eternal years of God are hers;
But Error, wounded, writhes with pain,
And dies among his worshippers.

58

- Art Buchwald
A Master of Political Satire
Born in 1925

1 There are too many people who think they are educated because they have a diploma. They aren't. You don't get educated; you prepare yourself for an education.

2 Laughter was the weapon I used for survival. All my life I have been able to sense a person's weak spot. I use humour as a way to insult.

3 Even a depression can be beneficial. If you do not hurt yourself, you can gain tremendous insights and empathy, find inner strengths and hidden talents. It's a mysterious process, but if you can hold on, you become a wiser and better person.

59

- Ole Bull
The Greatest Violin Virtuoso of His Time
1810 - 1880

1 It is not enough to tell me my faults. You must also teach me how to rid myself of them.

2 I think it is best that the critics write against me and I play against them.

3 My mission in the world is Norwegian music; I am no painter, no sculptor, no literary man. I am a musician.

4 I hear a wonderfully deep and characteristic sound vibrating within the Norwegian breasts. It has been the goal of my life to add strings to it so that it can speak out and its sonorous tones penetrate the temple as Norway's church music bears the words of the minister to the hearts of the congregation; that on the battlefield it may remind the country's defenders of their hearthstones; that it may be heard from our orchestras, sound from pianos round the land, cultivating , ennobling the family life more than all languages of the world.

5 Art is knowing the uninterrupted expression of an enthusiastic, genial will, and the genial will always achieves its purpose.

6 The skill in handling the violin is similar to that of a master barber who trims the beard without touching the skin.

60

- John Bunyan
The Author of The Pilgrim's Progress
1628 - 1688

1 He who bestows his goods upon the poor,
Shall have as much again, and ten times more.

2 He that is down needs fear no fall,
He that is low, no pride.

3 If we have not quiet in our minds, outward comfort will do no more for us than a golden slipper on a gouty foot.

4 In prayer it is better to have a heart without words than words without a heart.

5 One leak will sink a ship, and one sin will destroy a sinner.

61
- Luther Burbank
The Wizard of Cross Breeding of Plants
1849 - 1926

1 It is well for people who think to change their minds occasionally in order to keep them clean. For those who do not think, it is best at least to rearrange their prejudices once in a while.

2 If we had paid no more attention to our plants than we have to our children, we would now be living in a jungle of weeds.

3 If you violate nature's laws you are your own prosecuting attorney, judge, jury and hangman. Nature says you must eat sanely, sleep soundly, care for your body, avoid anger and hatred, be industrious, sober and self-respecting, and if you flaunt her laws you just naturally walk right into the jail of indigestion, nervous prostration, ill-health, a bad heart, worthlessness and failure.

62
- George Burns
A Master of the One-liner and Stand-up Comedy
1896 - 1996

1 You should retire only when you can find something you enjoy doing more than what you are doing now.

2 When you work too hard at a business you get tired; and when you get tired you get grouchy; and when you get grouchy you start fighting; and when you start fighting you are out of business.

3 It's fun to look back, if there isn't something cuter in front of you.

4 Our ability to bounce back from what might seem like the end of the world is absolutely amazing. And age has nothing to do with it. Whether you are 18 or 80, and whether you like it or not, you are going to go on living.

5 Whatever line of work you get into, or whatever you do, make sure it's something you love, something you enjoy doing. If you can accomplish this, you are bound to be successful.

6 The secret of feeling young is to make every day count for something.

7 I had a happy childhood. I thought everyone in the world was shining shoes. I did not think that I was the only one doing that.

8 By the time you are eighty years old you have learned everything; you only have to remember it.

9 I would rather be a failure in something that I love than a success in something that I don't.

63

1 If I were to name three most precious resources of life, I should say books, friends and nature; and the greatest of these, at least the most constant and always at hand, is nature.

2 I go to books and to nature as a bee goes to the flower, for a nectar that I can make into my own honey.

3 Nature teaches more than she preaches. There are no sermons in stones. It is easier to get a spark out of a stone than a moral.

4 Time does not become sacred to us until we have lived it.

5 It is always easier to believe than to deny. Our minds are naturally affirmative.

6 I was born with a chronic anxiety about the weather.

7 Writing is an unnatural business. It makes your head hot and your feet cold and it stops the digesting of your food.

8 Science I fold my hand and wait,
Nor care for wind or tide nor sea;
I have no more 'gainst time or fate
For lo! my own shall come to me.

9 Blessed is the man who has some congenial work, some occupation in which he can put his heart and which affords a complete outlet to all the forces there are in him.

10 I have enough to eat and wear, and time to see how beautiful the world is, and to enjoy it.

11 The secret of happiness is something to do.

12 The lure of the distant and the difficult is deceptive. The great opportunity is where you are.

64

1 The more I study religions the more I am convinced that man never worshipped anything but himself.

2 Morality, like consciousness, is both geographical and chronological; but strange and unpleasant truths progress slowly.

3 There are indeed only two efficacious forms of punishment all the world over, corporal for the poor and fines for the rich, the latter being the severer form.

4 Theologians everywhere and at all times delight in burdening human nature. Every race creates its own Deity after the fashion of itself. The heaven of all faiths, including Spiritualism, the latest development, is only an earth more or less glorified even as the Deity is humanity more or less perfected.

5 Women, all over the world, are what men make them.

6 Do what thy manhood bids thee do,
From none but self expect applause;
He noblest lives and noblest dies
Who makes and keeps his self-made laws.

65

- Leo Buscaglia
The Pioneer Advocate of the Power of Love
Born in 1925

1 Creating saints of our departed loved ones can help us to fill the void and make the parting better.

2 Acceptance and understanding can be expected only from the strong.

3 Don't waste time trying to reason with pain, suffering, life and death.

4 People are good if you give them a chance to be.

5 Cruelty is a sign of weakness.

6 Commitment and caring are the basic ingredients of love.

7 Love is indestructible and therefore the most powerful force.

8 People who think they know it all can be dangerous.

9 Death is a challenge. It tells us not to waste time. It tells us to tell each other right now that we love each other.

10 There are two big forces at work, external and internal. We have very little control over external forces such as tornadoes, earthquakes, floods, disasters, illness and pain. What really matters is the internal force. How do I respond to those disasters? Over that I have complete control.

11 We are no longer puppets being manipulated by outside powerful forces; we become the powerful force ourselves.

12 The fact that I can plant a seed and it becomes a flower, share a bit of knowledge and it becomes another's, smile at someone and receive a smile in return, are to me continual spiritual exercises.

13 If we wish to free ourselves from enslavement, we must choose freedom and the responsibility this entails.

14 Love is life, and if you miss love, you miss life.

15 Time has no meaning in itself unless we choose to give it significance.

66

- Richard Evelyn Byrd
Spent Five Months' Winter Alone Near South Pole
1888 - 1957

1 Few men during their lifetime come anywhere near exhausting the resources dwelling within them. There are deep wells of strength that are never used.

2 It is by struggle that we progress.

3 Give wind and tide a chance to change.

4 A man does not attend wisdom until he recognizes that he is no longer indispensable.

5 It was Jules Verne who really inspired me to go for the Poles.

6 Real peace comes from struggle that involves such things as effort, discipline, enthusiasm. This is also the way to strength. An inactive peace may lead to sensuality and flabbiness, which are discordant. It is often necessary to fight to lessen discord. This is a paradox.

67 - Michael Caine
Rose from Butcher Shop to International Celebrity
Born in 1933

1 I sweated blood for ten years in the theater and television and made an average of fourteen dollars a week.

2 When I was trying to get a leg up as an actor, I was shot down many times.

3 If I work fast enough, pack enough pictures in, I will be a star before anyone realizes I'm not a star material.

4 To be a movie star, you have to invent yourself.

5 There are secrets so close to you that they can alter the very foundations on which you have built your life.

68 - Mary Calderone
A Pioneer of Sex Education in American Schools
Born in 1904

1 Through all my career I've worked very slowly, taking small but strongly professional steps. I tried never to say something that I could not back or that's not based on research. I know who my authorities are and never claim to be one myself.

2 I have done everything I have done with as much honesty and integrity as I could manage - and I really like that in myself. It makes me feel I have lived up to myself, to the best in me, which is what has been expected of me by the people who went before me - my father, my teachers, the people who have loved me.

3 Each one of us is a unique sexual person. No one else in the world has had, or can have, the same exact combination of heredity, prebirth experience and learning and experience after birth. So, value yourself as a unique sexual person, and learn to be that person in the best way possible for you and those who love you.

4 Talent is something you have to share.

69

1 If I had measured my conception of success by the amount of money to be earned as a writer, rather than by a self-imposed standard of significant storytelling, I would have had good reason to abandon forever writing as an occupation. Somewhere along the way I had acquired the belief that it was best for me not to consider writing as a means of making money but instead to produce fiction that would be worthy of recompense.

2 Waiting, ever waiting, was an ordeal I probably imposed upon myself so as to generate enough fortitude and stamina to be able to endure the consequences of trying to become a published writer.

3 My goal from the beginning has been to be a writer of fiction that revealed with all my might the inner spirit of men and women as they responded to the joys of life and reacted to the sorrows of existence.

4 You have to create luck. It doesn't come to you. You have to recognize an opportunity, and when you see it, you foster it in some way. You use it as a springboard to something better or something higher.

5 I was always willing to undergo hardship or whatever it took to be able to stay with my work. I can eliminate anything in life that's going to interfere with what I am trying to do.

6 I am really not interested in what someone else would advise me to do. I like to take my own advice. I am sort of independent. I don't belong to a league.

7 Don't talk about your writing. It's better to let your writing speak for you.

8 I am a storyteller. The only sensationalism I'm after is to tell a sensationally good story.

70

1 Only a happy bird can sing.

2 The higher we go, the more is expected of us and the harder we must work.

3 I believe in preparation and in waiting for things. Money and success come much sooner if you are not in a big rush.

4 I try to impart to my students things that come to me naturally, and that may not be natural to others.

71

1 A man's life has a lot to do with his spirit.

2 There is a bit of the little boy in every good ballplayer.

3 I remember when I played not one game, not two games, but three games in a day, and all I got was a dollar and fifty.

72

- Glen Campbell
The Rhinestone Cowboy and Singer
Born in 1938

1 No matter how dire the circumstances, with faith and fortitude you can overcome them.

2 For every star in a show business there are a hundred people behind the scenes. Many of the folks behind the curtain are as important or more important than the celebrity out front, but the anonymous workers are often unrecognized by the famous.

3 Nothing can disarm a performer more than having something go wrong before he goes on stage.

4 Many miracles happen gradually, not instantly.

73

- Charles Camsell
The Greatest Authority of Canada's Northland
1876 - 1958

1 Geological notebooks, while useful to a degree, are a disappointing source for material of human interest. They contain primarily observations of scientific nature.

2 Explain it how you will, men - and also women - who have once tasted the life of the North never seem to be fully satisfied elsewhere.

74

- Chester Carlson
The Inventor of the Dry Photocopying Process
1906 - 1968

1 The most pleasure we get from life is sweating.

2 I would like to die a poor man.

3 I am not the father of the 914 as people generally call me. I am simply the midwife. I am not an inventor. I understand what is required to take a product that is a concept and help make that product a commercial reality.

1 Every noble work is at first impossible.

2 Blessed is the man who has found his work. Let him ask for no other blessedness.

3 Even in the meanest sorts of Labour, the whole soul of a man is composed into a kind of real harmony the instant he sets himself to work.

4 Our grand business is not to see what lies dimly in the distance, but to do what lies clearly at hand.

5 Endurance is patience concentrated.

6 A man without a purpose is like a ship without a rudder.

7 It is in general more profitable to reckon up our defects than to boast of our attainments.

8 The goal of yesterday will be the starting point of tomorrow.

9 A great man shows his greatness by the way he treats little men.

10 All that mankind has done, thought, gained or been, is lying as in magic preservation in the pages of books. They are the chosen possession of men.

11 In books lies the soul of the whole Past Time; the articulate audible voice of the Past, when the body and material substance of it has altogether vanished like a dream.

12 Blessings upon Cadmus, the Phoenicians, or whoever it was that invented books.

13 My books are friends that never fail me.

14 The history of the world is but the biography of great men.

15 Experience is the best of schoolmasters, only the school-fees are heavy.

16 No man lives without jostling and being jostled. In all ways he has to elbow himself through the world, giving and receiving offense.

17 Sincerity is the first characteristic of all men in any way heroic. All the great men I have ever heard of have sincerity as the primary material of them.

18 Before we censure a man for seeming what he is not, we should be sure that we know what he is.

19 The lightning spark of thought, generated in the solitary mind, awakens its likeness in another mind.

20 Silence is the element in which great things fashion themselves together.

21 Silence is more eloquent than words.

22 Silence is deep as Eternity; speech is shallow as Time.

23 I don't like to talk much with people who always agree with me. It is amusing to coquette with an echo for a little while, but one soon tires of it.

24 Make yourself an honest man, and then you may be sure that there is one fewer rascal in the world.

25 Earnestness alone makes the eternity.

26 Wondrous is the strength of cheerfulness, and its power of endurance. The cheerful man will do more in the same time, will do it better, will preserve it longer, than the sad or sullen.

27 Ill health, of body or mind, is defeat, Health alone is victory. Let all men, if they can manage it, contrive to be healthy.

28 The man who cannot laugh is not only fit for treason, stratagems and spoils, but his whole life is already a treason and a stratagem.

29 No man who has once heartily and wholly laughed can be altogether irreclaimably bad.

30 Debt is a bottomless sea.

31 Man is a tool-using animal.

32 Love is ever the beginning of knowledge, as fire is of light.

33 Clever men are good, but they are not the best.

34 The work an unknown good man has done is like a vein of water flowing hidden underground, secretly making the ground green.

35 The eternal stars shine as soon as it is dark enough.

36 The greatest of faults, I should say, is to be conscious of none.

37 The weakest living creature, by concentrating his powers on a single object, can accomplish something; whereas the strongest, by dispersing his over many, may fail to accomplish anything.

38 A man must get his happiness out of his work. Without work that he enjoys, he can never know what happiness is.

39 The king is the man who can.

40 Let each become all that he was created capable of being.

76

- Dale Carnegie
A Pioneer of Public Speaking Training
1888 - 1955

1 Don't try to be like anyone else. Just try to be like you.

2 One of the most tragic things I know about human nature is that all of us tend to put off living. We are all dreaming of some magical rose garden over the horizon, instead of enjoying the roses that are blooming outside our windows today.

3 If you do not feel like smiling, just force yourself to smile. If you are alone, force yourself to whistle or hum a tune or sing. Act as if you were already happy, and that will tend to make you happy.

4 You can make more friends in two months by becoming interested in other people than you can in two years by trying to get other people interested in you.

5 The royal road to a man's heart is to talk to him about the things he treasures most.

6 Criticism is futile because it puts a man on the defensive, and usually makes him strive to justify himself. Criticism is dangerous, because it wounds a man's precious pride, hurts his sense of importance, and arouses his resentment.

7 In dealing with people, let us remember we are not dealing with creatures of logic. We are dealing with creatures bustling with prejudices and motivated by pride and vanity.

8 The only way to get the best of an argument is to avoid it.

9 The difference between appreciation and flattery is that one is sincere while the other is insincere. One comes from the heart out, the other from the teeth out. One is unselfish, the other selfish. One is universally admired, the other is universally condemned.

10 It is the way we react to circumstances that determines our feeling.

11 Develop success from failures. Discouragement and failure are two of the surest stepping stones to success. No other element can do so much for a man if he is willing to study them and make capital out of them.

12 You never achieve real success unless you like what you are doing.

13 The successful man will profit from his mistakes and try again in a different way.

14 Do the thing you fear to do and keep on doing it; that is the quickest and surest way ever discovered to conquer fear.

15 There is only one way to get anybody to do anything; and that is by making the other person want to do it.

16 We all have possibilities we don't know about. We can do things we don't even dream we can.

77

- Wallace Hume Carothers
The Inventor of Synthetic Fibers
1896 - 1937

1 I never left a task unfinished or done in a careless manner. For me to begin a task was to complete it.

2 If I had to start over, I would devote my life to music.

78

- Rachel Carson
The Pioneer Crusader Against the Dangers of Chemical Pesticides
1907 - 1964

1 Man cannot control or change the ocean as, in his brief tenancy of earth, he has subdued and plundered the continents. In the artificial world of cities and towns, he often forgets the true nature of his planet and the long vistas of its history, in which the existence of the race of men has occupied a mere moment of time.

2 It is a wholesome and necessary thing for us to turn again to the earth and in the contemplation of her beauties to know the sense of wonder and humility.

3 Conservation is a cause that has no end. There is no point at which we will say, "our work is finished".

4 The balance of nature is built of a series of interrelationships between living things and between living things and their environment. This does not mean that we must not attempt to tilt that balance in our favour; but when we do make this attempt, we must know what we are doing. We must know the consequences.

5 A writer's occupation is one of the loneliest in the world and so I believe that only the person who knows and is not afraid of loneliness should aspire to be a writer.

6 If there is poetry in my book about the sea, it is not because I deliberately put it there but because one could not write truthfully about the sea and leave out the poetry.

7 There is one quality that characterizes all of us who deal with the sciences of the earth and its life - we are never bored. We can't. Every mystery solved brings us to the threshold of a greater one.

8 If I had influence with the good fairy who is supposed to preside over the christening of all children, I should ask that her gift to each child in the world be a sense of wonder so indestructible that it would last throughout life.

9 The pleasures of contact with the natural world are available to anyone who will place himself under the influence of a lonely mountain top - or the sea - or the stillness of a forest, or who will stop to think about so small a thing as the mystery of a growing seed.

79
- Henry Cartier-Bresson
The Master of the Expressive Documentary Photography
Born in 1908

1 I want to prove nothing, demonstrate nothing. Things and beings speak sufficiently.

2 To take a photograph is to recognize a fact in a split-second and to organize with vigor usually perceived forms which express and signify it. It means lining up brain, eye and heart for the purpose of taking aim at the target.

3 Technology levels individuals. Amateur find themselves solitary, unrecognized; professionals enter into the law of the jungle. One might almost say that now only children are still able to express themselves spontaneously.

80
- Enrico Caruso
One of the Greatest Operatic Tenors of All Time
1873 - 1921

1 The requisites of a singer - a big chest, a big mouth, 90 per cent memory, 10 per cent intelligence, lots of hard work, and something in the heart.

2 I always try to give my best in interpreting a part. I know that I am a singer and an actor but I give an impression of being neither but a real man conceived by the composer.

3 The difficulty does not lie in achieving perfection but in keeping it. As soon an artist achieves the pinnacle of his success, when he is at the top of his ladder, he is haunted by the terrible question - when will he start to go down? When will he fall? I can never take a step upon the stage without asking myself that.

4 I have been compared with the greatest artists; I have worked to become one of them. I don't believe I ever felt satisfied with a performance, no matter how much praise it brought; I always had the wish to make what I had done a little better the next time I tried, so I studied and practiced, and thought a good deal about everything connected with my art.

81

- Johnny Cash
A Famous Country Singer and Guitarist
Born in 1932

1 The longer I took pills, the more unpredictable and violent I got. My friends began to avoid me. I lost sight of my obligation to my audience.

2 There comes a time in every man's life when he realizes the need to try to accomplish one thing that will say to the world, "This is the best I had to offer. This is me. This is what I'd like my life to say."

3 I know that I must try to let a good light shine and try to live my daily life with charity and tolerance for those whose lives I touch, whether saint or sinner.

4 When you stand with Him, you must renew the stand daily; you must daily be on guard; the hounds of hell are not going to stop snapping at your heels. The devil and his demons aren't going to give up on you as long as they can find a vulnerable spot once in a while.

5 By doing a prison concert we were letting inmates know that somewhere out there in the free world there was somebody who cared for them as human beings.

6 The more mountains I am climbing, the more I enjoy the view from the top.

7 Daddy taught us many things, but the most important lesson was that hard work is good for you.

8 I am going to be true not only to those who believe in me and depend on me, but to myself and to God.

9 It all comes down to charity. It's the same old lesson: you gain by giving.

10 Beware that you brag about standing, lest you fall.

11 I must pity those who say they don't believe in God. Even the devil believes in God.

12 I hope that if I'm ever arrested for being a Christian, there'll be enough evidence to convict me.

13 The hard times, the torture and misery I put myself through, made me know pain and gave me tolerance and compassion for other people's problems.

14 You don't have to have lived in poverty in order to become a successful country singer, but it helps.

82

- Mary Cassatt
The Most Distinguished Woman Painter of Her Time
1847 - 1926

1 For me art is as essential as breathing.

2 In art what we want is the certainty that the one spark of original genius shall not be extinguished; that is better than average excellence, that is what will survive, what it is essential to foster.

3 How we try for happiness, poor things, and how we don't find it; the best cure is hard work - if only one has the health for it.

83

- Carrie Chapman Catt
The Founder of the League of Women Voters
1859 - 1947

1 When a just cause reaches its flood tide, whatever stands in the way must fall before its overwhelming power.

2 No written law has ever been more binding than unwritten custom supported by popular opinion.

3 Civilization is not produced by a single movement. It is rather a fabric woven of many threads each of which is necessary to its perfection. I do not feel that I want to pull on every thread. Each person must work for personally important causes; no one person or organization could accomplish everything.

4 What others endure, you can bear to know about.

5 A pacifist usually believes in defense. Aggression and defense may be interpreted to mean the other. Patriotism, that reverential love of home, flag and country, is flaunted to cover the fact that young men must kill other young men in its name. There is no book on defense that reveals the truth; a book that will clearly define when defense is defense and when it is aggression is needed. Apparently, no one yet knows the facts clearly enough to write that book.

6 Don't get frightened; think. Don't be intimidated; act.

84

- Miguel de Cervantes
The Creator of Don Quixote
1547 - 1616

1 The brave man carves out his fortune, and every man is the son of his own works.

2 Make it thy business to know thyself, which is the most difficult lesson in the world.

3 Never stand begging for that which you have the power to earn.

4 Tell me thy company and I will tell thee what thou art.

5 Make hay while the sun shines.

6 There is a time for some things, and a time for all things; a time for great things, and a time for small things.

7 Be slow of tongue and quick of eye.

8 A little in one's own pocket is better than much in another man's purse. It's good to keep a nest-egg. Every little makes a mickle.

9 A bird in the hand is worth two in the bush.

10 He preaches well who lives well.

11 Rome was not built in a day.

12 He who sings, frightens away his ills.

13 Every tooth in a man's head is more valuable than a diamond.

14 Forewarned, forearmed; to be prepared is half the victory.

15 The pen is the tongue of the mind.

16 One swallow never makes a summer.

17 The road is better than the inn.

18 No fathers or mothers think their children ugly; and this self-deceit is yet stronger with respect to the offspring of the mind.

19 Honesty is the best policy.

20 No man is more than another unless he does more than another.

21 Time ripens all things; no man is born wise.

22 The best sauce in the world is hunger.

85
- Marc Chagall
The First Living Artist to be Exhibited at the Louvre
1887 - 1985

1 What is essential is not to know everything, but to pulse with life's touch, not to oppose daily actions - which are often the most moving - with a scornful spirit.

2 Our whole inner world is reality - perhaps more real than the apparent world.

3 My pictures are painted collections of inner images which possess me.

4 When I was a small boy, I searched the heavens for a miracle. Since then I tried to find the miracle through my art.

5 Only the upright heart that has its own logic and its own reason is free.

86
- Wilt Chamberlain
The Breaker of More NBA Records Than Any Other Player
Born in 1936

1 Everything is habit forming, so make sure what you do is what you want to be doing.

2 Commonsense costs nothing, but if you use it you can make a mint.

3 The choosing of friends is the single most important thing one can do to enhance

one's well-being and help in leading oneself toward an honest, worthwhile and productive life.

4 Of all our faculties the most important one is our ability to imagine.

5 Compassion, goodwill, common sense, understanding and love are just a few of the things in life that are free. Use them.

6 People only see what they want to see.

7 The busier I am, the more projects I am able to take on and complete. When I am in one of those lazy moods and doing nothing, I can't find time to do anything.

8 We learn to act through our associations - observing, absorbing, then simulating the actions that appeal to us - and therefore our friends play a great role in determining what we become.

9 We are shaped by who we meet.

87

- Coco Chanel
A Revolutionary Fashion Designer
1883 - 1971

1 Until a fashion becomes popular, it is not a fashion but an eccentricity.

2 There are people who have money and people who are rich.

3 Adornment is never anything except a reflection of the heart.

4 Nature gives you the face you have at 20; it is up to you to merit the face you have at 50.

5 There is no time for cut-and-dried monotony. There is time for work and time for love. That leaves no other time.

6 Women are not flowers. Why should they want to smell like flowers?

7 He who does not enjoy his own company is usually right.

88

- Charlie Chaplin
Cinema's Most Celebrated Comedian-Director
1889 - 1977

1 Do not fear confrontation. Even when planets collide, out of the chaos comes the birth of a star.

2 Every art contributes to the biggest art of all - the art of living.

3 You have to believe in yourself, that's the secret. I had that exuberance that comes from utter confidence in yourself.

4 It is desire that creates something desirable. But if the world and I don't get along together, then the world must change.

5 There are more valid facts and details in works of art than there are in history books.

6 When you are alone, you are in good company.

7 I get shy when I don't know how to do something very well.

8 As I get older, I am more and more preoccupied with faith. You cannot practice art without religion.

9 In the end, everything is a gag.

10 I went into the business for the money, and the art grew out of it.

89

- Cesar Chavez
The Organizer of the First Effective Union of Farm Workers
1927 - 1993

1 Whatever you do, and no matter what reasons you may give to others, you do it because you want to see it done.

2 We shall overcome.

3 I would feel complimented if you called me a fanatic. The only ones who make things change are fanatics. If you are not a fanatic around here, you can't cut it.

4 You must stay with one thing and just hammer away, hammer away and it will happen.

5 Wherever I went, I saw problems, but no matter what happened, I learned.

90

- Anton Chekhov
A Foremost Playwright and Master of the Short-story
1860 - 1904

1 When one longs for a drink, it seems as though one could drink a whole ocean - that is faith; but when one begins to drink one can drink altogether two glasses - that is science.

2 Man is what he believes.

3 Everything in this world is beautiful except what we think and what we do once we forget life's superior aims and our human dignity.

4 I believe that closeness to Nature and leisure are the two elements indispensable for happiness - without them, happiness is impossible.

5 Everything I have written will be forgotten in a few years. But the paths I have traced will remain intact and secure, and there lies my only merit.

91

- Maurice Chevalier
The Most Popular French Entertainer of 20th Century
1888 - 1972

1 The women you kiss either lick you or stab you.

2 I wasn't cut out to be an artist.

3 Old age isn't so bad when you consider the alternative.

4 Love the public the way you love your mother.

92

1 I don't think necessity is the mother of invention. Invention, in my opinion, arises directly from idleness, possibly also from laziness - to save oneself trouble.

2 It is often difficult for persons who are themselves not imaginative writers to appreciate that writing an abridged version of a book conceived by an imaginative author is equivalent to mutilating his or her brain child, and this cannot be expected to give an author any satisfaction, no matter how keenly the operation and excision is performed.

3 A detective story is the direct successor of the old Morality Play. It is the triumph of good over evil - the deliverance of the innocent from the aggressor - that is what makes it exciting.

4 Idealism can arise from antagonism to injustice and to crass materialism - and is fed more and more by a desire to destroy. Those who get to love violence for its own sake will never become adults. They are fixed in their own retarded development.

5 I had a disastrous childhood. A lonely, heartbreaking, no-one-wanted-me kind of growing up.

6 An archeologist is the best husband any woman can have; the older she gets the more interested he is in her.

7 I have always believed in writing without a collaborator, because where two people are writing the same book, each believes he gets all the worry and only half the royalties.

93

1 No matter how proud I feel because the enterprise bears the name of Chrysler, I never fool myself that I did all this. Any great industrial corporation lives and grows only through the devoted services of many minds and talents pooled in a common effort.

2 There is no such thing as a big job. Any job, regardless of size, can be broken down into a number of small jobs which, when done, complete the larger job.

3 Nothing in my life has given me more cause for pride and satisfaction than my wife's faith in me through those years when I was a grease-stained roundhouse mechanic.

94

1 A man who has to be convinced to act before he acts is not a man of action.

2 Freedom is nothing in the world but the opportunity for self-discipline.

3 Winner is the man who can believe for a quarter of an hour longer than his enemy that he is not beaten.

4 War is too serious matter to be left to the generals.

5 I have been misunderstood by my own family, betrayed by my friends, abandoned by my party, ignored by the voters, suspected by my country. I have nothing left, nothing, nothing, nothing.

6 It is far easier to make war than to make peace.

95

1 I would forget to eat because of baseball.

2 All season, every season, every game I give everything I have to this game.

3 A manager is like a parent and he must never go against his players.

4 A man takes his childhood with him into his adult life.

96

1 My father never got to see me play. But I knew he was watching me, and I never let him down.

2 Baseball is not unlike a war. It is a game of matching trick against trick and of making opponents tremble with fear before they could make him tremble. In such a game, the base runner has the right of way and the man who blocks it does it at his own peril.

3 I never wagered on a game in my life, not even on our own club. I never liked horse races or prize fights on account of the betting angle.

4 When you get older, you wish for companionship. I was just a loner; I couldn't have that with my children.

5 To get along with me - don't increase my tension.

6 If you are .000 the first two times, you still have two chances left. It's simple to see that you can still be a .500 hitter in that game. That is, if you bear extra hard on those remaining chances.

7 My batting eye was almost as dependable as ever, but the legs wouldn't carry me around with speed and timing. Old wounds ached constantly. I literally had

to grit my teeth and force myself to run when the chance arose to bunt and beat it out, or stretch a single into a double. Luckily, I got out with no serious injuries.

8 You cannot eat baseball and sleep baseball and study baseball year after year and then just stop like that. It's in the bloodstream. You crave it. You can't get along without it.

9 After you give the pitcher the sign, reach down and grab a handful of dirt, as if you are drying off sweat. Now just before the ball gets to the plate, drop the dirt on the batter's feet. It will distract him just enough to make him flinch and take his eye off the ball.

97 - Jacqueline Cochran
The First Woman to Fly Supersonic
1912 - 1980

1 A formula for success has many components. It's never precisely the same mixture. And a drop of luck can substitute for a dash of opportunity. But in every well-balanced recipe for success, you will probably find honesty, determination, some skill and experience, as well as a lot of courage.

2 To live without risk, for me, would have been tantamount to death.

3 Given time enough, everything seems to come out right.

4 Happiness is a relative thing. A mangy cur with fleas in his fur will be happy and contented when the fleas are removed. But a Fido the Great may sulk until he gets his homogenized milk and ground porterhouse steak. Then he is happy too. But who is happier? The flea-free mutt or the well-fed Fido?

5 No one gets more nervous than a pilot when things are going wrong and he isn't at the controls.

6 What I have done, others can do also.

98 - Gabrielle Colette
One of the Most Famous French Women Writers of Her Day
1873 - 1954

1 What we write comes true.

2 Whether you are dealing with an animal or a child, to convince is to weaken.

3 You will do foolish things, but do them with enthusiasm.

99 - Christopher Columbus
The Discoverer of America
1451 - 1506

1 I would rather take a willing coward than an unwilling criminal.

2 I will continue until I find them.

3 Today we sailed West because that was our destination.

4 I have served their Highnesses with as great diligence and love as I might have employed to win paradise and more; and if in somewhat I have been wanting, that was impossible, or much beyond my knowledge and strength. God in such cases asketh nothing more of men than goodwill.

100

- Nadia Comaneci
The First Gymnast to Score a Perfect 10 in Olympics
Born in 1961

1 Pressure is a part of the game for all top athletes, in all sports, as it is for people at the top in any walk of life.

2 There is nothing wrong with children being encouraged to develop skills and talents - it is only when they are forced into something, whether out of motives of nationalistic or parental ambition, that we should worry.

3 Success in any sport, and I suppose in life itself, is all about confidence; recognize your limitations by all means, but work away at trying to push them further back all the time. It is unbelievable what can be achieved if you only try. Aim for the impossible. Failure is always easiest to bear when you know in yourself that you have given your best, and maybe a little extra.

4 A degree of risk is inherent in most sports and if a ban was placed on every sport that endangers life and limb, there won't be many left. All that can be done is to try and prevent any unnecessary risk creeping into the sport.

5 I owe a great deal to my country, for allowing me to pursue my chosen sport. I have worked very hard for my achievements, but without the enthusiasm and support of a dedicated gymnastics administration it's quite likely my talents would have gone unfulfilled.

6 I am not nearly as cool and unflappable as many people tend to believe.

7 One of the sad things about competing is that you miss almost everything else that is going on in the hall. Total concentration is required throughout the time that you are in the arena, so you are unaware of other athletes' performances. One momentary lapse can cost you a lot.

8 At the top level of many sports, gymnastics included, the psychological demands are greater than the physical. Single-minded determination and total self-control give you the edge in a close fight.

101

- Maureen Connolly
The Winner of the Grand Slam of Tennis at Age 19!
1934 - 1969

1 All I ever see is my opponent. You could set off dynamite in the next court and I would not notice.

102

1 The mind of man is capable of anything - because everything is in it, all the past as well as all the future.

2 We live, as we dream - alone.

3 There is no rest for the messenger till the message is delivered.

4 Only in men's imagination does every truth find an effective and undeniable existence. Imagination, not invention, is the supreme master of art as of life.

5 Vanity plays lurid tricks with our memory.

6 A man's real life is that accorded to him in the thoughts of other men by reason of respect or natural love.

7 No woman is ever completely deceived.

103

1 Nothing in the world can take the place of persistence. Talent will not; nothing is more common than unsuccessful men with talent. Genius will not; unrewarded genius is almost a proverb. Education will not; the world is full of educated derelicts. Persistence and determination alone are omnipotent. The slogan *Press on* has solved and always will solve the problem of the human race.

2 If you see 10 troubles coming down the road, you can be sure that 9 will run into the ditch before they reach you.

3 All growth depends upon activity. There is no development physically or intellectually without effort, and effort means work. Work is not a curse; it is the prerogative of intelligence, the only means to manhood, and the measure of civilization.

4 Few men are lacking in capacity, but they fail because they are lacking in application.

5 No person was ever honoured for what he received. Honour has been the reward for what he gave.

6 There is no dignity quite so impressive, and no independence quite so important, as living within your means.

7 The man who saves is the man who wins.

8 I am for economy. After that I am for more economy.

9 I have never been hurt by anything I did not say.

10 After order and liberty, economy is one of the highest essentials of a free government. Economy is always a guarantee of peace.

11 The people cannot look to legislation for success. Industry, thrift, character are not conferred by act or resolve. Government cannot relieve from toil. It can provide no substitute for the rewards of service.

12 We do not need more intellectual power; we need more spiritual power. We do not need more of the things that are seen; we need more of the things that are unseen.

13 No enterprise can exist for itself alone. It ministers to some great need, it performs some great service, not for itself, but for others; or failing therein, it ceases to be profitable and ceases to exist.

14 Knowledge comes, but wisdom lingers. It may not be difficult to store up in the mind a vast quantity of facts within a comparatively short time, but the ability to form judgments requires the severe discipline of hard work and the tempering heat of experience and maturity.

104

- Gary Cooper
A Foremost American Screen Hero
1901 - 1962

1 The only achievement I am really proud of is the friends I have made in this community.

2 I have taken acting seriously. I'm not very good. You've got to have a fire under you. When you're new, a beginner, you've got a fire under you all the time. Now when I read stories, I try to keep in mind whether or not it would sell at the box office. Pictures run in cycles. I like to do something different not to startle the world with an artistic floperoo. I just want to do something that isn't running in any other theater.

3 I have no regrets. It's been full and rich, a wonderful life. The choices I've made in my personal life haven't always been the happiest ones, but they were, in retrospect, the right ones.

105

- James Fenimore Cooper
The First Successful American Novelist
1789 - 1851

1 Society cannot exist without wholesome restraints.

2 I owe all my success to a steady mind, a sober judgment, fortitude, perseverance and, above all, common sense.

3 Choice supposes a preference, and preference inequality of merit or of fitness.

4 Individuality is the aim of political liberty.

5 I care nothing for criticism, but am not indifferent to slander.

6 The public press is a power for life or death of a nation.

106

- Peter Cooper
The Builder of the First US Steam Locomotive Tom Thumb
1791 - 1883

1 The Wheel of fortune is turned by common sense applied to common events.
2 I have always recognized that the object of business is to make money in an honourable manner.
3 There is no peace to the wicked.

107

- Nicolaus Copernicus
The Founder of Modern Astronomy
1473 - 1543

1 All important matters take time. It took several hundred years for the Ten Commandments to develop into the Sermon on the Mount.
2 My greatest joy in planting is not to pluck my own fruits but to provide them for others.
3 The voice of reason is heard, not in the thunder or the whirlwind, but in the quieter moments of life. Noise is painful and people try to forget it as soon as possible after it subsides.
4 People usually fear things they cannot comprehend.
5 It is the part of wisdom to seek the truth.
6 One must have a universal mind. One must see the world as a united whole and not as conglomeration of divided parts. The scientist who would examine the various phenomena individually, without regard to the order and close dependency among them, might be compared to an artist who would borrow fragments, such as hands and feet and other parts of the body which, though truly painted by a master's hand, represented different bodies: and these incongruous fragments, when put together, would rather fit the picture of a monster than that of a man.
7 The basic pattern of the universe is not war, but peace.
8 Most of our arrogance, including my own, is due to our ignorance. And most of our ignorance is due to the brevity of our life. We die when we have just begun to learn, and before we have had a chance to evaluate our own little contribution to the wisdom of the world.

108

- Ezra Cornell
The Founder of Western Telegraph Union & Cornell University
1807 - 1874

1 Wealth is only a means to useful ends.
2 The first step towards improvement is to find out our present position.
3 It is not the fact of an animal being recorded in the herd book that gives him value, but the character of the pedigree there recorded. The book of nature is a good authority, but is not proof against the art and intrigue of man.

109

- Bill Cosby
The First Black Actor in a Weekly TV Dramatic Series
Born in 1937

1 A father's job is not to get tired of. A father has to keep hanging around and loving and knowing that his baby needs guidance because her own rudder hasn't started working yet. Keep trying and keep having patience. That is fatherhood.

2 No matter how hopeless or copeless a father maybe, his role is simply to *be* there.

3 Raising children is an incredibly hard and risky business in which no cumulative wisdom is gained; each generation repeats the mistakes the previous one made.

4 No matter how much money you have, you will never be able to buy your kids everything they want. The great American trap is trying to make a child happy by buying something.

5 No matter what you tell your child to do, he will always do the opposite. Even though your kids will consistently do the exact opposite of what you tell them to do, you have to keep loving them just as much.

6 Nothing is harder for a parent than getting your kids to do the right thing. Although we try hard to inspire our kids to do good work on their own, the motivation for such work always has to come from inside them; and if the kids really don't want to study, don't want to achieve, then we must not feel guilty; we are not at fault.

7 Forget about the celebrities. We are not gods; we are not perfect and we have our problems.

8 The only reason we had children was to give them love and wisdom and then freedom. But it's a package deal: the first two have to lead to the third.

9 In order to be regarded as an individual, rather than a representative of a race, one must first be that individual.

110

- Norman Cousins
One of America's Remarkable Journalists
1915 - 1990

1 The starting point for a better world is the belief that it is possible. Civilization begins in the imagination. The wild dream is the first step to reality. Visions and ideas are potent only when they are shared. Until then, they are merely a form of daydreaming.

2 The management of our natural resources begins with the management of our human resources.

3 To talk about the need for perfection in man is to talk about the need for another species. The essence of man is imperfection. Imperfection and blazing contradictions - between mixed good and evil, altruism and selfishness, cooperativeness and combativeness, optimism and fatalism, affirmation and negation.

4 Death is not the greatest loss in life. The greatest loss is what dies inside us while we live.

111

1 Sometimes we are lucky enough to know that our lives have been changed. It happened to me that summer's day when my eyes opened to the world beneath the surface of the sea.

2 I am obstinate, when I have something in mind. I make a list of things I would like to play with: the Amazon, Haiti, the windship. I try, and I don't get the money. I try again, and I don't get the money, and after 10 years, I get it.

3 My life has been spent playing with nuts and bolts. I am passionate to play. I don't live anywhere. I have a hand in a Concorde, a toe in the 747, my lungs in the Calypso and my heart in the water.

4 I have many houses and I travel all over the world, but I really live only when I'm on the *Calypso*.

5 People do not realize that all pollution ends up in the sea. The earth is less polluted. It is washed by rain, which carries everything into the oceans where life has diminished by 40 percent in last 20 years.

6 When one is an officer, even of a defeated force, one tries to do something.

7 I have a very irregular life. I think a regular life is a step to the tomb.

8 The sea is not a bargain basement. The greatest resource of the ocean is not material but the boundless spring of inspiration and well-being we gain from her. Yet we risk poisoning the sea forever just when we are learning her science, art, and philosophy and how to live in her embrace.

9 Biological sciences will in the end take lead, for without life, there is no science.

112

1 A time comes to us all when we must put our theories to the test and let action attest belief.

2 No one can move events faster than the tide, but there are always those who must ride the first waves.

3 I will agree to any fair proposal to remove my school, but my right to teach coloured pupils, if I see fit, I will not relinquish.

4 Darkness is a worthy cloak.

5 Learning is a virtue only if it leads to wisdom and usefulness. Your aim should be to learn, not for the purpose of exhibiting your knowledge, but to help others.

6 There are some seeds for whom germination is long and difficult.

113

1 I got where I am, not just by ambition, but by the desire to do my best - in roles, in my appearance, in interviews, in everything.

2 I love competition. Competition is one of the great challenges of life. We must have competition or we don't grow.

3 Every experience I had and every mistake I had during my nightclub career has helped, if only to show me the things which I should avoid in the future.

4 I carry myself regally. I am only five feet and four and a half inches but I look much taller. I always wear three and a half inch heels and I never even slump mentally. I walk tall.

5 Never marry out of loneliness.

114

1 I like to be alone once in a while - everybody does. You think better when you are alone; you can't think when you are talking. I like to read a lot. I like to go out to a movie alone; entertain myself. I don't have to have people, but I enjoy company with people when there is something to do, something to say. I don't like small talk. I am not very good at it.

2 I would rather sing than eat.

3 A star's success is often short-lived.

115

1 After depending on the crutches for nearly three years I figured out that if I ran, or sort of hippety-hopped along, I would concentrate so much on what I was doing that I would forget about the pain.

116

1 The many preceding disappointments had depressed me so much that I was no longer capable of feeling excited about it.

2 A secret known to many is no longer a secret.

117

1 Cooking is very close to painting. When you are making a dish, you add a little of this and a little of that. It's like mixing paints.

2 It is difficult to hold the world's interest for more than half an hour at a time. I myself have done so successfully every day for twenty years.

3 The hermit sees in the clouds the paranoiac hallucinations of his temptation. The elephants carry on their backs erotic fountains, obelisks, churches, escurials. Elephants stride on almost invisible legs of spiders of desire. With outstretched arm, the saint bears his cross to exorcise the vision.

4 Sleep is a state of equilibrium, a kind of monster in which your body disappears. Nothing is left then but the head supported by a subtle host of crutches. It is only when all the crutches are balanced that the god of sleep can take possession of you.

5 Sexual obsessions are the basis of artistic creation.

118

1 He who sees a need and waits to be asked for help is as unkind as if he had refused it.

2 Those who live by intellect and reason and who are endowed with a certain divine liberty are not constrained by any custom because these men are not guided by the laws, but rather the laws by them.

3 Like a pilgrim who is traveling on a road where he hath never been before, who believes that every house which he sees from a far is the hostel, and finding that it is not directs his belief to another, and so from house to house until he comes to the hostel, so our soul, so soon as it enters upon the new and never-yet-made journey of life, directs its eyes toward the goal of its supreme good, and therefore whatever it sees that appears to have some good in it, it thinks to be it. And because its knowledge is at first imperfect, through having no experience or instruction, little goods appear great to it. And so we see little children intensely longing for an apple, and then going on further, longing for a little bird, and then further on longing for fine clothes, and then a horse, and then a mistress. And this comes to pass because in none of these things does he find that which he is ever searching. But in truth we may lose this way in error, just as we may lose the paths of earth.

4 Providence has set two ends before man to be contemplated by him; the blessedness, to wit, of this life, which consists in the exercise of his proper power and is figured in the terrestrial paradise, and the blessedness of eternal life, which consists in the fruition of the divine aspect, to which his proper power may not ascend unless assisted by the divine light. And this blessedness is given to be understood by the celestial paradise.

119

1 The highest possible stage in moral culture is when we recognize that we ought to control our thoughts.

2 A man who dares to waste one hour of his life has not discovered the value of life.

3 I have always maintained that, excepting for fools, men did not differ much in intellect, only in zeal and hard work.

4 I have never been an atheist. I may say that the impossibility of conceiving that this grand and wondrous universe, with our conscious selves, arose through chance seems to me the chief argument for the existence of God.

5 I would far rather be descended from a monkey on both my parents' side than from a man who uses his brilliant talents for arousing religious prejudice in discussions of subjects about which he knows nothing.

6 Man with all his noble qualities still bears in his bodily frame the indelible stamp of his lowly origin.

120

1 You cannot be a success if everyone likes you.

2 I always make it a point to speak grammatically. Who knows? It might become popular.

3 When they see me on the screen, they're seeing 45 years of sweat. They pay for my experience and if that loses its importance, I might as well get lost. I survived because I was tougher than anybody else. You learn the hard way and that's the only way.

4 I have always found it difficult to find the right man because when challenged by an equal, most men back off.

5 Apart from my children, my work has been the big romance in my life. No question about it. It really stands by you. You have your disappointments in your work and your ups and downs, but it is there when all else fails.

6 I am a woman meant for a man, but I never found a man who could compete.

7 Never see your rushes. You will get depressed about how you look and you won't be able to do anything about it.

8 You won't be a star if you don't look like one.

121

1 You want somebody to treat you good, you better treat them good.

2 Money don't make you free. Popularity don't make you free. Sure I live in Beverly Hills, but I am shackled by the same thing that happened to the brother in Watts. People still see me a Black.

3 The ultimate mystery is one's own self.

4 In the same way that live performance is an impermanent art, a star is an impermanent illusion who lives only in the memory of those who have seen him and then dies with them. He is carried on people's shoulders and he falls on his face, all within a minute. He is an insecure egocentric, a tyrant and a teddy bear.

5 A star is the fool who will try anything in public and the genius when it works. He has a thick skin that you can pierce with a frown.

6 The fear of losing success begins when you become entrenched with it.

7 Being a star has made it possible for me to get insulted in places where the average Negro could never hope to get insulted.

122

1 The older I get the more I feel that faithfulness and perseverance are the greatest of virtues.

2 To have a good thought means to act.

3 Only prayer helps keep a balance.

4 I never considered myself a liberal. I considered myself a radical.

5 All the way to heaven is heaven. Hell is not to love any more.

123

1 There is something magnificent about having the courage to stand with a few and for a principle and to fight for it... no matter whose respect you may forfeit as long as you keep your own.

2 When great changes occur in history, when great principles are involved, as a rule the majority is wrong. The minority is right.

3 I have never advocated violence. I have always believed in education, in intelligence, in enlightenment, and I have always made my appeal to the reason and conscience of the people.

4 While there is a lower class, I am in it. While there is a criminal element, I am in it. While there is a soul in prison, I am not free.

124

1 I honestly think of running as an art form. Watching a race is like looking at a pretty picture. But it is also something that requires total dedication. I want to give one hundred percent to my sport.

2 The pain of not competing is even greater than the physical pain. The only time I feel bad is when I can't go out and run.

3 When you want to do something so bad and you can't do, then it hurts badly.

4 When I began to train my hardest lesson was to learn how not to train.

5 I always try to get to know all of my fellow runners, male or female. What's the fun of racing if we can't be friends?

6 The more I win, the more I want to win.

7 At sixteen I was already a has been.

8 What's the use of doing something if you don't try to be the best?

125

1 To be a success in any line of work requires courage, persistence, a willingness to pinch and go without many pleasures and pastimes while you are young and getting a good start in life.

2 I appropriated most of my discoveries from the works of others.

3 Confidence and courage are the essentials of success in carrying out any plan. You must have faith; you must not be stampeded by rumours and guesses. Work together in banishing fear. Together you cannot fail.

126

1 It takes great passion and great energy to do anything creative, especially in the theater. You have to care so much that you can't sleep, you can't eat, you can't talk to people. It's just got to be right. You can't do it without that passion.

2 I've never had any theories. I don't have any favorite kind of dancing. A good work of art is a good work of art and I don't care if it's made out of jackstraws, marble or gesso.

3 The difference between an artist and a non-artist is that the artist will not settle for anything less than the truth as far as he can sense it, or feel it, or perceive it, whatever the medium. He doesn't know what the truth is ever - he senses it. He has to feel toward it. Art always has an element of personality, of involvement, of sincerity, and the individual gives into it and gets out of it the best that he can.

4 People in the theater take advantage of everybody they can.

127

- Daniel Defoe
The Author of Robinson Crusoe
1661 - 1731

1 You cannot do a kindness too soon, for you never know how soon it will be too late.

2 Friends are good - good if well chosen.

3 I am most entertained by those actions which give me light into the nature of man.

4 Law is the result of reason, and the sovereignty of reason over all the actions of men cannot be invaded, but the laws offered by whatever society of men against reason are void of course.

5 You would not only eat your neighbour's bread but your neighbour himself, rather than starve, and your honesty would all shipwreck in the storm of necessity.

6 Of all the writings delivered in a historical manner to the world, none certainly were ever held in greater esteem than those which give us the lives of distinguished private men at full length; and as I may say, to the life.

7 Preaching of sermons is speaking to a few of mankind; printing of books is talking to the whole world.

8 The best of men cannot suspend their fate; the good die early, and the bad die late.

9 Nature has left this tincture in the blood, that all men would be tyrants if they could.

10 Wherever God erects a house of prayer, the Devil always builds a chapel there; and it will be found, upon examination, that the latter has the larger congregation.

128

- Demosthenes
One of the Greatest Orators of Ancient Greek
384 B.C. - 322 B.C.

1 Small opportunities are often the beginning of great enterprises.

2 You cannot have a proud and chivalrous spirit if your conduct is mean and paltry; for whatever a man's actions are, so must be his spirit.

3 Nothing is easier than self-deceit. For what each man wishes, that he also believes to be true.

4 As a vessel is known by the sound, whether it be cracked or not, so men are proved by their speeches, whether they be wise or foolish.

5 Everything great is not always good, but all good things are great.

6 What we have in us of the image of God, is the love of truth and justice.

7 We are all human beings and therefore should make only such proposals and only such laws as will arouse the indignation of no one; but whatever may come, we should accept it as human.

8 The most formidable enemy that threatens Athens is not the King of Macedonia, but your own supineness.

9 There is one safeguard known generally to the wise, which is an advantage and security to all, but especially to democracies against despots - suspicion.

129

- Jack Dempsey
The All-time Boxing Champion for Drawing Crowds
1895 - 1983

1 There is often more pleasure in pursuit than in possession.

2 If you want to win, you must develop your ability to concentrate and to perform almost automatically. If you have to stop to figure out what you are going to do, you are too late.

3 No fighter has everything. Hit a fellow on the chin and if he doesn't blink, hit him in the belly. It is as simple as that.

4 I started fighting when I was eight. I had an elder brother who was a boxer, so I got a pair of boxing gloves and started practicing with four or five kids in our neighbourhood. When I fought Willard at the age of twenty-four, I had already had sixteen years' boxing experience.

5 When I started, I decided to put all I had on offense and let the defensive side of boxing take care of itself. I studied that phase more than most people know.

6 Every time I got hit, I learned something and found ways to improve my defense that wouldn't weaken my attack. I built up my punching power largely through a heavy bag. I don't believe many people appreciate how hard and how long I worked slugging away at that big bag. That wasn't a matter of a few weeks but a hard, steady grind for several years.

130

- Charles Dickens
One of the Greatest English Writers
1812 - 1870

1 Whatever I have tried to do in my life, I have tried with all my heart to do well.

2 I should never have made my success in life if I had not bestowed upon the last thing I have ever undertaken the same attention and care that I have bestowed upon the greatest.

3 There is no substitute for thorough-going, ardent and sincere earnestness.

4 Industry is the soul of business and the keystone of prosperity.

5 Reflect upon your present blessings, of which every man has many, not on your past misfortunes, of which all men have some.

6 A word in earnest is better than a speech.

7 I would rather have the affectionate regard of my fellowmen than I would have heaps and mines of gold.

8 A loving heart is the truest wisdom.

9 Charity begins at home, and justice begins next door.

10 I never could have done what I have done without the habits of punctuality, order and diligence, without the determination to concentrate myself on one subject at a time.

11 Nature gives to every time and season some beauties of its own.

1 Tell all the truth, but tell it slant.

2 There is no frigate like a book
To take us lands away.
Nor any coursers like a page
Of prancing poetry.

3 If I can stop one heart from breaking,
I shall not live in vain.
If I can ease one life the aching,
Or cool one pain,
Or help one fainting robin
Unto his nest again,
I shall not live in vain.

4 The pedigree of honey does not concern the bee;
A clover, any time, to him is aristocracy.

5 Remorse is memory awake.

6 Success is counted sweetest
By those who ne'er succeed.

7 Truth is such a rare thing, it is delightful to tell it.

8 My friends are my estate.

9 Fame is a bee.
It has a song.
It has a sting.
Ah, too, it has a wing.

10 Faith is the Pierless Bridge
Supporting what We see
Unto the Scene that We do not.

11 I argue thee that love is life
And life hath immortality.

12 To be alive - is power -
Existence - in itself -
Without a further function -
Omnipotence - enough.

13 Luck is not chance -
It's toil -
Fortune's expensive smile
Is earned -

132

- Marlene Dietrich
Hollywood's Sex Goddess of Her Time
1902 - 1992

1 The average man is more interested in a woman who is interested in him than he is in a woman with beautiful legs.
2 I never took my career seriously. That does not mean that I did not perform very correctly, that I did not do my duty. But I was never impressed by my work.
3 Beauty comes from within. The idea might seem horrible but it's true.
4 Children give you a reason to go on living. There is always the possibility that they might need you. Without them you might as well not exist.
5 There are no Ten Commandments when it comes to love; there is only one: to love unconditionally.

133

- Phyllis Diller
The Funniest Woman of the World of 1960s and 70s
Born in 1917

1 It's a good thing that beauty is skin deep, or I'd be rotten to the core.
2 My stage character is a cartoon. Everything I say on stage is in a bubble over my head.
3 I am a word girl.
4 I bury a lot of my ironing in the backyard.

134

- Joe DiMaggio
One of the Greatest Center Fielders of 1930s and 40s
Born in 1914

1 Base-hits are my job. When I am not hitting them, I worry, same as any businessman who's not doing much business.
2 A man is never satisfied. You go up there and get four hits and you want five so bad you can taste it.
3 I am just a ballplayer with only one ambition, to give all I've got to help my club win. I've never played any other way.
4 I once made a solemn promise to myself that I wouldn't try to hang on once the end was in sight. I've seen too many beat-up players struggle to stay up there, and it was always a sad spectacle.
5 When baseball is no longer fun, it's no longer a game.

135

1 You may not realize it when it happens, but a kick in the teeth may be the best thing in the world for you.

2 Don't pretend to know more than you do. Own up to your ignorance honestly, and you will find people who are eager to fill your head with information.

3 There are two kinds of people: the first kind are kicked and licked if they can't get a job. The second kind are sure that even if jobs are scarce they can always do something.

4 Exercise is needed to develop minds as well as bodies.

5 Your imagination may be creaky or timid, or dwarfed or frozen at the points. The Readers' Digest can serve as a gymnasium for its training.

6 There is more treasure in books than in all the pirates' loot on Treasure Island and best of all, you can enjoy these riches every day of your life.

7 A buck is something to be spent creating. It's not what you have, but how much you can borrow that's important in business.

8 All our dreams can come true - if we have the courage to pursue them.

9 When youngsters get into serious trouble, it is generally the parents who are delinquent, not the children. If you will look a little deeper, when some unpleasant incident occurs, you'll find that there's usually something wrong in the domestic menage. In too many cases, the parents are the ones who are in trouble and the parents are the ones who need help.

10 Every child is born blessed with a vivid imagination. But just as a muscle goes flabby with disuse, so the bright imagination of a child pales in later years if he ceases to exercise it.

136

1 Read no history, nothing but biography, for that is life without theory.

2 Perseverance and tact are the two great qualities most valuable for men who would mount, but especially for those who have to step out of the crowd.

3 Little things affect little minds.

4 Every production of genius must be the production of enthusiasm.

5 There is no education like adversity.

6 Patience is a necessary ingredient of genius.

7 The secret of success is constancy of purpose.

8 The secret of success in life is for a man to be ready for his opportunity when it comes.

9 Man is not the creature of circumstances. Circumstances are the creatures of men.

10 We make our fortunes and we call them fate.

11 Next to knowing when to seize an opportunity, the most important thing in life is to know when to forego an advantage.

12 The more extensive a man's knowledge of what has been done, the greater will be his power of knowing what to do.

13 Action may not always bring happiness, but there is no happiness without action.

14 Everything comes if a man will only wait.

15 Without tact you can learn nothing.

16 Predominant opinions are generally the opinions of the generation that is vanishing.

17 There can be no economy where there is no efficiency.

18 Despair is the conclusion of fools.

19 To be conscious that you are ignorant is a great step to knowledge.

20 It is much easier to be critical than to be correct.

21 Talk to a man about himself and he will listen for hours.

22 Candor is the brightest gem of criticism.

23 Critics are the men who have failed in literature and art.

24 Variety is the mother of Enjoyment.

25 There is no index of character as sure as the voice.

26 Propriety of manners and consideration for others are the two main characteristics of a gentleman.

27 What we anticipate seldom occurs; what we least expect generally happens.

28 Seeing much, suffering much and studying much are the three pillars of learning.

29 The health of the people is really the foundation upon which all their happiness and all their powers as a State depend.

30 Justice is truth in action.

31 I believe that heroic makes heroes.

32 All my successes have been built on my failures.

33 A human being with a settled purpose must accomplish it; nothing can resist a will which will stake even existence upon its fulfillment.

34 We are all born for love. It is the principle of existence and its only end.

35 As a general rule the most successful man in life is the one who has the best information.

36 No government can be long secure without a formidable opposition.

137

1 God requires no more to be accomplished than He gives time for performing.

2 I saw the path marked out for me and what I have done in it, as it were, has been done by itself.

3 We must see what can be done.

4 No one will consider the day ended until the duties it brings are discharged.

5 I advocate the cause of the much suffering insane throughout the entire length and breadth of my country. I ask relief for the East and for the West, for the North and for the South. I ask for the people that which is already the property of the people.

6 I am not ambitious of nominal distinction, and notoriety is my personal aversion. Reputation I prize above all present good and would not exchange it for fame or transient popular applause.

7 I think, even lying in bed, I can still do something.

8 Heaven has greatly blessed my labours. I feel truly more and more that a leading Providence defines my path in the dark valleys of the world.

9 My success and influence are evidence to my mind that I am called by Providence to the vocation to which life, talents and fortune have surrendered these many years.

138

1 In order to achieve in the marketplace you have to have a sizable ego.

2 The hardest lesson I had to learn in journalism was the meaning of *power on the job*.

3 Since spanking and verbal criticism have become, to many parents, more important tools of child rearing than approval, we should not be surprised that countless young men and women enter adulthood with negative feelings about themselves. No wonder, positive reinforcement is so often lacking between boss and subordinate, teacher and student.

4 To a journalist, good news is often not news at all. In the news business, tragedy is good news; the bloodier, the better. The more horrible the story, the greater the chance to demonstrate ability. A reporter's heart beats faster en route to a murder than it does en route to a City Hall meeting, and a journalist on television is more likely to receive an Emmy for covering mass murder than for covering local politics.

5 The men who manage America's seven-hundred-plus television stations are almost always models of the American success story. In most cases, they preside over enterprises that make money even when badly managed.

139

1 Knowledge can be obtained under difficulties; poverty may give place to competency; obscurity is not an absolute bar to distinction; and a way is open to welfare and happiness to all who will resolutely and wisely pursue that way.

2 No man can put a chain about the ankle of his fellow man without at last finding the other end fastened about his own neck.

3 My joys have far exceeded my sorrows and my friends have brought me far more than my enemies have taken from me.

4 The doctrine that submission to violence is the best cure for violence did not hold good between slaves and overseers.

5 In my childhood I wished that it was possible for me to remain small all my life, knowing that the sooner I grew large the shorter would be my time to remain with my grandparents.

6 It was the boast of slave holders that their slaves enjoyed more of the physical comforts of life than the peasantry of any country in the world. My experience contradicts this.

140

1 Beliefs held by the multitude and their leaders are likely to be wrong. Beliefs held by the unconventionalists which fly in the face of orthodoxy are probably right.

2 I may talk pessimism, but I never cease to fight forward.

3 The mystery of life - its inexplicability, beauty, cruelty, tenderness, folly etc., etc. - has occupied the greater part of my waking thoughts; and in reverence or rage or irony, as the moment or the situation might dictate, I have pondered and even demanded of cosmic energy to know why.

141

1 It has taken me long years to find even one absolutely true movement.

2 Virtuous people are simply those who have either not been tempted sufficiently, because they live in a vegetative state, or because their purposes are so concentrated in one direction that they have not had the leisure to glance around.

3 The most terrible part of a great sorrow is not the beginning, when the shock of grief throws one into a state of exaltation which is almost anesthetic in its effects, but afterwards, long afterwards, when people say, "Oh, she has gotten over it" or "She is all right now, she outlived it."

4 I have only made movements which seem beautiful to me.

5 My life has known but two motives - Love and Art - and often Love destroyed Art, and often the imperious call of Art put a tragic end to Love.

6 I wanted to write about my art mostly, but my publishers were not interested, and I needed the money desperately. Therefore I wrote mostly about my love affairs. It's a crazed century that can only find interest in me as a female Casanova.

7 *Natural dancing* should only mean that the dancer never goes against nature, not anything is left to chance.

8 I shall never hear of money in exchange for my work. I want a studio-workshop, a house for myself and pupils, simple food, simple tunics and the opportunity to give our best work. I want to dance for the masses, for the working people who need my art and have never had the money to come and see me and I want to dance for them for nothing.

9 A great dancer can give to the people something that they will carry with them forever. They can never forget it, and it has changed them, though they may not know it.

10 My gods are *Beauty* and *Love*; there are no others.

142
- Jimmy Durante
One of the Greatest Clowns of the Era
1893 - 1980

1 Be nice to people on your way up, because you meet them on your way down.

2 The song gotta come from da heart.

3 Having true-blue friends is the strongest thing a person can have going for him in the whole world.

4 Every couple needs time to learn each other's faults.

143
- Amelia Earhart
The First Woman to Fly Solo Across Atlantic
1898 - 1937

1 Courage is the price that Life exacts for granting peace,
The soul that knows it not, knows no release
From little things;
Knows not the livid loneliness of fear,
Nor mountain heights where bitter joy can hear
The sounds of wings.
How can life grant us boon of living, compensate
For dull grey ugliness and pregnant hate
Unless we dare
The soul's dominion? Each time we make a choice, we pay
With courage to behold the restless day,
And count it fair.

2 I want to do it because I want to do it. Women must try to do things as men have tried. When they fail, their failure must be but a challenge to others.

3 When I go, I'd like best to go in my plane; quickly.

4 Just becoming a parent doesn't necessarily make a person a good parent.

144

- Mary Baker Eddy
The Founder of the Christian Science
1821 - 1910

1 Pride is ignorance; those assume most who have the least wisdom or experience; and they steal from their neighbour, because they have so little of their own.

2 Disease is an experience of so called mortal mind. It is fear made manifest on the body. Christian Science takes away this physical sense of discord, just as it removes any other sense of moral or mental inharmony.

3 The daily ablutions of an infant are no more natural nor necessary than would be the process of taking a fish out of water every day and covering it with dirt in order to make it thrive more vigorously in its own element. Water is not the natural habitat of humanity.

4 The noblest charity is to prevent a man from accepting charity; and the best alms are to show and to enable a man to dispense with alms.

145

- Thomas Edison
One of the Greatest Inventors of the World
1847 - 1931

1 Genius is one percent inspiration, ninety-nine percent perspiration.

2 There is no substitute for hard work.

3 Success is based on imagination plus ambition and the will.

4 The three great essentials to achieve anything worth while are: hard-work, stick-to-itiveness and common sense.

5 I never did anything worth doing by accident, nor did any of my inventions come by accident; they came by work.

6 Ideas are in the air, and if I did not catch it, someone else will.

7 To do much clear thinking a man must arrange regular periods of solitude when he can concentrate and indulge his imagination without distraction.

8 Show me a thoroughly satisfied man and I will show you a failure.

9 Waste is worse than loss. The time is coming when every person who lays claim to ability will keep the question of waste before him constantly. The scope of thrift is limitless.

10 Restlessness and discontent are the first necessities of progress.

11 When down in the mouth, remember Jonah, he came out all right.

12 I am not a genius. I'm just a sponge. I absorb ideas and put them in use. Most of

my ideas were thought of by somebody else, who never bothered to develop them.

13 Many people think of inventions as coming on a man in one piece. Things don't happen that way, much. The phonograph, for example, was a long time coming, and it came step by step. For my own part, it started way back in the days of the Civil War, when I was a young telegrapher in Indianapolis.

14 Work heals and ennobles. Work brings out the secrets of nature and applies them for the happiness of men.

15 Everything comes to him who hustles while he waits.

16 If we were to do all we are capable of doing, we would literally astonish ourselves.

17 I am wondering what would have happened to me if some fast talker had converted me to the theory of the 8-hour day, and convinced me that it was not fair to my fellow workers to put forth my best efforts in my work. I am glad that the 8-hour day had not been invented when I was a young man. If my life had been made up of 8-hour days, I do not believe I could have accomplished a great deal.

18 The best thinking has been done in solitude.

19 I never did a day's work in my life - it was all fun.

20 God invented the talking machine. I invented the first one that can be shut off.

21 I will try anything. I will try Limburger cheese.

22 I am not discouraged, because every wrong attempt discarded is another step forward.

23 Concentration is the ability to apply your physical and mental energies to one problem incessantly without growing weary.

24 I start where the last man left off.

25 One might think that the money value of an invention constitutes its reward to the man who loves his work. But, speaking for myself, I can honestly say this is not so. I continue to find my greatest pleasure, and so my reward, in the work that preceded what the world calls success.

26 Nearly every man who develops an idea works it up to the point where it looks impossible, and then gets discouraged. That's not the place to become discouraged.

27 There is far more opportunity than there is ability.

146

- Dwight Eisenhower
The Commander of the Allied Forces in World War II
1890 - 1969

1 We succeed only as we identify in life, or in war, or in anything else, a single overriding objective, and make all other considerations bend to that one objective.

2 In the final choice a soldier's pack is not so heavy a burden as a prisoner's chain.

3 I don't waste a single minute thinking about a person I don't like.

4 Leadership is the ability to decide what is to be done and to get others to want to do it.

5 Leadership is the art of getting someone else do something that you want done because he wants to do it.

6 Peace and justice are two sides of the same coin.

7 There is no victory at bargain basement prices.

147

- Lee Elder
The Best Black-American Golfer until 1982
Born in 1934

1 I wasn't born with talent; I developed it, worked at it.

2 After turning professional I spent many sleepless nights wondering how I was going to pay the hotel bill and how I was going to eat the following day. I did not always win; I did not always play guys I could beat one-handed.

3 There were instances when winning left me with a sense of guilt. I knew it was dishonest to trick players into a bet, but there are times when you have to forget about honesty if you want to survive.

148

- George Eliot
One of England's Foremost Women Novelists
1819 - 1880

1 No great deed is done by falterers who ask for certainty.

2 What we call despair is often only the painful eagerness of unfed hope.

3 It's but little good you will do watering the last year's crop.

4 It is no use filling your pocket with money if you have got a hole in the corner.

5 The beginning of compunction is the beginning of a new life.

6 The reward of one duty is the power to fulfill another.

7 One must be poor to know the luxury of giving.

8 People glorify all sorts of bravery except the bravery they might show on behalf of their nearest neighbours.

9 Nothing is so good as it seems beforehand.

10 It seems to me we can never give up longing and wishing while we are thoroughly alive. There are certain things we feel to be beautiful and good, and we must hunger after them.

11 Animals are such agreeable friends - they ask no questions, they pass no criticisms.

12 What do we live for, if it is not to make life less difficult to each other?

13 He was like the cock who thought the sun had risen to hear him crow.

14 I am not denying the women are foolish: God Almighty made them to match the men.

149

-Duke Ellington
The Most Important Figure in the History and Evolution of Jazz
1899 - 1974

1 If you are going to play good jazz, you have got to have a plan of what's going to happen. There has to be intent. It's like an act of murder. You play with intent to commit something.

2 Nothing is worth worrying about. I never worry, but I do become concerned.

3 Music is my mistress and she plays second fiddle to no one.

4 *Love* is supreme and unconditional; *like* is nice but limited.

5 Any time friends have to be careful of what they say to friends, friendship is taken on another dimension.

6 New York is a place where the rich walk, the poor drive Cadillacs, and beggars die of malnutrition with thousands of dollars hidden in their mattresses.

7 Cacophony is hard to swallow.

8 A man's education doesn't start until he finds what he wants to learn.

150

- Ralph Waldo Emerson
One of America's Most Prominent Writers of 19th Century
1803 - 1882

1 Beware of what you set your heart upon, for it shall surely be yours.

2 What lies behind you, and what lies in front of you, pales in comparison to what lies inside of you.

3 Every great achievement is the story of a flaming heart.

4 Finish each day and be done with it. You have done what you could. Some blunders and absurdities no doubt crept in; forget them as soon as you can. Tomorrow is a new day; begin it well and serenely and with too high a spirit to be encumbered with your old nonsense.

5 Every really able man, if you talk sincerely with him, considers his work, however much admired, as far short of what it should be. What is this Better, this flying Ideal, but the perpetual promise of his Creator.

6 They conquer who believe they can. Do the thing you fear and the death of fear is certain.

7 It is easy in the world to live after the world's opinions; it is easy in solitude to live after our own; but the great man is he who, in the midst of the crowd, keeps with perfect sweetness the independence of solitude.

8 Don't spend your time in doubts and fears; spend yourself in the work before you, well assured that the right performance of this hour's duties will be the best preparation for the hours or ages that follow it.

9 If a man has good corn, or wood, or boards, or pigs to sell, or can make better chairs or knives, crucibles, or church organs, than anybody else, you will find a broad, hard-beaten road to his house, though it be in the woods.

10 One of the illusions of life is that the present hour is not the critical, decisive hour. Write it on your heart that every day is the best day of the year. He only is rich who owns the day, and no one owns the day who allows it to be invaded with worry, fret and anxiety. Finish every day, and be done with it. You have done what you could.

11 Who so would be a man must be a non-conformist.

12 For every thing you have missed, you have gained something else; and for everything you gain, you lose something.

13 He only is a well-made man who has a good determination.

14 The frost which kills the harvest of a year, saves the harvests of a century, by destroying the weevil or the locust.

15 The best lightning-rod for your protection is your own spine.

16 Every artist was first an amateur.

17 The shoemaker makes a good shoe because he makes nothing else.

18 Fear always springs from ignorance.

19 All great men come out of the middle classes.

20 When nature adds difficulties, she adds brains.

21 The sun shines after every storm. There is a solution for every problem, and the soul's highest duty is to be a good cheer.

22 There is no defeat except from within. There is really no insurmountable barrier save your own inherent weakness of purpose.

23 Concentration is the secret of strength in politics, in war, in trade, in short, in all management of human affairs.

24 The power of a man increases steadily by continuance in one direction.

25 A man is what he thinks all day long.

26 The characteristic of heroism is its persistence.

27 Most people are brave only in the dangers to which they accustom themselves, either in imagination or in practice.

28 The ancestor of every action is thought.

29 A man is a hero, not because he is braver than anyone else, but because he is brave for ten minutes longer.

30 The world belongs to the energetic.

31 The task ahead of us is never as great as the power behind us.

32 We are born to grow rich through the use of our faculties.

33 All I have seen teaches me to trust the Creator for all I have not seen.

34 If you would lift me, you must be on a higher ground.

35 Ideas must work through the brains and the arms of good and brave men, or they are no better than dreams.

36 God offers to every mind its choice between truth and repose. Take which you please, - you can never have both.

37 A man should study ever to keep cool. He makes his inferiors his superiors by heat.

38 Trust men, and they will be true to you; treat them greatly and they will show themselves great.

39 Many times the reading of a book has made the future of a man.

40 If we encountered a man of rare intellect, we should ask him what books he read.

41 A man who buys a book is not just buying a few ounces of paper, glue and printer's ink; he may be buying a whole new life.

42 A great part of courage is the courage of having done the thing before.

43 Make yourself necessary to somebody.

44 All life is an experiment. The more experiments you make, the better.

45 The great men of the past did not slide by any fortune into their high place. They have been selected by the severest of all judges, Time.

46 Little minds have little worries; big minds have no time for worries.

47 If you would rule the world quietly, you must keep it amused.

48 Frankness invites frankness. So of cheerfulness, or a good temper, the more it is spent, the more of it remains.

49 Nature arms each man with some faculty which enables him to do easily some feat that is impossible to any other man.

50 That which befits us is cheerfulness and courage.

51 To make knowledge valuable, you must have the cheerfulness of wisdom. Goodness smiles to the last.

52 Self-trust is the essence of heroism.

53 Consideration is the soil in which wisdom may be expected to grow, and strength be given to every up-springing plant of duty.

54 That which we are we are all the while teaching, not voluntarily, but involuntarily.

55 Nothing great was ever achieved without enthusiasm.

56 An actually existing fly is more important than a possibly existing angel.

57 Great geniuses have the shortest biographies.

58 An institution is the lengthened shadow of one man.

59 Hitch your wagon to a star.

60 The things taught in schools and colleges are not an education, but the means of education.

61 The first wealth is health.

62 Our knowledge is the amassed thought and experience of innumerable minds.

63 If a man owns land, the land owns him.

64 Adopt the pace of nature; her secret is patience.

65 Steam is no stronger now than it was a hundred years ago, but it is put to better use.

66 Nothing can bring you peace but yourself.

67 What you are speaks so loudly that I cannot hear a word what you say.

68 The grandest homage we can pay to truth is to use it.

69 Every violation of truth is a stab at the health of human society.

70 The sense of being perfectly dressed gives us a feeling of inward tranquillity.

71 The education of the will is the object of our existence.

72 Happiness lies only in the triumph of principles.

73 Trust the instinct to the end, though you can render no reason. It is vain to hurry it. By trusting it to the end, it shall ripen into truth and you shall know why you believe.

74 The wise man throws himself on the side of his assailants. It is more his interest than it is theirs to find out his weak points.

75 Our chief want is someone who will inspire us to be what we know we could be.

76 A man's style is his mind's voice.

77 Science does not know its debt to imagination.

78 The measure of mental health is the disposition to find good everywhere.

79 No accomplishment, no assistance, no training, can compensate for lack of belief.

80 Trust thyself. Every heart vibrates to that iron string.

81 Enthusiasm is the leaping lightning, not to be measured by the horse-power of the understanding.

82 For every minute you remain angry, you give up 60 seconds of peace of mind.

83 Use what language you will, you can never say anything to others but what you are.

84 One of the most beautiful compensations of this life is that no man can sincerely try to help another without helping himself.

85 Cause and effect, means and ends, seed and fruit, cannot be severed. The effect already blooms in the cause, the end pre-exists in the means, the fruit in the seed.

86 If you serve an ungrateful master, serve him the more. Put God in your debt. Every stroke shall be repaid. The longer the payment is withheld, the better for you; for compound interest on compound interest is the rate of this exchequer.

87 A man should learn to detect and watch that gleam of light which flashes across his mind from within.

88 Not gold, but only man can make
A People great and strong - Men who, for truth and honor's sake,

Stand fast and suffer long.
Brave men who work while others sleep,
Who dare while others fly -
They build a nation's pillars deep
And lift them to the sky.

89 Man cannot discover new oceans until he has the courage to lose sight of the shore.

90 No facts are to me sacred, none are profane; I simply experiment, an endless seeker, with no Past at my back.

91 To be great is to be misunderstood.

92 A man's action is only a picture book of his creed.

93 When it is dark enough, you can see the stars.

94 Courage consists in equality to the problem before us.

95 We are the prisoners of ideas.

96 All great masters are chiefly distinguished by the power of adding a second, a third and perhaps a fourth step in a continuous line. Many a man had taken the first step. With every additional step you enhance immensely the value of your first.

97 There is nothing capricious in nature and the implanting of a desire indicates that its gratification is in the constitution of the creature that feels it.

98 For the resolute and determined there is time and opportunity.

99 There is always a best way of doing everything.

100 There is a time when a man distinguishes the idea of felicity from the idea of wealth; it is the beginning of wisdom.

101 You cannot do wrong without suffering wrong.

102 The essence of greatness is the perception that virtue is enough.

103 We are always getting ready to live, but never live.

104 There is no prosperity, trade, art, city, or great material wealth of any kind, but if you trace it home, you will find it rooted in a thought of some individual man.

105 The key to every man is his thought. Sturdy and defying though he look, he has a helm which he obeys, which is the idea after which all his facts are classified. He can only be reformed by showing him a new idea which commands his own.

106 Be an opener of doors.

107 I know of no such unquestionable badge and ensign of a sovereign mind as that of tenacity of purpose.

108 No one can cheat you out of ultimate success but yourself.

109 Nothing is more simple than greatness; indeed, to be simple is to be great.

110 Nature pardons no mistake; her yea is yea, and her nay is nay.

111 Life is a succession of lessons which must be lived to be understood.

151

1 Everything good takes time.

2 If you're gonna play, then play to win.

3 You can become even better than you think you can be. You got to want it to happen and be prepared to put the effort.

4 No matter how young you are, you got to warm up in order to prevent muscle pulls and other injuries.

5 The single most important thing in basketball is superior conditioning. You got to be in better shape than the guy who is guarding you.

6 If you are worn out, you are not going to win no matter what kind of skill you got.

7 If you don't believe in yourself, if you don't set goals and strive for them, you will never make it happen.

8 Whether it is dunks or special moves, free throws or defense, you got to set goals and then motivate yourself to reach them. It takes plenty of discipline and hard work.

9 I always believed in myself. Even when I was a kid, before I started playing basketball. I was always small. Yet I always had big hands and could jump, so I learned to be trickier than bigger guys. I liked to experiment. I loved to watch guys and what they'd do in emergency situations. When I practiced, I worked on ways to take advantage of my advantages.

152

1 I have made it a rule to adopt the method of ignorance. I read very little. Instead of turning over the leaves of books, an expensive method which is not within my means, and instead of consulting others, I set myself obstinately face to face with my subject until I contrive to make it speak.

2 No, I don't *believe* in God. I *see* Him everywhere.

3 Life has unfathomable secrets. Human knowledge will be erased from the world's archives before we know the last word concerning a knat.

4 The sum of all my work has been but to shift a few grains of sand upon the shore of knowledge and it is useless for me to endeavour to sound the mysteries of life.

5 It is He that hath made us and not we ourselves.

6 See first; you can argue later.

7 The more I observe and experiment, the more I feel rising before me, in the cloudy blackness of the possible, a vast note of interrogation.

8 We can say excellent things without using a barbarous vocabulary. Lucidity is the sovereign politeness of the writer. I do my best to achieve it.

153 - Michael Faraday
The Bookbinder Who Became an Extraordinary Scientist
1791 - 1867

1 Anyone can become a philosopher and scientist. All that is needed is to get rid of any ideas or thoughts that may influence the thought process. A person's mind must be a blank page, awaiting the arrival of new thoughts and ideas.

2 It is the duty of a philosopher to challenge accepted ideas and, in doing so, to help the world to grow and change.

3 Anyone who can resist prejudice can be as successful as I am.

4 The way a person comes to a discovery is often more important than the discovery itself.

5 Facts come first. Theories are constructed.

6 Time is all that I require.

7 I have lived my life as a plain person and I shall die as a plain person.

154 - James Farley
An Extraordinary Campaigner
1888 - 1976

1 The best advice I can give to any young person upon graduation from school can be summed up in exactly eight words: be honest with yourself and tell the truth.

155 - David Farragut
One of the Most Courageous Naval Officers of American Civil War
1801 - 1870

1 I believe in celerity.

2 Anyone wearing a sword ought to be ashamed not to be proficient in its use.

3 I have made it the rule of my life to ask no official favours, but to await orders and obey them.

4 He who dies in doing his duty to his country, and at peace with God, has played the drama of life to the best advantage.

5 Damn the torpedoes! Go ahead.

156 - Federico Fellini
Italy's Most Famous Film Maker of His Time
1920 - 1993

1 I make movies in the same way that I talk to people - whether it's a friend, a girl, a priest, or anyone; to seek some clarification. That is what neo-realism means to me, in the original, pure sense - a search into oneself, and into others; in any direction, any direction where there is life.

2 I don't believe that rational understanding is an essential element in the reception of any work of art. Either a film has something to say to you or it hasn't. If you are moved by it, you don't need to have it explained to you. If not, no explanation can make you moved by it.

3 I have always liked the world of the spectacle, from both sides of the footlights, either as a child watching my first sepia-tinted film about gladiators or making my own puppets at home.

4 Freedom, especially a woman's freedom, is a conquest to be made, not a gift to be received. It isn't granted. It must be taken.

5 It is more worthwhile to look directly at what is happening, instead of hiding behind morality.

6 All art is autobiographical; the pearl is the oyster's autobiography.

7 One should never think of a title first, only last, and it should be as encompassing as possible of its subject. If you limit yourself too early with a title, you will find what you look for instead of what is really interesting; so you have to go into with an open mind. A title doesn't help you, it leads you.

8 Real life isn't what interests me. I like to observe life, but to leave my imagination unfettered. Even as a child, I drew pictures not of a person, but of the picture in my mind of the person.

9 When you are struggling, what is most difficult is to keep respect for yourself.

10 The person that I respect most is the one who is able to fail repeatedly and still has the persistence to keep trying.

11 Establishing contact with another human being is the most precious thing in life.

12 Happiness cannot be a constant. There is no way to hold on to it tightly. In fact, when you clutch too tightly, it seems more likely to disappear. We can be perfectly happy only if we can take happiness for granted, and since that can never be, one element of happiness has to be lacking - security.

13 Put yourself into life and never lose your openness, your childish enthusiasm throughout the journey that is life, and things will come your way.

157

- Cyrus Field
The First Person to Lay Telegraph Cable Across Atlantic
1819 - 1892

1 When a thing is dead it is difficult to galvanize it to life. It is more difficult to revive an old enterprise than to start a new one. The freshness and novelty are gone and the feeling of disappointment discourages further effort.

2 We have had many difficulties to surmount, many discouragements to bear, and some enemies to overcome, whose very opposition has stimulated us to greater exertion.

3 To no one man is the world indebted for this achievement; one may have done more than another, this person may have a prominent and that a secondary part, but there is a host of us who have been engaged in the completion of the work.

4 If they bring me bad news I shall not sleep if I read them, and if the news is good, it will keep until morning.

5 Even though I keep telling men it's possible, it's still unbelievable. It takes a lot of believing to make it happen. Believing is a lonely business.

158
- Marshall Field
A Pioneer of the Wholesale Business
1834 - 1906

1 Goodwill is the one and only asset that competition cannot undersell nor destroy.

2 Those who enter to buy, support me. Those who come to flatter, please me. Those who complain teach me how I may please others so that more will come. Only those hurt me who are displeased but do not complain. They refuse me permission to correct my errors and thus improve my service.

3 I have tried to make all my acts and commercial moves the result of definite consideration and sound judgment. There were never any great ventures or risks. I practiced honest, slow-growing business methods, and tried to back them with energy and good system.

4 Do the right thing, at the right time, in the right way; do some things better than they were ever done before; eliminate errors; know both sides of the question; be courteous; be an example; work for the love of work; anticipate requirements; develop resources; recognize no impediments; master circumstances; act from reason rather than rule; be satisfied with nothing short of perfection.

5 Right or wrong, the customer is always right.

159
- W. C. Fields
One of the Classic American Comedians
1879 - 1946

1 A man who overindulges, lives in a dream. He becomes conceited. He thinks the whole world revolves around him - and it usually does.

2 Horse sense is what a horse has that keeps him from betting on people.

3 If I don't make it in one field, I will make it in another. All I know is that I am going to make it.

4 Never try to impress a woman, because if you do, she will expect you to keep up to the standard for the rest of your life.

160

- Bobby Fischer
The Youngest World Champion of Chess
Born in 1943

1 It takes a certain amount of adversity to develop character.

2 Practice, Study and Talent helped me become a good chess player.

3 Fancy rooms, views and cultural sideshows like school, poetry and concerts are contemptible distractions when you are trying to accomplish more than anyone else in the history of your art.

4 Once you think that your own mind is not your friend anymore, you are on your way to insanity.

5 Don't even mention losing to me. I can't stand to think of it.

6 I give 98 percent of my mental energy to chess. Others give only 2 percent.

7 Psychologically, you should have confidence in yourself and this confidence should be based on fact.

8 I prepare myself well. I know what I can do before I go in. I'm always confident.

9 Your body has to be in top condition. Your chess deteriorates as your body does. You can't separate body from mind.

10 I really love the dark of the night. It helps me to concentrate.

11 You have to have the fighting spirit. You have to force moves and take chances.

12 I don't believe in psychology. I believe in good moves.

161

- F. Scott Fitzerald
The Leading Writer of America's Jazz Age
1896 - 1940

1 No grand idea was ever born in a conference, but a lot of foolish ideas have died there.

2 Optimists are contented small men in high offices.

3 You don't write because you want to say something; you write because you've got something to say.

4 The victor belongs to the spoils.

162

- Henry Fonda
One of the Finest Actors of His Time
1905 - 1982

1 I haven't ever done anything except by other people. It ain't really Henry Fonda! Nobody could be. Nobody could have that much integrity.

2 Oh, God. Make me a good movie actor! Make me one of the best! For Jesus' sake, amen.

3 Most of us instantly recognize truth and forthrightness, in the theater and out of it. This does not mean that an actor must always be himself, but he must not lose

himself in his role. Being on stage is no excuse for not behaving like a human being.

4 There is no sense in using too much voice, and you don't need any more expression on your face than you'd in your everyday life.

163

- **Henry Ford**
The Inventor of the Assembly Line Production
1863 - 1947

1 Obstacles are those frightful things you see when you take your eyes off your goal.

2 Whether you think you can or think you can't, you're right.

3 To make your life a success, finish what you start.

4 You can do anything if you have enthusiasm. It is the yeast that makes your hopes rise to the stars. It is the spark in your eye, the swing in your gait, the grip of your hand, the irresistible surge of your will and your energy to execute your ideas. Enthusiasts are fighters. They have fortitude. They have staying qualities. Enthusiasm is at the bottom of all progress. With it there is accomplishment. Without it there are only alibis.

5 You cannot build a reputation on what you are going to do.

6 It is usual to associate age with years only because so many men and women somewhere along in, what is called middle age, stop trying.

7 Nobody can think straight who does not work. Idleness warps the mind.

8 Work does more than getting us our living; it gets us our life.

9 Thinking is the hardest work there is, which is the probable reason why so few engage in it.

10 The man who will use his skill and constructive imagination to see how much, instead of how little, he can give for a dollar, is bound to succeed.

11 Success is not rare - it is common. Very few miss a measure of it. It is not a matter of luck, or contesting - for certainly no success can come from preventing the success of another. It is a matter of adjusting one's efforts to obstacles and one's abilities to a service needed by others. There is no other possible success. But most people think of it in terms of getting; success, however, begins in terms of giving.

12 He who would really benefit mankind must reach them through their work.

13 Failure is only the opportunity to begin again, more intelligently.

14 I am convinced, by my own experience and that of others, that if there is any secret of success, it lies in the ability to get the other person's point of view and to see things from his angle as well as your own.

15 Even a mistake may turn out to be the one thing necessary to a worthwhile achievement.

16 Coming together is a beginning; keeping together is progress; working together is success.

17 One of the great discoveries a man makes, one of his great surprises, is to find that he can do what he was afraid he couldn't do.

18 Life is a series of experiences, each one of which makes us bigger, even though sometimes it is hard to realize this. For the world was built to develop character, and we must learn that the setbacks and griefs which we endure, help us in our marching forward.

19 There is joy in work. There is no happiness except in the realization that we have accomplished something.

20 There is no such thing as no chance.

21 Nothing is particularly hard if you divide it into small jobs.

164

- George Foreman
The Oldest Champion of World Heavyweight Boxing
Born in 1947

1 Life is like boxing. You've got only so many punches to throw and you can only take so many.

2 Life can end as quickly as a smile.

3 When you start trying to help people, it can get rough. You waste so many years helping yourself, you don't know that one day you're going to realize you need to help other people. And then you don't have it to give.

165

- Ben Franklin
One of the Best Role Models of All Time
1706 - 1790

1 If you would not be forgotten as soon as you are dead, either write things worth reading or do things worth writing.

2 Little strokes fell great oaks.

3 Carelessness does more harm than a want of knowledge.

4 The man who does things makes many mistakes, but he never makes the biggest mistake of all - doing nothing.

5 He that can have patience can have what he will.

6 Never leave that till tomorrow which you can do today.

7 A ploughman on his legs is higher than a gentleman on his knees.

8 A great bank account can never make a man rich. It is the mind that makes the body rich. A man is rich or poor according to what he is, not according to what he has.

9 Money never yet made a man rich, and there is nothing in its nature to produce happiness.

10 He does not possess wealth that allows it to possess him.

11 Well done is better than well said.

12 Those things that hurt, instruct.

13 When you are good to others, you are best to yourself.

14 The most acceptable service of God is doing good to man.

15 Empty the coins of your purse into your mind, and your mind will fill your purse with gold.

16 An investment in knowledge pays the best interest.

17 He that is good for making excuses, is seldom good for anything else.

18 He that is of the opinion that money will do everything may well be suspected of doing everything for money.

19 The way to wealth is as plain as the way to market. Waste neither time, nor money, but make the best use of both.

20 Dost thou love life? Then do not squander time, for that is the stuff life is made of.

21 Beware of little expenses; a small leak will sink a great ship.

22 He that goes a borrowing goes a sorrowing.

23 If you know how to spend less than you get, you have the philosopher's stone.

24 One today is worth two tomorrows.

25 To lengthen thy life, lessen thy meals.

26 Human felicity is produced not so much by great pieces of good fortune that seldom happen, as by little advantages that occur every day.

27 He who falls in love with himself will have no rivals.

28 Let honesty and industry be thy constant companions, and spend one penny less than thy clear gains; then shall thy pockets begin to thrive; creditors will not insult, nor want oppress, nor hunger bite, nor nakedness freeze thee.

29 If you would have a faithful servant, and one that you like, serve yourself.

30 Truth and sincerity have a certain distinguishing native lustre about them which cannot be perfectly counterfeited; they are like fire and flame that cannot be painted.

31 To cease to think creatively is but little different from ceasing to live.

32 Many a man thinks that he is buying pleasure, when he is really selling himself to it.

33 Make haste slowly.

34 If you argue and rankle and contradict, you may achieve a victory sometimes, but it will be an empty victory because you will never get your opponents goodwill.

35 I will speak ill of no man, and speak all the good I know of everybody.

36 It is easier to suppress the first desire than to satisfy all that follow it.

37 Fear not death; for the sooner we die, the longer we shall be immortal.

38 Write injuries in dust, benefits in marble.

39 The heart of the fool is in his mouth, but the mouth of the wise is in his heart.

40 There is much difference between imitating a good man, and counterfeiting him.

41 Work as if you were to live 100 years. Pray as if you were to die tomorrow.

42 None preaches better than the ant, and she says nothing.

43 Eat to please thyself, but dress to please others.

44 The eyes of other people are the eyes that ruin us. If all but myself were blind, I should want neither fine clothes, fine houses, nor fine furniture.

45 Early to bed and early to rise, makes a man healthy, wealthy and wise.

46 Three can keep a secret if two of them are dead.

47 Fatigue is the best pillow.

48 There are no gains without pains.

49 If passion drives you, let reason hold the reign.

50 There are two ways of being happy: we must either diminish our wants or augment our means.

51 Who is rich? he that rejoices in his portion.

52 Wealth is not his who has it, but his that enjoys it.

53 Money never made a man happy yet, nor will it. The more a man has, the more he wants. Instead of filling a vacuum, it makes one.

54 He who multiplies riches, multiplies cares.

55 The proof of gold is fire.

166

- Joe Frazier
Became the World Boxing Champion Despite Many Odds
Born in 1944

1 Music has soul. It gives you a feeling of belonging. It gets you with life. It is power, strength and stamina. It moves every bit of you and the audience, too. It is real. It makes you feel you are going places.

2 You can do anything you want to do, if you really put your heart and soul and mind into it. When I started boxing I had two jobs, a wife, a couple of kids and I had to train. But if you put your right foot in front of you and the left behind, somebody will give you a hand.

3 I really never strayed too far from boxing. When I wasn't performing, or in New York, I was back in Philadelphia at Joe Frazier's Gym.

4 A lot of heavyweights that are hot stuff in the amateurs, where a pure boxer has an edge in the way a bout is scored, don't cut it as pros. Pros is a tougher game for heavyweights. Pros is more physical, brutalizing deal. You can only go so far with slip-and-slide jive as a professional heavyweight.

5 You don't go to General Motors, build a car and say it's yours. Same thing at my gym. If you come here and learn, I want to make money back. You belong to us.

6 Mostly tired people make mistakes and healthy bodies seldom do.

7 We need to build our youth and care about our youth - for without them, there can be no future.

1 The world is full of willing people - some willing to work, the rest willing to let them.

2 Education is the ability to listen to almost anything without losing your temper or your self-confidence.

3 The reason why worry kills more people than work is that more people worry than work.

4 Before I built a wall I'd asked to know what I was walling in or walling out.

5 I have promises to keep, and miles to go, before I sleep.

6 There are tones of voice that mean more than words.

7 Happiness makes up in height for what it lacks in length.

8 We have to have frustrations. You just have to learn how to live with them. Sometimes you win, and sometimes you lose; but don't allow yourself to be made a fool by either success or failure. It's religion to be able to rise above both success and failure.

9 Always fall in with what you are asked to accept. Take what is given, and make it your way. My aim in life has always been to hold my own with whatever is going; not against but with.

10 We people are thrust forward out of the suggestions of form in the rolling clouds of nature. In us, nature reaches its height of form and through us exceeds itself. When in doubt, there is always form for us to go on with. Anyone who has achieved the least form to be sure of it, is lost to the larger excruciations.

11 Two roads diverged into a wood. I took the one less traveled by and that has made all the difference.

12 The best way out is always through.

13 There ought to be, in everything you write, some sign that you come from almost anywhere.

14 Home is the place where, when you have to go there, they have to take you in.

15 Nobody takes up poetry. You drift into it by little things.

16 The brain is a wonderful organ; it starts working the moment you get up in the morning and does not stop until you get into the office.

17 By working faithfully eight hours a day, you may eventually get to be a boss and work twelve hours a day.

18 A bank is a place where they lend you an umbrella in fair weather and ask for it back again when it begins to rain.

19 In three words I can sum up everything I've learned about life. It goes on.

20 Freedom lies in being bold.

168

1 Even acting right will sometimes bring dissensions in a family.

2 To make any reform effective, we must keep the subjects employed. We may instruct as we will, but if we allow them their time and they have nothing to do, they naturally must return to their evil passions.

3 When thee builds a prison, thee had better build with the thought ever in thy mind that thee and thy children may occupy the cells.

169

1 As the component parts of all new machines may be said to be old, the mechanic should sit down among levers, screws, wedges, wheels etc., like a poet among the letters of the alphabet, considering them as the exhibition of his thoughts, in which a new arrangement transmits a new idea to the world.

2 The inhabitants of all countries receive their ideas and prejudices from the established customs which surround them in youth, the customs that plunge them into vice or lead them on to virtue.

3 There should be no hereditary legislators. Wisdom is the friend of man; hence genius should have an equal claim to rise to the seat of power where talents might exert their full force for the good of the citizens.

4 There is no honour to be acquired but in following such pursuits as tend to harmonize men and nations and multiply the necessary and rational enjoyments of life.

170

1 Money and fame don't bring happiness.

2 We all have a contract with the public; in us they see themselves or what they would like to be.

3 During the war I saw so much in the way of death and destruction that I realized that I hadn't been singled out for grief - that others were suffering and losing their loved ones just like I lost my wife.

171

1 I give thanks to God, who has been pleased to make me the first observer of marvelous things unrevealed to bygone ages. I have ascertained that the moon is a body similar to earth. I have beheld a multitude of fixed stars never before seen. But the greatest marvel of all is the discovery of four new planets (four satellites of Jupiter). I have observed that they move around the sun.

2 Though scriptures cannot err, its expounders and interpreters are liable to err in many ways.

3 You cannot teach a man anything. You can only help him to discover it within himself.

172

1 Strength does not come from physical capacities, it comes from an indomitable will.

2 Never use violence of any kind. Never threaten violence in any way. Never even think violent thoughts. Never argue because it attacks another's opinion. Never criticize because it attacks another's ego. And your success is guaranteed.

3 A leader is useless when he acts against the promptings of his own conscience.

4 If I had not used humour, I would have gone insane a long time ago.

5 There is more to life than increasing its speed.

6 Faith must be enforced by reason. When faith becomes blind, it dies.

7 The moment the slave resolves that he will no longer be a slave, his fetters fall. Freedom and slavery are mental states.

8 Satisfaction lies in the effort, not in the attainment. Full effort is full victory.

9 Where there is love, there is life.

10 Hatred can be overcome only by love.

11 I have not the shadow of a doubt that any man or woman can achieve what I have, if he or she would make the same effort and cultivate the same hope and faith.

12 I have learnt through bitter experience the one supreme lesson: to conserve my anger, and as heat conserved is transmuted into energy, even so our anger controlled can be transmuted into a power which can move the world.

13 Joy lies in the fight, in the attempt, in the suffering involved, not in the victory itself.

14 To forget how to dig the earth and tend the soil is to forget ourselves.

15 One man cannot do right in one department of life whilst he is occupied in doing wrong in any other department. Life is one invisible whole.

16 All your scholarship, all your study of Shakespeare and Wordsworth would be vain if at the same time you did not build your character and attain mastery over your thoughts and your actions.

17 Purity of life is the highest and truest art.

18 Love is the subtlest force in the world.

19 It does not require money to be neat, clean and dignified.

20 Strength of numbers is the delight of the timid. The valiant in spirit glory in fighting alone.

21 If we have listening ears, God speaks to us in our own language, whatever that language be.

22 Prayer is not asking. It is a longing of the soul. It is daily admission of one's weakness. It is better in prayer to have a heart without words than words without a heart.

23 A man who throws himself on God ceases to fear man.

24 If we will take care of today, God will take care of the morrow.

25 God answers prayer in His own way, not ours.

26 A man with a grain of faith in God never loses hope, because he ever believes in the ultimate triumph of Truth.

27 Close the day with prayer so you may have a peaceful night, free from dreams and nightmares.

173

- Greta Garbo
Hollywood's First Major Romantic Idol
1905 - 1990

1 Anyone who does a job properly has a right to privacy.

2 I never said "I want to be alone". I only said "I want to be let alone."

3 We have to have some resemblance to understand each other truly or to develop a friendship. But we have to be really different to love each other.

4 Every one of us lives his life just once; if we are honest, to live once is enough.

5 In view of our short lives, it is not important who is writing or talking about others in derogatory terms. Death will crush the good and the bad, but history will select whom she wants.

6 Money gave me material independence but ruined me spiritually because I did not know how to use it. The question of keeping my money occupied my mind more than anything else. Throughout my entire life in Hollywood I had listened to the MGM bosses, and I had done what they had asked me to do.

7 Sometimes I consider myself a wise person who was afraid to discuss herself before the eyes and ears of others who would soon discover her to be an ignorant person.

8 If you're going to die on screen, you've got to be strong and in good health.

9 Life could be so wonderful, if we only knew what to do with it.

174

1 It is better to fail and do it independently than to succeed after being fitted to the conventional mould by others who have been shaped by the same process.

2 The rule of jotting down your thought on the instant does not apply merely to ideas that come as inspirations, or thoughts suggested by what you read or see, but it applies especially to the ideas that come to you at the time you give yourself up to concentrated thinking on play production.

3 The journey of a thousand miles must begin with a single step:
Plan each day's work to get results;
Start working;
Think on the typewriter;
Get it on paper.

175

1 A pound of pluck is worth a ton of luck.

2 Ideas control the world.

3 By saving nickels and dimes thrifty persons lay the foundation of fortunes.

4 Things don't turn up in this world until somebody turns them up.

5 Poverty is uncomfortable, as I can testify; but nine times out of ten the best thing that can happen to a young man is to be tossed overboard and compelled to sink or swim for himself.

6 If wrinkles must be written upon our brows, let them not be written upon the heart. The spirit should not grow old.

7 Commerce links all mankind in one common brotherhood of mutual dependence and interests.

8 The riders in a race do not stop short when they reach the goal. There is a little finishing canter before coming to a standstill. There is time to hear the kind voice of friends and to say to one's self, "The work is done."

176

1 You have only one life to live.

2 It never occurred to anybody that I might have feelings.

3 In the silence of night I have often wished for just a few words of love from one man, rather than the applause of thousands of people.

177

1 The best way to learn is to be on the set. You make one mistake and you won't forget it.

2 I don't act, I react to what someone else does. People want to see someone on the screen who they enjoy. I've tried to give them that by being natural and part of the scene whether it was in films, television or on the stage. If an audience gets the idea that you're acting, you're finished. You've got to look real and I think that comes from being real.

3 I don't know when to stop. When I make a commitment, it is to the end. They can put me in my grave and I'll still be trying to commit.

4 I don't do futuristic pictures. I don't have any particular sense of my image, but whatever I do has to have a sense of humour about it. There is nothing worse than the steely-eyed sheriff. Brave bores me. Smart intrigues me. I'm very wry and off-beat. I'm not going to make you fall down and laugh. I don't do comedy. I do humour.

178

1 The success of any great moral enterprise does not depend upon numbers.

2 All men are created equal, and all oppression is odious in the sight of God. Confine me as a prisoner, but bind me not as a slave. Punish me as a criminal, but hold me not as a chattel. Torture me as a man, but drive me not like a beast. Doubt my sanity, but acknowledge my immortality.

3 Wherever there is a human being, I see God-given rights inherent in that being, whatever may be the sex or complexion.

4 Since the creation of the world there has been no tyrant like Intemperance, and no slave so cruelly treated as his.

5 I am in earnest. I shall not excuse; I shall not equivocate; I shall not retreat a single inch; and I shall be heard.

6 With reasonable men, I will reason; with humane men I will plead; but to tyrants I will give no quarter, nor waste arguments where they will certainly be lost.

7 We may be personally defeated, but our principles never.

8 The history of mankind is a record of the saddest mistakes, the wildest aberrations, the most melancholy inconsistencies, the bloodiest crimes.

9 Every moral and religious reform is struggling against the wind and the tide of popular clamor.

179

- Paul Gauguin
A Leading French Painter of Postimpressionist Period
1848 - 1903

1 Life is hardly more than a fraction of a second. Such a little time to prepare oneself for eternity.

2 The work that we love brings us happiness.

3 It is possible, at any time, to change one's career and goals and way of life.

4 To draw freely is not to lie to oneself.

5 If we will look carefully, we will enjoy endless pleasure.

6 When extreme emotions blend in the depths of a person, when they burst out and when the entire mind flows like lava from a volcano, the cold calculations of reason have not presided over this emission, and who knows, where or when the work was started?

7 Many excellent cooks are spoiled by going into the arts.

180

- Lou Gehrig
The Only Person to Play 2130 Consecutive Professional Baseball Games
1903 - 1941

1 Baseball is hard work and the strain is tremendous. Sure, it's pleasurable, but it's tough.

2 Ballplayers can last just as long as their legs last.

3 I may have been given a bad break, but I have an awful lot to live for. With all this, I consider myself the luckiest man on the face of this earth.

4 This is an important work, too. I have a great responsibility because I am dealing with the lives of young men - many of them little more than boys.

181

- Bob Geldoff
The Man Who Raised $100 Million for Famine Relief in Africa
Born in 1954

1 I seem rude and surly to a lot of people, but I seemed that way at 18. I am dogmatic - always talking about things in terms of black and white.

2 Always go right to the top.

3 We could spend our money tomorrow, and it could keep thirty million people alive, for seven weeks, and then they would die. Or, we can build wells and give them a life. I prefer to do that.

4 It's not just a moral requirement that you should give more aid to Africa. It is also a sound economic one. You need the African market as much as they need your food.

1 I was really a genius, without knowing it. I never thought that it could happen to a Canadian.

2 In the theater, where the word is king, one reaches the heart mainly by passing through the ears. What is the use of finding the precise word, the correctly constructed phrase, if the idea which you expose, or the feelings you express, finds no correspondence in the thoughts and the hearts of your audience?

3 Theater is the marriage of two essential elements: the stage and the audience. In order to be fully consummated, marriage requires not only the coming together of the constituent parties, but also their total union. Therefore, audience and stage must necessarily melt into each other in order for the principle of the theater to be realized.

4 The theater is an art form whose joys are essentially collective. I can very well imagine you all by yourself in your living room, becoming enthused over the reading of a poem or listening to a symphony, but I cannot at all visualize you as a solitary spectator in an empty theater, throwing your programme up into the air in a delirium of enthusiasm after the curtain call has fallen on a dramatic masterpiece.

5 The ideal dramatic form must be the one which will interest the audience in its totality, the one which will reach not only the most numerous, but also the most diversified public.

6 The dramatist facing an audience finds himself, in my opinion, in the same situation as a student of mathematics whose professor has asked him to find the common denominator of a series lined up on the blackboard. For the dramatic author, this common denominator means the heart of his spectators, for it is a fact that just about everybody carries a heart in his bosom, but very few people have a head on their shoulders. And if the conflict of the two opposing passions can be understood by all, it is only a minority who will be able to follow the logical development of a reasoning process.

1 Conversation enriches the understanding, but solitude is the school of Genius.

2 The winds and waves are always on the side of the ablest navigators.

3 Every man has two educations: one which he receives from others; and one, more important, which he gives himself.

4 My early and invincible love of reading .. I would not exchange for the treasures of India.

5 History is indeed little more than the register of the crimes, follies and misfortunes of mankind.

184

-Althea Gibson
The First Black Person to Win Major Titles in Tennis
Born in 1927

1 Winning at Wimbledon was wonderful, and it meant a lot to me. But there is nothing quite like winning the championship of your own country. That's what counts the most with anybody.

2 You got to know your opponent. You got to know their strengths, their weaknesses.

185

- Lillian Gilbreth
The Foremost Woman Industrial Engineer of Her Time
1878 - 1972

1 It's better to be envied for what you are than for what you own.

2 The emphasis in successful management lies on the man, not on the work. Efficiency is best secured by modifying the equipment, materials and methods to make the most of the man.

3 God made each of us different from everyone else in the world. Because of this uniqueness we can learn something from everybody. Even from a mentally retarded person, we can perhaps learn how to help him and others; and from a crushing bore, how not to be a crushing bore.

4 Some people get pleasure out of owning things and that's very fine for them. But I find that owning expensive things doesn't bring me pleasure at all - just displeasure. You worry for fear you will be careless and lose them; you worry for fear you haven't locked them up properly and they will be stolen; you have to go to the trouble of insuring them; and if you are not careful, people who don't have things as nice as yours will envy you.

186

- Joe Girard
America's Top Car Salesperson for 12 Consecutive Years
Born in 1928

1 However I feel about myself or whoever I am with, I don't let my feelings get in the way. Selling is an important profession and those people, those prospects, those customers are the most important thing in the world to us, to each of us. They aren't interruptions or pains in the ass. They are what we live on. And if we don't realize that, as a hard business fact, then we don't know what we are doing. I am not talking about some of them or most of them. I am talking about all of them.

2 Whatever you are selling, there is probably somebody else out there selling one exactly like it.

3 Nobody can be a great salesman without wanting - wanting something very much. And the more you want, the more you drive yourself to do what it takes to sell.

4 You have to want something and you have to know what it is and you have to see every move you make as a way of getting whatever you want. Knowing what you want will power your drive.

5 You can't sell a scared person; he will run away from you. You can't sell a mooch; he will pick up how you feel about him. You can only sell to a human being.

6 People talk a lot to other people what they buy and what they plan to buy. Others are always offering advice about where to buy what and how much to pay. Every time you turn off one prospect, you turn off 250 more.

7 What counts most is how you work, not where you work.

8 If you throw enough spaghetti against the wall, some of it has got to stick.

9 Take some time every morning and decide what you are going to do that day and then you must do it.

10 A small piece of something is better than a big piece of nothing.

187

-Stephen Girard
A Great American Merchant and Banker of His Time
1750 - 1831

1 Labour is the price of life, its happiness, its everything. To rest is to rust. Every man should labour to the last hour of his ability.

2 I do not value fortune. The love of labour is my highest ambition.

3 The secret of my success was the fact that work was my only pleasure.

4 I work all day so I might sleep at night.

5 If I have the misfortune to be overcome by the fatigue of my labours, I shall have the satisfaction of having performed a duty which we owe to one another.

188

- Lillian Gish
The First Female Celebrity of the Screen
1896 - 1993

1 A happy life should be in balance. One must live equally in the mind, body and spirit. Those who are lacking in one of these three attributes cannot be totally happy. It is only by keeping all three nourished through the rich resources at our call that we can help tap the true source of our strength.

2 I never wanted to own anything but books and have always been curious and had the energy to pursue my interests.

3 My films are my children.

4 I was merely taught to speak clearly and loudly so the audience could understand. And it did not matter what I felt or how I felt - it was the audience that counted.

189

1 An actor's security and the eye of a hurricane have a great deal in common.

2 If I did not have a super ego, how the hell could I be a performer?

3 Don't try to fool the people. They sense what you are and it is foolish to try to con them into believing anything else.

4 I have never been a modest man and I have always been suspicious of an actor's modesty. I don't want my success to be admired - just the incongruity of it.

5 From having nothing, I have been given everything. I try not to let money mean anything, otherwise you're beaten at the start.

6 I sometimes wish I had the capacity to do all the things they say I do. I'd have a lot more fun out of life. For six weeks at a crack, I live between my hotel and the studio. I do my show and am so exhausted I walk right home. I'm not ashamed of anything I've ever done.

7 Thin people are beautify but fat people are adorable.

190

1 It is difficult to say what is impossible; for the dream of yesterday is the hope of today and the reality of tomorrow.

2 Every vision is a joke until the first man accomplishes it.

3 There can be no thought of finishing; for *aiming at the stars*, both literally and figuratively, is a problem to occupy generations, so that no matter how much progress one makes, there is always the thrill of just beginning.

191

1 The worst crime against working people is a company which fails to operate at a profit.

2 Be devoted to your work.

3 Permanent changes and progress must come from within man. You can't save people; they must save themselves.

4 It is our duty to live our lives as workers in the society in which we live, and not to work for the downfall or the destruction, or the overthrow of that society, but for its further development and evolution.

192

1 Marriage and tennis are hard to mix.

2 Tennis is my whole life and I cannot imagine any other.

193

1 People become what they think they are.

2 Money is only a part of value. Value is everything you have - your team, people who know you and love you.

3 A child's name helps shape his or her personality. A name is something we wear throughout our lives. It has its own power. The sound, the personality and the meaning all affect both our perception of ourselves and others' perception of us.

4 When you feel like a star, you act and spend like one, racking up bills you can't afford.

5 Anything is only worth what somebody else is willing to pay for it.

6 You are you
That's all that matters to me.
You are you
And only you can be the one I love and yearn for,
The one that my heart burns for.
Yes, you are you
And that makes you best of all.
Never wished that you were more beautiful
More lovely or a star
For God made all your features
I love you as you are.
Yes, you are you
And that makes you best of all.

7 It is easier to stay out of drugs than to get out.

8 No winning formula lasts forever.

194

1   I gathered impressions both from life and from books. The first group of impressions may be compared to raw material, the second to a semi-manufactured product.

2   Many truths are best not recalled, especially those that only degrade people.

3   I often play the role of the holy fool who does not understand his own deeds; that helps me a lot in distancing myself from the banal and the petty.

4   In the nature that surrounds us and is hostile to us, there is no beauty. Beauty is created by man and from the depths of his soul. It is born out of man's desire to perceive it.

5   Essential romanticism is an active attitude towards reality, a program of work and a method for educating the people's will to life; it is a formula for building the new forms of life and a system of hatred towards the evils of the old world, whose cruel heritage is still perceived by men.

6   All parties are lifeless affairs which contain a good deal more of the self-pride of untalented people than of the spirit of men fired with the desire to build a new, free life for people, upon the ruins of the old, restricted life.

7   To meet a man does not always imply danger; still, one ought to be more careful in the choice of one's acquaintances.

8   Only he knows what toothache means who had had it, and then only while the tooth is actually aching. When it is over, a man forgets how tormenting it can be. It would be an admirable thing if the whole population of the earth could have toothache for at least several hours a month, all at the same time. That alone would teach people to understand one another.

195

1   Integrity means a man is the same on the inside as he claims to be on the outside.

2   There is nothing wrong with men possessing riches but the wrong comes when riches possess men.

3   I do not know what the future holds. But I know who holds the future.

4   The foundations of civilizations are no stronger than the corporate integrity of the homes on which they rest. If the home deteriorates, civilization will crumble and fall.

5   I don't think this or any other country is going in the right direction. We should be headed in the direction of goodness and righteousness, away from crime and immortality, and towards helping one's neighbours who are in need.

6   I believe there is hope for the future. I don't wring my hands and give up. I believe it is possible for us to grapple with the problems of the cities, the nation,

and the world and solve them. As long as men and women provide spiritual leadership, there is hope.

7 Personal security means knowing and accepting who we are and where we are going. That comes not from careers alone, but from diversifying our emotional portfolio. The only lasting peace and security is God Himself.

8 The only limit to the power of God lies within you.

196

- Martha Graham
One of the Most Influential Dancers of 20th Century
1894 - 1991

1 Your goal is freedom, but freedom can be achieved only through self-discipline.

2 There is no competition. Your only competition is the person you can become.

3 Everyone is born with a genius but most people keep it for only a brief moment.

4 Every individual has talents, but very few people know how to use them.

5 Each of us is unique and if you don't fulfill that uniqueness in whatever course your life may take, in whatever position you may hold, it is lost for all time. It is man's privilege and terror and job to reveal himself, to BE himself.

6 I want to make people feel intensely alive. I would rather have them against me than indifferent.

7 Nothing is more revealing than movement.

197

- U. S. Grant
The General Who Won the American Civil War for the North
1822 - 1885

1 Labour disgraces no man; unfortunately you occasionally find men disgrace labour.

2 Save! You will find the little treasure a faithful servant.

3 I have never advocated war, except as a means of peace.

4 I have known a few men who were always aching for a fight when there was no enemy near and who were as good as their word when the battle did come.

5 The will of the people is the best law.

6 I know no method to secure the repeal of bad or obnoxious laws so effective as their stringent execution.

7 I propose to fight it out on this line, if it takes all summer.

198

1 I never considered myself handicapped. All I ever wanted to do was play baseball.

2 I had always dreamed of becoming a major-leaguer.

3 I never wanted any favours. All I wanted was an opportunity to make the team of the major league.

199

1 The darkest hour in any man's life is when he sets down to plan how to get money without earning it.

2 Talent without tact is only half talent.

3 Abstaining is favourable both to the head and the pocket.

4 Fame is a vapour; popularity an accident; riches take wings; and the only certainty is oblivion.

5 The illusion that times that were are better than those that are, has probably pervaded all ages.

200

1 It is courage the world needs, not infallibility.

2 Courage is always the surest wisdom.

3 Not to love, not to serve, is not to live.

4 Everything worthwhile in the world has been accomplished notwithstanding.

5 Christ ever meant to me a peerless Leader, whose challenge was not to save ourselves, but to lose ourselves; not to understand Him, but to have the courage to follow Him; treading in the footsteps of Christ explains the meaning of life.

6 It would be the negation to me of the whole spirit of foreign missions if we do not send young men and women, as we do, into places where danger is great. We can only bring out good in people by trusting them.

7 I don't personally regard the hospital work as the first work of the mission, and never did. I am far more interested in making a new man than a new body. The message of the love of God to my mind lies in the orphanage and dock and industrial work and in gardens more than in the hospitals. This is the attitude of God that makes the mission appeal where others don't.

8 Whatever you do, do it heartily.

1   When I was a kid, I wanted to play, talk, shoot, walk, eat, laugh, look and be like Gordie Howe. He was far and away my favorite player. He is still the best player ever.

2   Whenever I was down, what kept me going was one thing my father drilled into us as kids, that what we started we had to finish. I didn't want to quit on myself or on him, so I decided to keep going.

3   I think I worry more about equipment than anybody in the league. My sticks have almost no curve. I don't have a great slapshot anyway, so I don't need a curve for that. And with a straighter blade I can stickhandle better and control my backhand better. I use one of the three heaviest sticks in the NHL because my wrists aren't strong enough to use a whippy stick. As the season goes on, I use shorter and shorter sticks. By the end of the year, it's one and a half inch shorter than it was in October. I figure I'm getting more and more tired as the year goes on and little extra lightness might get me a couple of pucks come April. I baby my sticks. I tape them all by myself and that's a lot of sticks. The night I broke Gordie's points record I used fourteen sticks. My blade is as wide as it can possibly be. You can blindfold me and hand me a stick that's quarter of an ounce off and I can tell it's not my stick.

4   I have always skated in very tight skate. I think it gives me more control.

5   My dad always taught me to wear the lightest equipment they make. It's a feel game and you can't feel the stick with riot gear on. So I always wear the lightest gloves and the lightest pads I can. I might be cold when I get in, but a couple of goals will warm you right up.

6   People ask me about all the records I set. They mean a lot, obviously, but I know most of them will be broken. When Gordie set all his records, nobody figured they'd be broken. Somebody will come along and break most of my records as well.

7   Hockey teaches you humility.

8   The best way to deal with people with disabilities is to just be yourself.

1   When you get what you are after, it's worth whatever it costs, no matter what.

2   The main difference between a good and a bad picture is timing and tempo.

3   What you get is a living. What you give is a life.

4   No man drinks for the sake of drinking. He drinks because he has no place to go.

5   Man is a moving animal. The bigger the man, the more he has the need for activity. It isn't so much with women.

6   The sense of beauty is developed by environment.

7   A picture is the universal symbol and a picture that moves is a universal language.

8   Any actress can look good at any age, if she is good enough and still holds interest, whereas mere beauty fades away and grows dull.

9   The camera opens and shuts, opens and shuts with equal timing - so half of everything you do isn't seen. Then take away the sound, and you lose another quarter. What's left on the screen is a quarter of what you felt or did. Therefore, your expression must be four times as deep and true as it would be normally, to cover with full effect to your audience.

203

- Sarah Grimké
Pioneer of Women's Rights and Abolition
1792 - 1873

1   I ask no favours for my sex; all I ask is that they take their feet off our necks.

2   Death is so beautiful a transition to another and a higher sphere of usefulness and happiness, that it no longer looks to me like passing through a dark valley, but rather like merging into sunlight and joy.

Angela Grimké
Pioneer of Woman's Rights and Abolition
1805 - 1879

3   If persecution is the means which God has ordained for the accomplishment of this great end, *Emancipation*, then, is dependence upon Him for strength to bear it; I feel as if I could say, *Let It Come!* for it is my deep, solemn, deliberate conviction that *this is a cause worth dying for.*

4   The artificial distinctions in society, the separation between the higher and the lower orders, the aristocracy of wealth and education, are the very rock of pauperism and the only way to eradicate this plague from our land will be to associate with the poor, and the wicked too.

5   Slavery always has, and always will produce insurrections wherever it exists, because it is a violation of the natural order of things, and no human power can much longer perpetuate it.

204

- Johan Gutenberg
The Inventor and Developer of Printing from Movable Type
1397 - 1468

1   I have found it necessary to be favoured with quiet and seclusion in pursuing any new branch of business, and I cannot succeed in this unless it be kept a profound secret.

2   There is nothing like trying.

3   I claim no powers of magic; it is simply patience that has done it.

4   We must expect difficulties and seek to overcome them. We must make more fresh type until we contrive a way of hardening the wood.

205

- Janet Guthrie
The First Woman to Compete in Indy 500
Born in 1938

1 Racing is a matter of spirit, not strength. It is a matter of doing your best each little moment. There is never a break. You must have a desire, a very intense desire to keep going.

2 There is almost nothing as challenging as racing. You have to extend yourself beyond what you can normally do and that makes everything in life more exciting. When I drive a really good race, everything else in the world feels better, and tastes better.

3 I am a good driver, but I am no superwoman. No driver can afford to get angry behind the wheel. A good driver needs emotional detachment, concentration, good judgment and desire.

4 My passion for racing came close to destroying me psychologically. I lived in terrible quarters and spent all my money on cars. I was suffering from severe depression. It was really rough at the end of 1975.

206

- Alice Hamilton
The Founder of Industrial Medicine in America
1869 - 1970

1 Taking part in a new and expanding discipline brings out the best in one.

2 If you are going to sketch me, I'll take off my hat, for nothing dates one so much as a hat, and I refuse to be dated.

3 Employers and doctors both appeared more willing to listen to me as I told them their duties than they would have been if I had been a man. It seemed natural and right that a woman should put care of the producing workman ahead of the value of the thing he was producing.

4 Personal liberty is the most precious thing in life.

5 It is all right to be modest, but one does not want to be anonymous.

207

- Scott Hamilton
The World Champion Figure-Skater
Despite a Severe Childhood Disease
Born in 1958

1 To win you have to forget winning and skate for something else.

2 It takes time to get things you work for.

3 I want to be a person that someone can turn to when they need help.

4 Smiling helps. Your marks come easier. If you are smiling, it looks like you are not working as hard and things are coming natural to you.

208

1 A profound silence is a much more proper expression of deep distress in tragedy than all the noisy applause which is so much in vogue - no matter how great the authority of custom may be for it.

209

1 Look at the work that awaits you. Write if you will; but write about the world as it is and as you think it *ought* to be and must be - if there is to be a world. Write about all the things that men have written about since the beginning of writing and talking - but write to a point. Work hard at it, *care* about it. Write about *your people*; tell their story. You have something glorious to draw on begging for attention. Don't pass it up.

2 Life has within it that which is good, that which is beautiful and that which is love.

3 I think that the highest gift that man has is art, and I am audacious enough to think of myself as an artist - that there is both joy and beauty and illumination and communion between people to be achieved through the dissection of personality. That is what I want to do. I want to reach a little closer to the world, which is to say to the people, and see if we can share some illuminations together about each other.

4 There are great plays and lousy plays and reasonably good plays; when the artist achieves a force of art which is commensurate with his message - he hooks us.

5 The most ordinary human being has within him elements of profundity, of profound anguish.

6 In life, adequate respect must be paid to the tenacity of the absurd in both human and natural affairs.

210

1 From the first day in hospital I had set myself goals. I had promised myself I would be out of that Stryker bed for my birthday, August 26, and I was.

2 I was optimistic, but I wasn't stupid. All my life I had felt that if you worked hard enough you could get what you wanted. I wanted to walk again, I was working my butt off - and there was no improvement. Worse than that, nobody would tell me anything, not even my friends, the student nurses. So I broke into the files to find out.

3 I thought of quitting lots of time. It was a rotten environment, and I knew that

any time I felt like it, I could just walk away. But every time I had asked myself, "Is all this BS worth the end result?" And I could never quite bring myself to say *No*.

4 Hey, we are out here. We have got lives and hopes and dreams like everyone else. Don't just look at our chairs - look at us.

211

- Thomas Hardy
A Major English Novelist of Late 19th Century
1840 - 1928

1 The old husk drops off because it has long withered and you discover that beneath it is a sound and vigorous growth of genuine conviction.

2 I may have higher aim someday but, for the present, circumstances lead me to wish merely to be considered a good hand at a serial.

3 My only ambition was to have some poem in a good anthology such as Francis Palgraves's *Golden Treasury*.

212

- William Harvey
The Discoverer of the Correct Theory of Blood Circulation
1578 - 1657

1 People prefer the familiar because it is comfortable.

2 Little is ever accomplished by bitter controversy.

3 Without frequent observation and reiterated experiment the mind goes astray after phantoms and appearances.

4 Often, many men lacking in experience get an idea of another's probable view, and later give it out boldly as definitely true. Hence it comes about that they not only err themselves, but lead imprudent other people astray.

5 It is often much better to grow wise at home and in private, than by publishing what you have amassed with infinite labour, to stir up tempests that may rob you of peace and quiet for the rest of your days.

6 Search out and study the secret of nature by experiments.

213

Nathaniel Hawthorne
A Preeminent 19th Century American Novelist
1804 - 1864

1 No man can be a poet and a bookkeeper at the same time.

2 No man, for any considerable period, can wear one face to himself and another to the multitude without finally getting bewildered as to which may be true.

3 Every individual has a place to fill in the world, and is important in some respect, whether he chooses to be so or not.

4 The best things come, as a general thing, from the talents that are members of a

group. Every man works better when he has companions working in the same line. Great things, of course, have been done by solitary workers; but they have usually been done with double the pains they would have cost if they had been produced in more genial circumstances.

5 We sometimes congratulate ourselves at the moment of waking from a troubled dream; it may be so the moment after death.

214

- Franz Haydn
A Great Composer of the Classical Period in Music
1732 - 1809

1 Often when I was wrestling with obstacles of every kind, when my physical and mental strength alike were running low and it was hard for me to persevere in the path on which I had set my feet, a secret feeling within me whispered: "There are so few happy and contented people here below, sorrow and anxiety pursue them everywhere; perhaps your work may, some day, become a spring from which the careworn may draw a few moment's rest and refreshment." And that was a powerful motive for pressing onward.

2 The mind and soul must be free.

3 I never had a proper teacher. I started with the practical side, first in singing, then in playing instruments and later in composition. I listened more than I studied. I listened attentively and tried to turn to good account what most impressed me. In this way my knowledge and ability were developed. I heard the finest music in all forms that was to be heard in my time, and of that there was much in Vienna.

4 What I am is all the result of the direst need.

5 Art is free, and should be fettered by no mechanical regulations. The educated ear is the sole authority on all these questions, and I think I have as much right to lay down the law as anyone.

6 A harmonious song was all my life.

215

- William Herschel
The Discoverer of the Planet Uranus
1738 - 1822

1 The most likely way of making important discoveries is to systematically observe every heavenly body and noting interesting features and relative positions.

216

1 If you want to make money, you must do things in a large way.

2 Idleness is the devil's workbench.

217

1 Oceans have not kept people apart, as many scientists believe. Instead, oceans have helped to bring people together.

2 The ocean cannot absorb all the chemical waste we dump into it. Life in the ocean is dying. If it died, life on the earth would soon die too.

3 I am not an adventurer, but I don't turn an adventure down when it comes my way.

4 Those who plow across the sea with roaring engines, and then come back and say there is nothing to see far out on the ocean, can have no conception of the surprises that await him who drifts along slowly on the surface.

5 Somewhere along the way the modern man has made a mistake by failing to acknowledge the huge difference between progress and civilization.

6 There is only one ocean. We speak of seven, but they are part of the same sea, and the continents are islands.

7 Take away our hundreds of generations of accumulated inheritance, and then compare what is left of our abilities with those of the founders of the Indus civilization... The citizens of Mohenjo Daro and their uncivilized contemporaries would have learnt to drive a car, turn on a television set and knot a neck-tie as easily as any African or European today. In reasoning and inventiveness little has been gained or lost in the build up of the human species during the last five millennia. With this in mind a visitor to Mohenjo Daro will be left with the impression that the creators of this city had either surpassed all other human generations in inventiveness, or that they were immigrants bringing with them centuries of cultural inheritance.

8 Human history has no known beginning. As it stands, it begins with civilized mariners coming in by sea. This is no real beginning. This is the continuation of something lost somewhere in the mist. Is it still hidden under desert sand, as was Sumerian civilization itself, remaining unknown to science until discovered and excavated in southern Iraq in the last century? Was it buried by volcanic eruption, as was the great Mediterranean civilization on the island of Santorini, unknown until discovered in our own time under fifty feet of ashes? Or could it possibly be submerged in the ocean that covers two-thirds of our restless planet, as suggested by the hard-dying legend of Atlantis?

9 The modern man has his brains stuffed full, not so much with his own experience, but with opinions and impressions derived from books, magazines, radio and motion pictures. The result is an over-loaded brain and reduced

powers of observation. The primitive man, on the other hand, was an extrovert and alert, with keen instincts and all his senses alive.

10 The civilization may be compared with a house full of people who have never seen outside the building. None of them know what their house looks like, although they live in it. It is necessary to go outside to see the house as it really is.

218

- James Jerome Hill
The Builder of the Great Northern Railway
1838 - 1916

1 Tilling the soil is the basis of every human achievement.

2 If you want to know whether you are destined to be a success or a failure in life, you can easily find out. The test is simple and infallible. Are you able to save money? If not, drop out. You will lose.

219

- Napoleon Hill
A Pioneer Researcher of the Law of Success
1883- 1970

1 Eat sparingly, work enthusiastically and love generously.

2 Most real failures are due to limitations which men set up in their own mind. If they had the courage to go one step farther, they might discover their error.

3 Fear is nothing but faith in reverse gear. The foundation on which both faith and fear rests is belief in something.

4 No man has a chance to enjoy permanent success until he begins to look in a mirror for the real cause of all his mistakes.

5 If a man has built a sound character, it makes but little difference what people say about him, because he will win in the end.

6 One of the surest ways to find happiness for yourself is to devote your energies toward making someone else happy. Happiness is an elusive, transitory thing. And if you set out to search for it, you will find it evasive. But if you try to bring happiness to someone else, then it comes to you.

7 Until a man selects a definite purpose in life, he dissipates his energies and spreads his thoughts over so many subjects, and in so many different directions that they lead not to power, but to indecision and weakness.

8 Success comes to those who set goals and pursue them regardless of obstacles and disappointments.

9 All outstanding successes can be attributed to knowing how to tap and use invisible sources of intelligence, sources which have no relationship to formal education.

10 A man is never so near success as when that which he calls failure has overtaken him, for it is on occasions of this sort that he is forced to THINK. If he thinks accurately and with persistence, he discovers that so-called failure is usually nothing more than a signal to rearm himself with a new plan or purpose.

11 The waste of life lies in the love we have not given, the powers we have not used, the selfish prudence that will risk nothing and which, shirking pain, misses happiness as well.

12 Every adversity carries in itself the seed of an equal or better advantage.

13 Effort only fully releases its reward after a person refuses to quit.

14 What the mind of man can conceive and believe, the mind of man can achieve.

15 You are searching for the magic key that will unlock the door to the source of power; and yet you have the key in your own hands, and may make use of it the moment you learn to control your thoughts.

16 It is always your next move.

17 If you do not conquer self, you will be conquered by self.

18 It is literally true that you can succeed best and quickest by helping others to succeed.

19 When your desires are strong enough you will appear to possess superhuman powers to achieve.

20 Through some strange and powerful principle of mental chemistry which she has never divulged, Nature wraps up in the impulse of strong desire, that something which recognizes no such word as impossible and accepts no such reality as failure.

21 The starting point of all achievement is desire. Keep this constantly in mind. Weak desires bring weak results, just as a small amount of fire makes a small amount of heat.

22 No man can succeed in a line of endeavour which he does not like.

23 Everyone enjoys doing the kind of work for which he is best suited.

24 Success in its highest and noblest form calls for peace of mind and enjoyment and happiness which come only to the man who has found the work that he likes best.

25 Select your environment with the greatest care, for it is the mental feeding ground out of which the food that goes into your minds is extracted.

26 You can start where you stand, and apply the habit of going the extra mile by rendering more service and better service than you are now being paid for.

27 When defeat comes, accept it as a signal that your plans are not sound; rebuild those plans, and set sail once more toward your coveted goal.

28 No man ever achieved worthwhile success who did not, at one time or another, find himself with at least one foot hanging well over the brink of failure.

29 You give before you get.

30 There is one quality which one must possess to win, and that is definiteness of purpose, the knowledge of what one wants, and a burning desire to possess it.

31 The world has a habit of making room for the man whose words and actions show that he knows where he is going.

32 Strength and growth come only through continuous effort and struggle.

33 You are constantly punishing yourself for every wrong you commit and rewarding yourself for every act of constructive conduct in which you indulge.

34 Capability means imagination.

35 The imagination is literally the workshop wherein are fashioned all plans created by man.

36 Your big opportunity may be right where you are now.

37 Create a definite plan for carrying out your desire and begin at once, whether you are ready or not, to put this plan into action.

38 All achievement, all earned riches, have their beginning in an idea.

39 More gold has been mined from the thoughts of men than has ever been taken from the earth.

40 Think and grow rich.

41 Opportunity often comes disguised in the form of misfortune, or temporary defeat.

42 The majority of men meet with failure because of their lack of persistence in creating new plans to take the place of those which fail.

43 No man is ever whipped, until he quits - in his own mind.

44 Every well built house started in the form of a definite purpose plus a definite plan in the nature of a set of blueprints.

45 Reduce your plan to writing. The moment you complete this, you will have definitely given concrete form to the intangible desire.

46 Nature cannot be tricked or cheated. She will give you the object of your struggles only after you have paid her price.

47 All great truths are simple in final analysis, and easily understood; if they are not, they are not great truths.

48 A man should always do his best, regardless of how much he receives for his services, or the number of people he may be serving or the class of people served.

49 Any idea, plan or purpose may be placed in the mind through repetition of thought.

50 Cherish your visions and your dreams as they are the children of your soul, the blueprints of your ultimate achievements.

51 All great men picture themselves doing what they desire and tell themselves they will be able to do it.

52 Believe you can do what you want, because you have nothing to lose.

53 Faith is a state of mind, induced or created by affirmation or repeated instructions to the subconscious mind.

54 In order to believe, one must desire. In order to desire one must decide what one wants. By repeating the belief *emotionally* the subconscious mind seeks out the opportunities that consciously a person misses. The thoughts or affirmations, when mixed with emotions, magnetically attract similar or related thoughts.

55 In order to reach your ultimate goal, you must form a group of people with ambitions like your own, but differing in specialized knowledge. Together, the group can solve problems that no one person alone could solve.

220

1 We can do more good by being good than in any other way.

221

1 People are pretty much the same, and their taste and desires are too.
2 Cost must be controlled every day, every week, every month.
3 Be big, think big, act big, dream big.
4 Success seems to be connected with action. Successful men keep moving. They make mistakes, but they don't quit.

222

1 There are three things the public never begins to pay the value of: bread, milk and the daily paper.
2 I never had work that I did not like.
3 Standardizing men and women leads as a rule to appalling mediocrity.

223

1 If you stick to something long enough, eventually somebody takes notice.
2 It is in the ordinary things around us that menace and danger lurk, and perhaps our ultimate destruction.
3 I am really quite sensitive and cowardly about many things. You would never believe it, but I am terrified of policemen and entanglements with the law even though I make my living dramatizing such situations.
4 Self-plagiarism is style.
5 Imagine three men sitting in a room in which a bomb is planted. If the audience does not know the bomb is there and neither do the men, when bomb goes off everyone is stunned. If, however, the audience knows the bomb is there but the men don't, the audience's reaction is quite different.
6 I am only a visual storyteller.
7 Movies are delightfully simple. What you do is take a piece of time, add colour and pattern and you have a movie.

8 Critics don't bother me. They did not like *Psycho*, but ten years later they called it a classic.

9 Drama is life with the dull bits cut out.

224

- Ho Chi Minh
A Very Influential Communist Leader of 20th Century
1890 - 1969

1 I have got used to being an old revolutionary. The one thing old revolutionaries have to be is optimistic. You wait and see.

2 Colonialism is a leech with two suckers, one of which sucks the metropolitan proletariat and the other that of the colonies. If we want to kill this monster, we must cut off both suckers at the same time.

3 We will never agree to negotiate under the threat of bombing.

225

- Dustin Hoffman
One of the Most Consistently Interesting Actors of His Generation
Born in 1937

1 Success can really cripple you. We live in a culture based on success. But life isn't for that.

2 I try to be as personal as I can in my work - by being personal to be able to bring to it a truth in what I observe and what I feel.

3 A very good story told in a mediocre way works, while even a very good job done on something that lacks a story, doesn't.

226

- Ben Hogan
The Most Remarkable Comeback-Player in Golf's History
Born in 1912

1 No man accomplishes anything by himself.

2 The perfect round of golf has never been played. It's eighteen holes-in-one. I almost dreamt it once, but I lipped out at eighteen.

3 I have had to fight for everything I ever got.

227

- Robert Hooke
An Ingenious Scientific-Experimenter of All Time
1635 - 1703

1 I never began to make any draught until, by many examinations in several lights and in several positions to these lights, I had discovered the true form.

2 There is nothing as conducive to the advancement of philosophy as the examining of hypotheses by experiments and the inquiry into experiments by hypothesis.

3 The natural philosopher must first collect the data and later try explaining the how and why of the facts. This is the true method of coming to the knowledge of all operations of Nature and therefore whoever goes the other way to work, begins a priori to this first of the Cause and then deduces the Effects from it, begins at the wrong end.

228

- Herbert Hoover
A Role Model of Efficiency and Individual Integrity
1874 - 1964

1 No difficult or simple job ever gets done until someone decides *right now* to do what it takes to get the job done. Unfortunately, too many people stand by ready to carry the stool when there is piano to be moved.

2 A boy has two jobs. One is just being a boy. The other is growing up to be a man.

3 Honest differences of views and honest debate are not disunity. They are the vital process of policy-making among free men.

4 All progress and growth is a matter of change, but change must be growth within our social and government concepts if it should not destroy them.

5 The glory of the nation rests in the character of her men. And character comes from boyhood. Thus every boy is a challenge to his elders. It is for them that we must win wars. It is for them that we need a just and lasting peace. For the world of tomorrow, about which all of us are dreaming and planning, will be carried forward by the boys of today.

6 The primary duty of organized society is to enlarge the lives and increase the standards of living of all the people.

7 If the law is upheld only by the government officials, then all law is at an end.

229

- Bob Hope
The All-Time Master of Monologues
Born in 1903

1 Nothing gives me stage fright like an empty seat.

2 I have only been serious about one thing in life. And that is a good laugh.

3 If you have not got any charity in your heart, you have the worst kind of heart trouble.

4 Me retire? I'd die before I'd give up hearing an audience laugh. It's the greatest tonic, the greatest medicine, in the world.

5 Middle age is when your age starts to show around your middle.

230

1 A kind of lameness since birth had made physical tasks painful for me and it had motivated me to seek some less arduous work to earn my living. One day, after overhearing a heated discussion between my employer and a patron on the impossibility of inventing a sewing machine and how lucrative its invention might be, if it could be invented, I determined to accept that challenge and to devote all my energy and skill to the inventing of such a machine. After many years of hardship and starvation I finally succeeded in inventing the machine but its marketing proved to be far harder than that of inventing it.

231

1 Nothing can replace blood kin.

2 I like to earn things, to be on the ice and sweat and bleed with the boys.

3 Have you ever done something where you feel you've been there before? The first time's an accident, the second time you are stupid. So the second time, I didn't want to be stupid.

232

1 The most dangerous thing for an actor is to refuse to listen to anyone else, to feel you know more than anybody. You become your own worst enemy. I am sure it's a manifestation of insecurity. It takes a great deal of security to say, "I don't know" without feeling embarrassed, or "What does that word mean?" or "I don't understand". Most insecure people say "Yes, I know all about that", thereby shutting off learning. They are losers.

2 Fright is one of the worst things in the world. I have been plenty frightened at times. I don't like things that I can't control.

3 Acting is something more than the ability to memorize lines.

4 Nobody is *discovered*, ever. There are too many interesting-looking people on earth for that to ever happen. The movies themselves have created this myth. It's been fictionalized a thousand times.

5 There is a tremendous difference between television and movies. In television the enemy is time. Everything is done so hurriedly, there is no time to do good work. You have to exist in mediocrity. In a movie you may shoot two or three pages a day. On a television series you do twelve pages a day. In television you have to remember that what you are doing will come out of a little box. So you have to exaggerate and play everything bigger than life. You can't be subtle, or

your character will be lost. In a movie, on a big screen, the slightest move - the lifting of an eyebrow, the curling of a lip - comes across like a blasting horn, because it's magnified twenty times. The same thing would register zero on television.

233

- Alexander von Humboldt
The Founder of Modern Geography and Geophysics
1769 - 1859

1 I lay very little stress either upon asking or giving advice. Generally speaking, they who ask advice know what they wish to do and remain firm in their intentions. A man may allow himself to be enlightened on various points, even upon matters of expediency and duty, but after all he must determine his course of action for himself.

2 Only what we have wrought into our character during life can we take away with us.

3 To me Nature is not a mere objective phenomenon, but a mirror image of the spirit of man.

4 Exploration is an act of complete dedication, of reverences.

234

- H. L. Hunt
One of the Richest Persons of America of His Time
1889 - 1974

1 A company is like any other living organism. It is constantly changing. If it ever ceases to change, it's dead.

2 I have never made a decision that, if everything went against me, I could not keep right on going.

3 You minimize your risk by doing as much home work as possible, and by spreading risk. Then, every once in a while, you will stumble into something that makes you go boom.

4 There is nothing complicated about the oil business. You use the buck-and-bit method. Put up a buck and sink a bit in the ground. Do that often enough where you have reason to believe there's oil, and you can't lose.

5 Every person is responsible for his own actions.

235

- Zora Hurston
A Prominent Writer of Afro-American Culture
1901 - 1960

1 Nothing that God ever made is the same thing to more than one person.

2 No matter about the difficulties past and present, step on it.

3. I see nothing but futility in looking back over my shoulder in rebuke at the grave of some white man who has been dead too long to talk about. That is just what I would be doing in trying to fix the blame for the dark days of slavery and the Reconstruction.

4. There has been no proof in the world so far that you would be less arrogant if you held the lever of power in your hands.

5. With tolerance and patience we godly demons may breed a noble world in a few hundred generations or so.

236

- Aldous Huxley
A Famous Satirist of 20th Century
1894 - 1963

1. The most valuable of all education is the ability to make yourself do the thing you have to do, when it has to be done, whether you like it or not.

2. Experience is not what happens to a man. It is what a man does with what happens to him.

3. Those who believe that they are exclusively in the right are generally those who achieve something.

4. Life has to be lived forwards, but it can only be understood backwards. I suppose that's why we always make the important discoveries too late.

5. Every man who knows how to read has it in his power to magnify himself, to multiply the ways in which he exists, to make his life full, significant and interesting.

6. The inspiring talker produces zeal, whose intensity depends not on the rationality of what is said or the goodness of the cause being advocated, but solely on the speaker's skill in using words in exciting way.

7. The secret of genius is to carry the spirit of the child into old age, which means never losing your enthusiasm.

8. Men and women are capable of being devils and lunatics. They are no less capable of being fully human.

9. The proper study of mankind is books.

10. There is no substitute for talent. Industry and all the virtues are of no avail.

11. Sanity is a matter of degree.

12. Facts do not cease to exist because they are ignored.

13. To his dog, every man is Napoleon, hence the popularity of dogs.

14. From family to nation, every human group is a society of island universes.

15. After silence that which comes nearest to expressing the inexpressible is music.

16. It is a little embarrassing that after forty-five years of research and study, the best advice I can give to people is to be a little kinder to each other.

17. Silence is as full of potential wisdom and wit as the unhewn marble of great sculpture.

237

1 As you go through life, there are thousands of little forks in the road, and there are a few really big forks - those moments of reckoning, moments of truth.

2 There are times in everyone's life when something constructive is born out of diversity. There are times when things seem so bad that you have got to grab your fate by the shoulders and shake it.

3 The Lord makes everything turn out for the best.

4 The primary skill of a manager consists of knowing how to make assignments and picking the right people to carry out those assignments.

5 The kind of people I look to fill top management spots are the eager beavers, the mavericks. These are the guys who try to do more than they're expected to do - they always reach.

238

1 The strongest man is the one who stands most alone.

2 Look into any man's heart you please, and you will always find, in every one, at least one black spot which he has to keep concealed.

3 There can be no freedom, or beauty about a home life, that depends on borrowing and debt.

4 The spirit of truth and the spirit of freedom - they are the pillars of society.

5 The public doesn't require any new ideas. The public is best served by the good, old-fashioned ideas it already has.

239

1 There is nothing that keeps up my spirits more than hard work.

2 Great minds have purposes, others have wishes. Little minds are tamed and subdued by misfortunes, but great minds rise above them.

3 There is a certain relief in change, even though it be from bad to worse; as I have found in travelling in a stagecoach, that it is often a comfort to shift one's position and be bruised in a new place.

4 A sharp tongue is the only edge tool that grows keener with constant use.

5 Honest good humour is the oil and wine of a merry meeting, and there is no jovial companionship equal to that where the jokes are rather small and the laughter abundant.

6 Whenever a man's friends begin to compliment him about looking young, he may be sure that they think that he is growing old.

240

- Andrew Jackson
The First Publicly-Elected American President
1767 - 1845

1 One man with courage makes the majority.

2 Save your money and thrive; or pay the price in poverty and disgrace.

3 Every good citizen makes his country's honour his own, and cherishes it not only as precious but as sacred. He is willing to risk his life in its defense and is conscious that he gains protection while he gives it.

4 You must pay the price if you wish to secure the blessing.

241

William James
A Leading American Philosopher and Psychologist
1842 - 1910

1 Wherever you are, it is your friends who make your world.

2 Need and struggle are what excite and inspire us.

3 It is our attitude at the beginning of a difficult undertaking which, more than anything else, will determine its successful outcome.

4 If you only care enough for a result, you will almost certainly attain it. If you wish to be rich, you will be rich. If you wish to be learned, you will be learned. If you wish to be good, you will be good. Only you must really wish these things and wish them exclusively, and not wish at the same time a hundred incompatible things just as strongly.

5 Compared to what we ought to be, we are only half awake. Our fires are dampened, our drafts are checked. We are making use of only a small part of our mental capacities.

6 Since you make them either evil or good, by your own thoughts about them, it is the ruling of your thoughts that proves to be your main concern.

7 The greatest discovery of my generation is that human beings can alter their lives by altering their attitudes of mind.

8 We become how we act. So if we wish to conquer undesirable emotional tendencies in ourselves, we must go through the outward movements of the kind of tendencies we wish to cultivate.

9 Action seems to follow feeling. But really action and feeling go together. By regulating the action, which is under more direct control of the will, we can indirectly regulate the feeling, which is not.

10 Belief creates the actual fact.

11 Confident thoughts make the real things.

12 We forget that every good that is worth possessing must be paid for in strokes of daily effort. We postpone and postpone until those smiling possibilities are dead.

13 The minute a man ceases to grow, no matter what his years, that minute he begins to be old.

14 The art of being wise is the art of knowing what to overlook.

15 Genius means little more than the faculty of perceiving in an unhabitual way.

16 The great use of a life is to spend it for something that outlasts it.

17 Nothing is so fatiguing as the eternal hanging on of an uncompleted task.

18 There is no more miserable human being than one in whom nothing is habitual but indecision.

19 The deepest principle in human nature is the craving to be appreciated.

20 To study the abnormal is the best way of understanding the normal.

21 Be not afraid of life. Believe that life is worth living, and your belief will help create the fact.

22 Habit is the enormous flywheel of society, its most precious conservative agent. It alone is what keeps us all within the bounds of ordinance.

23 A new position of responsibility will usually show a man to be a far stronger creature than he was supposed.

24 I don't sing because I am happy. I am happy because I sing.

25 As we become drunkard by so many separate drinks, so we become saints and authorities and experts by so many separate acts and hours of work.

26 Give up the feeling of responsibility. Let go your hold. Resign the care of your destiny to higher powers. Be genuinely indifferent as to what becomes of it all.

27 Just for today I will exercise my soul in three ways; I will do somebody a good turn and not get found out; I will do at least two things I don't want to do.

28 We are all ready to be savage in some cause. The difference between a good man and a bad one is the choice of the cause.

29 Acceptance of what has happened is the first step to overcoming the consequences of any misfortune.

242

- Edward Jenner
The Conqueror of Smallpox
1749 - 1823

1 Fame is a gilded butt, forever pierced with the arrows of malignancy.

2 Throughout my life I sought the lowly and sequestered paths of life - the valley and not the mountain. The fortune that flew in through my profession had always been sufficient to gratify my riches. My ambitions, and those of my nearest connections, were always very limited.

3 I am not surprised that men are not thankful to me; but I wonder that they are not grateful to God for the good which He made me the instrument of conveying to my fellow creatures.

243

1 Nothing is impossible to the power of God.

2 I would rather die than do anything contrary to the will of God.

3 Beware of saying that you are my judge, for you are assuming a great responsibility, and you burden me too much.

4 I would be the most miserable person in the world if I knew I were not in the grace of God.

5 Everything that I have done is at our Lord's command, and if He ordered me to do otherwise, I would obey, since it would have been at His command.

6 I know nothing, but rely entirely on God.

7 I trust in my judge, the King of Heaven and earth.

8 I have a good master, that is, God, whom I trust in everything, and not anyone else.

244

1 The important thing is to take risk, to go out and try to see what works.

2 Enlightenment is the highest level of intellectual achievement.

3 Intuition and enlightenment are more important than intellectual understanding.

245

1 I never lost my desire to win, no matter what I was doing.

2 In everything I have done, God has directed me. Knowing this, how can I look at my infection as anything other than an opportunity to do something that might even overshadow my playing career? Sure, I was convinced that I would never catch the AIDS virus and that it was going to happen to someone else. But I am actually glad it happened to me. I think I can spread the message concerning AIDS better than almost anyone.

3 Even as a fierce competitor I try to find time for a smile.

4 I believe in working hard. Chances are that anything you see me do during a game I've done a thousand times in practice.

5 The will to win is the greatest strength of a player.

6 Each day, every one makes decisions that affect their future - whether for good or for bad.

7 When I'm playing basketball, I'm playing to win and nothing else; not to score, to rebound, or to excel in one particular area of the game, but to win. That means I'm a rebounder, a scorer, a passer, even a cheerleader. I try to be an example to my teammates of what having a winning attitude is all about.

8 I have a burning desire to be the very best player on the best team.

9 I try to maintain an attitude of unselfishness that keeps me craving for more of the rewards of success, more championships for my team, not glory for myself.

10 During every practice I set an example by practicing longer and harder than anybody else.

11 I listen to the coaches and follow their instructions down to the last detail.

12 I am an intense competitor who plays fair and respects everybody on the floor - my teammates, the opposition, the coaches, the referees and the fans - but hates to lose.

13 I always set goals and challenge myself.

14 I never think that there is something I can't do, whether it's beating my opponent one-on-one or practicing another hour because something about my game isn't right. But I also remember my limitations and stay within the role the coaches design for me.

15 I play the inner game within myself, not against someone else.

16 Winners neither accept nor make excuses.

246

- Howard Johnson
A Pioneer of the Restaurant Business
1898 - 1972

1 I always considered my business as my life.

247

- Pauline Johnson
The Canadian Poetess and Princess
1862 - 1913

1 If I had only two dollars and I knew they would be my last, I would spend half on my body and half on my soul. With one dollar I would buy a whacking good meal and with the other a dozen cut carnations. Then I would die happy looking at my lovely flowers.

2 Friendship is the power of heat, of light, of strength. Without the sun of friendship the heart of mankind would be the bleached, colourless, bloodless thing that a plant is when grown in the dark.

3 Why is it that we rejoice when a soul is born into this world of sorrow and mourn when one passes through to the Happy Hunting Grounds?

248

1 Marriage keeps me single; it keeps me from getting married again. If I had come into show business as a single man, I might have got married six or seven times by now, but I was already married so I could not.

2 To be born in Wales is not to be born with a silver spoon in your mouth; it is to be born with music in your heart and poetry in your soul.

3 When you come from a working-class family there is not much chance of you dying from an overdose of any bloody thing because you don't have it.

4 You have to learn that the body can take only so much and that over-indulgence in anything can kill you.

249

1 It is the duty of the man of letters to record the sudden spiritual manifestations (whether in the vulgarity of speech or in a memorable phase of the mind itself) with extreme care, seeing that they themselves are the most delicate and evanescent of moments.

2 Nations, races and individual men are unified by an image, or bundle of related images, symbolic or evocative of the state of mind, which is of all states of mind not impossible, the most difficult to that man, race or nation; because only the greatest obstacle that can be contemplated without despair rouses the will to full intensity.

3 Set down in their Sahara, men must, of course, make the map according to their lights and instruments in order to preserve their integrity.

4 Don't make a hero out of me. I'm only a simple, middle-class man.

5 I never met a bore.

250

1 There are two cardinal sins from which all the others spring: impatience and laziness.

2 Youth is happy because it has the ability to see beauty. Anyone who keeps the ability to see beauty never grows old.

3 The true way goes over a rope which is not stretched at any great height but just above the ground. It seems more designed to make people stumble than to be walked upon.

4 One tends involuntarily to judge things from a more private point of view at night.

5 The crows maintain that a single crow could destroy the heavens,. There is no doubt of that, but it proves nothing against the heavens, for heaven simply means: the impossibility of crows.

251

- Karen Kain
Canada's Première Ballerina
Born in 1951

1 I was lucky; on the night of my eighth birthday I knew I wanted to be a ballerina.

2 All stages are slippery, one way or another.

3 The spotlight is a lie detector. Every thought is transmitted to the audience: every quiver betrays your doubts; every smile lends confidence - unless, of course, it's not an honest smile but that tout facsimile you sometimes paste on to hide the fear. You know that the audience can sense the falseness of that smile and the knowledge makes you all the more nervous.

4 More often than not, the people who will make the most extraordinary roles in your life don't make much of a first impression.

5 The first and foremost basic requirement for every professional dancer is a strong, healthy body, but ironically that's one of the hardest things to achieve and maintain. A proper diet, well-planned supplementary exercises, the judicious care of massage therapists, physiotherapists, and prompt medical attention when problems arise are absolute essentials if we are to dance at all, let alone dance well.

6 One of the most difficult things about being a dancer is adapting to the profession's unnatural weight demands.

7 True sensitivity to music involves much more than dancing on the beat. The music comes first, no matter how difficult the accompanying steps. Musical inventiveness characterizes the greatest dancing; depending on what the steps are saying, on the style and on your mood, you can dance on, before or after the music.

8 I am always nervous backstage. I am waiting for my cue, and trying to focus my concentration. In the last few moments before I make my entrance, I try to erase my doubts and fears and to muster all my courage to convince myself that I am really capable of achieving what I am about to attempt.

9 Preparing a role is never easy, and it doesn't get any easier even when you have been a principal dancer for twenty years.

10 The hardest thing for any performing artist is to find real contentment in private life.

252

- Wassily Kandinsky
The Founder of Russian Academy of Artistic Science
1866 - 1944

1 The impact of an acute angle of a triangle on a circle produces an effect no less powerful than the finger of God touching the finger of Adam in Michelangelo; and if fingers are not just anatomical or physiological, but something more, a triangle or circle is something more than geometry.

2 Experiencing the works of others is in the broadest sense like experiencing nature.

3 For many years I was like a monkey in a net; the organic laws of construction entangled me in my desires and only with great pain, effort and struggle did I break through these walls around art.

4 The realm of art, which like that of nature, science, political forms etc., is a realm into itself; it is governed by its own laws proper to it alone.

253

- Paul Kane
The First Artist to Paint the Aborgines of Canadian West
1810 - 1871

1 I determined to devote whatever talents and proficiency I possessed to the paintings of a series of pictures illustrative of the North American Indians and scenery. The subject was one in which I felt a deep interest in my boyhood. I had been accustomed to see hundreds of Indians about my native village, but the face of the red man is no longer seen. All traces of his footsteps are fast being obliterated from his once favorite haunts, and those who would see the aborigines of this country in their original state, or seek to study their native manners and customs, must travel far through the pathless forest to find them. The principal objective in my undertaking was to sketch pictures of the principal chiefs, and their original costumes, to illustrate their manners and costumes, and to represent the scenery of an almost unknown country. These paintings, however, would necessarily require explanations and notes, and I accordingly kept a diary of my journey.

2 Few, who read this journal, surrounded by the comforts of civilized life, will be able to imagine the heartfelt satisfaction with which we exchanged the wearisome snowshoes for the comfortable boats, and the painful anxiety of half-satisfied appetites for a well-stocked larder.

3 The *mal de racquet* tortured me at every step; the soles of my feet were terribly cut and wounded from the ice which formed inside my stockings occasioned by the freezing of the perspiration. It breaks in small pieces and is like so much sharp gravel in the shoes; and I was weak from the want of food; but the hope of reaching a place of safety kept me up and I toiled on over the ice ridges.

4 My return journey, from Sault Saint Marie to Toronto, was performed on board steamboats; and the greatest hardship I had to endure was the difficulty of trying to sleep in a civilized bed.

1 It is rarely possible to repay directly those who have rendered us great personal kindness. But it is also futile to rationalize and say that the time for sacrifice, to repay just moral debts, is past - for I do not believe that time ever passes. Nature does not often collaborate with men to permit simple repayment, whether the debt is from son to father, from soldier to comrade, or from pupil to master. We may never be able to pay directly for the gifts of true friendship - but pay we must - even though we make our payment to someone who owes us nothing, in some other place and at some other time.

2 To make enduring photographs, one must learn to see with the mind's eye, for the heart and the mind are the true lens of the camera.

3 Since we worked by natural light in those days, and stopped long before dusk, I had many opportunities to hear the stimulating conversations of Garo's friends - all prominent in music, letters, art and the theater - who would gather in his studio. My narrow world broadened. My education was augmented. It was in Garo's studio that I first set my heart on photographing those men and women who leave their mark on the world. Full of ambition, I prepared for an independent career.

4 It is the artist's job to accomplish at least two things - to stir the emotions of the viewer and to lay bare the soul of his subject. When my own emotions have been stirred, I hope I can succeed in stirring those of others. But it is the mind and soul of the personality before my camera that interests me most, and the greater the mind and soul, the greater my interest.

5 We still have not secured an acceptance of photography as an art form in the sense that painting has been accepted. Photography can be appreciated; it has its impact; it serves a great purpose. Yet rarely is a print purchased in order that it may be hung and lived with as a work of art.

6 The most important skill for a photographer to develop, be he amateur or professional, is that of being able to see his subject through his eyes before he sees it through his camera.

7 Although I am not interested in the mechanics or chemistry of photography, I have never delegated the development of my negatives or the preparation of my master prints. The very thought of a production-line operation in the Karsh studio is anathema to my soul.

8 I prefer to work alone during the sitting, and my assistant is not normally in the room when I am actually making the portrait. The relationship between photographer and subject, in my view, is similar to the relationship between physician and patient. A man can hardly be expected to bare his soul in an interview when a third party is present.

9 I am invariably in a state of great mental tension when the sitting begins, yet it is imperative that my sitter should not be aware of this. I observe constantly the composition as it is, or as it might be, and as I chat together, I continue to observe. Never do I use the phrase "Hold it"; it is not in my vocabulary. When everything is ready, the raising of my finger, a smile to the subject, perhaps

nothing at all, will mark the moment to be captured by the camera. Talk is suspended, the camera clicks, and our conversation continues immediately.

10 I have often experienced special problems when photographing actors, because it is immensely difficult to keep an actor from acting, especially when a camera is present.

11 Art is not accidental, but it is sometimes enhanced in unexpected ways. The failure of one flash bulb will usually ruin a picture; on rare occasions it can create one.

12 The preference of the subject concerning what to wear for the picture may be different from that of the photographic artist, and sometimes a considerable amount of diplomacy may be required - especially when his subject is a personality accustomed to the battlefield or quarterdeck.

13 I approach great personalities with a deep sense of appreciation of their accomplishments, of the ways in which they have enriched the lives of all of us. But I do not think I have ever been unduly awed by an important person who has come before my camera just because he was important. My temperament, my nature, compel me to approach all people with consideration, but I have a tremendously strong ally beside me when I am carrying out my duty, for my companion is my camera, which will never forget. I must feel that I am master of the occasion, or my subject will feel insecure. Nothing in this attitude towards my subject diminishes my genuine curiosity or my desire to learn more about the personality I am going to photograph.

14 Creating the atmosphere during the sitting consists of not only the mood for the making of the photograph but also a mood within the composition in which the viewer can subsequently share. To share in the music of Pablo Casals, to hear the sweet, sonorous tones given forth by his cello as he draws his bow across the strings - you can hear such things in a photograph if they belong in it. Yet if you were to encounter this little old man smoking his pipe in a bistro, you would not necessarily be attracted to him at all.

15 If some of us were to be judged by our physical appearances alone, we would not fare too well.

16 The problem of how to avoid being repetitious in the composition is one that has haunted me more than any other. My subjects are all different, and I believe I am deeply aware of these differences. But in a superficial way they are all the same. A man sitting across the table from you will hold his hands or rest his elbow in roughly the same way that half the world would under similar circumstances. A photographer can easily contrive to break this monotony if he is dealing, say, with fashion models or if his sole function is to startle. But these are not solutions for the portraitist. I have sought to minimize repetitiveness.

255

- Legson Kayira
Walked 2000 Miles Pursuing His Dream to Reach America
Born in 1939

1 The main driving force behind my success was my daily affirmation *I will keep trying.*

256

- Kip Keino
One of the Greatest Runners of All Time
Born in 1940

1 You must believe in your own ability.

2 When I feel confident I will win, I take off the cap and throw it.

3 I returned from the 1964 Olympic Games disappointed because I hadn't won a gold medal but was heartened by the realization that international games were not as difficult as I had imagined. That experience became the turning point in my career, giving me new inspiration as a runner.

4 I feel when you are in front you control the race. Those people who run behind cannot run fast.

257

- Helen Keller
The First Blind-Deaf to Communicate with Millions of People
1880 - 1968

1 Keep your face to the sunshine and you cannot see the shadow.

2 The most pathetic person in the world is someone who has sight but has no vision.

3 The best and most beautiful things in the world cannot be seen or even touched. They must be felt with the heart.

4 Life is nothing if not an adventure.

5 I long to accomplish a great and noble task, but it is my chief duty to accomplish small tasks as if they were great and noble.

6 One can never consent to creep when one feels an impulse to soar.

7 Character cannot be developed in ease and quiet. Only through experiences of trial and suffering can the soul be strengthened, vision cleared, ambition inspired and success achieved.

8 Your success and happiness lie in you. Resolve to keep happy, and your joy and you shall form an invincible host against difficulties.

9 I do not want the peace which passeth with understanding, I want the understanding which bringeth peace.

10 Literature is my Utopia. Here I am not disfranchised. No barrier of the senses shuts me out from the sweet, gracious discourse of my book friends. They talk to me without embarrassment or awkwardness.

11 I thank God for my handicaps, for through them I have found myself, my work, and my God.

12 The marvellous richness of human experience would lose something of rewarding joy if there were no limitations to overcome. The hilltop hour would not be half so wonderful if there were no dark valleys to traverse.

13 If the blind put their hand in God's, they find their way more surely than those who see but have not faith or purpose.

14 Life is a succession of lessons which must be lived to be understood.

15 There is no king who has not had a slave among his ancestors, and no slave who has not had a king among his.

16 Truly each book is as a ship that bears us away from the fixity of our limitations into the movement and splendor of life's infinite ocean.

17 Security is mostly superstition.

18 Toleration is the greatest gift of mind; it requires the same efforts of the brain that it takes to balance oneself on a bicycle.

19 Although the world is very full of suffering, it is also full of the overcoming of it.

20 The welfare of each is bound up in the welfare of all.

258 - John F. Kennedy
The Youngest, and the First Roman Catholic, President of USA
1917 - 1963

1 Our task now is not to fix the blame for the past, but to fix the course for the future.

2 Efforts and courage are not enough, without purpose and direction.

3 All of us do not have equal talent, but all of us should have an equal opportunity to develop our talents.

4 Let us never negotiate out of fear, but let us never fear to negotiate.

5 Leadership and learning are indispensable to each other.

6 If a free society cannot help the many who are poor, it cannot save a few who are rich.

7 Victory has a hundred fathers, and defeat is an orphan.

8 The time to repair the roof is when the sun is shining.

9 Happiness is the full use of your powers along lines of excellence in a life affording scope.

259 - Elizabeth Kenny
The Discoverer of the Hot-Pack Treatment for Polio
1886 - 1952

1 If I had a sixpence for every mistake I made, I'd be a millionaire.

2 I am correct and the rest of the world is wrong. I cannot deny what my eyes see. I have a message to give the world, and I shall not be thwarted. I am engaged in a terrible struggle. I have to have the bulldog courage to hear the cries of the afflicted children.

3 I am getting older and weary of hardships, insults, disappointments, frustrations, heartbreak and humiliation. I want the whole world to use the Kenny treatment. I am going to campaign for that until I die. Don't think I'm getting too old. I have work to do and I shall finish it. Thirty years I fought, and I am beginning to win.

4 I refused a fanfare and official welcome. I preferred the money be used for polio work.

5 No man, not even a doctor, ever gives any definition of what a nurse should be than this - *devoted and obedient*. This definition would just as well do for a porter. It might even do for a horse. It will not do for a nurse.

260 - Johannes Kepler
The Discoverer of the Three Laws of Planetary Motion
1571 - 1630

1 If God is concerned with astronomy, which piety desires to believe, then I hope I shall achieve something in this domain, for I see how God let me be bound with Tycho through an unalterable fate and did not let me be separated from him by the most oppressive hardships.

2 I feel carried away and possessed by an unutterable rapture over the divine spectacle of the heavenly harmony.

3 I measured the skies, now the shadows I measure, sky-bound was the mind, earth-bound the body rests.

261 - Andre Kertesz
One of the Inventors of Modern Photojournalism
1894 - 1985

1 The camera can be used in direct response to how one feels about the world.

2 I always maintained the one-to-one relationship with my subject and the art. I never veered from this, even to please my peers or to elicit recognition.

3 I am an amateur and intend to be one all my life. For me, photography should capture the true personality of things... Remember, the reporters and the amateurs - both of them want only to make a souvenir or a document; that is pure photography.

262 - Charles Kettering
An Extraordinary Inventor
1876 - 1958

1 The opportunities of man are limited only by his imagination. But so few have imagination that there are ten thousand fiddlers to one composer.

2 Don't be afraid to stumble. Any inventor will tell you that you don't follow a plan far before you strike a snag. If, out of 100 ideas, you get one that works, it's enough.

3 Learn how to fail intelligently.

4 Every great improvement has come after repeated failures. Virtually nothing comes out right the first time. Failures, repeated failures, are finger posts on the road to achievement.

5 A problem well stated is a problem half solved.

6 If you want to kill any idea in the world today, get a committee working on it.

7 We can communicate an idea around the world in 70 seconds, but sometimes it takes years for an idea to get through quarter inch of human skull.

8 Suppose a half dozen of us are seated around the walls of a very dark room. We are told that somewhere in the open middle space is a chair. Who could find it? Not those of us who sat still and philosophized about where chairs are placed in rooms. The fellow who would locate it is the one who'd get up, then walk and stumble around until he discovered it. Nobody ever found anything while sitting down.

9 Research is an organized method of trying to find out what you are going to do after you cannot do what you are doing now. It may also be said to be the method of keeping a customer reasonably dissatisfied with what he has. That means constant improvement and change so that the customer will be stimulated to desire the new product enough to buy it to replace the one he has.

10 We work day after day, not to finish things, but to make the future better.

11 Anyone who wants to be a scientist must be willing to fail 99 times before he succeeds once, and suffer no ego damage.

12 The process of research is to pull the problem apart into its different elements, a great many of which you already know about. When you get it pulled apart, you can work on the things you don't know about.

13 We tried one thing after another for about 6 years, until the engine itself finally told us exactly what it wanted.

14 Do not bring me your successes; they weaken me. Bring me your problems; they strengthen me.

15 Problems are the price of progress. Don't bring me anything but trouble. Good news weakens me.

16 No one ever would have crossed the ocean if he could have gotten off the ship in the storm.

17 There is a great difference between knowing a thing and understanding it. You can know a lot and not really understand anything.

18 The first essential of being an engineer is knowing a lot about mechanisms just from your observations of them; the second is to form a picture of some new form of mechanism in your mind and the third is to have enough mathematics and physics to be able to calculate whether or not this new mechanism would work satisfactorily.

19 If I want to stop a research program, I can always do it by getting a few experts to sit on the subject, because they know right away that it is a fool thing to try in the first place.

20 If I have any success, it's due to luck, but I notice the harder I work, the luckier I get.

21 A research problem is not solved by apparatus; it is solved in a man's head.

22 Industries are like some watches; they have to be shaken hard every so often to keep them going.

23 A bean is pretty smart. Nature provides the bean with a quantity of nourishment

to keep it going until it gets a start in life. When planted in the ground, it sends up a sprout to take a look around. There it could say, "I'll just grow in this lovely sunshine and put out a lot of leaves. I have plenty of bean meat to keep me going for a while." But the bean, being smart, does no such thing. Instead, it uses its store of nourishment to send roots deep into the earth. Only then is it ready to put out leaves in the sunshine.

24 We should all be greatly concerned about the future and try to make it the best possible, for it is where we are all going to spend the rest of our lives.

25 God gave you hands to use them. No matter how much you have in your head, it will be of no use to you whatsoever until you learn how to use your hands and to know what your hands are for.

26 The difference between intelligence and education is this: intelligence will make you a good living.

263

- Jean Claude Killy
The Second Person to Win 3 Gold Medals in Olympic Alpine Skiing
Born in 1943

1 Desire is that extra thing that makes a champion. You must have the desire to win and think only about winning. A second place for me is nothing. I have to be the first. It is not just a matter of pride, or even money.

2 The important thing is to be happy and to be happy I need challenges.

3 Ski racing is an art. I do not really ski to hear the crowd cheer or for the pay cheques. All I want to do is ski the perfect race.

4 I take all the risks. I have always skied on an instinct. If people say I look pretty in a race, then I know I am not winning.

5 I am determined. I have the will to win. I think only about winning. That's why I work harder than anyone I know when I train. I just can't accept the idea of losing. I refuse to accept defeat.

6 I like to have people rooting for me. Most important are the kids who come to see me race. When I can make them happy, it gives me a good feeling. I want to give something back to the sport that gave me so much.

7 The biggest grief in my life is that I have not had more schooling. That is why I often try to read books.

8 When I ski, I am alone with the mountain. I leave everything else aside. Being a champion has its moments. But the fun of skiing, it's good for a lifetime. Skiing is a world in itself. It is close to nature. I enjoy skiing for its own sake. It is not an escape from anything.

264

1 Everyone is different in some way. People should not label anyone.

2 The main thing is to care. Care very hard, even if it is only a game you are playing.

3 You are wisest only to keep two rules in mind: (1) close the gate; and (2) the match is not over till you shake hands at the net.

4 At my funeral, no body is going to talk about me. They're all just going to stand up and tell each other where they were on the night I beat Bobby Riggs.

5 You have to think about solutions all the time. Very few people have vision. They can't perceive the future, or the consequences of an action, a change. They can't visualize, they can't imagine. Imagination is probably the most powerful thing we have and yet how few people ever use it!

6 Pressure really juices me up.

7 It should just kill you to lose to anyone, no matter how good he is.

265

1 People can develop only along the lines of their own development.

2 The final objective of all human desire is a knowledge of the nature of God.

3 Except a living man, there is nothing more wonderful than a book! - a message to us from the dead - from human souls we never saw, and who lived perhaps thousands of miles away; and yet these words on those little sheets of paper speak to us, amuse us and comfort us.

266

1 More important than the big break is the readiness - being ready for opportunity when it occurs, if it occurs.

2 The beauty of dropping to the bottom is that it wipes the slate clean.

3 When I went into this business, I was committing my life to be a songwriter.

4 If I did not have hope, I would not get out of bed. I feel like a person can make a difference and that it matters to try and make a difference.

5 Freedom is just another word for nothing left to lose.

1 Sometimes the simplest things in life seem like the most difficult.

2 Business means competition, dedication and drive.

3 Doing what one enjoys is the way to be happy.

4 Find out where your talents lie and then do whatever you are doing better than anybody else. But be willing to pay the price of accomplishment.

5 Intelligence does not necessarily make for a restaurant's success; rather, it is application, dedication and hard work.

6 Give quality and value in pleasant surroundings; that includes pleasant employees.

7 The most important asset of a salesman is a knack of putting himself in the position of his customers and addressing their needs and interests, not his own.

8 A company must be ready to react quickly to unforeseen changes in its market, even when they require a completely new course.

9 To succeed in sales, find a way to make your customers successful with your product.

10 Believe in what you are selling and develop the ability to communicate that belief.

11 When you are green, you are growing. When you are ripe, you rot.

12 It takes a certain kind of mind to see beauty in a hamburger bun. Yet, is it any more unusual to find grace in the texture and softly curved silhouette of a bun than to reflect lovingly on the arrangement of textures and colours in a butterfly's wing?

1 A man who does not change his mind, does not think.

2 Once I have made up my mind I am very unswerving.

3 No business ever expanded by contraction.

1 A good marriage, it is said, is made in heaven. This might be true, but the maintenance work must be done right down here. A successful marriage is not a gift, it is an achievement. No real marriage can exist without differences in opinion and the ensuing battles. But battles can be healthy. They bring to marriage the vital principle of equal partnership. If there is a secret to making marriage work, it is "Never go to bed mad."

2 If you have a good name, if you are right more often than you are wrong, if your children respect you, if your grandchildren are glad to see you, if your friends can count on you and you can count on them in time of trouble, if you can face your God and say, "I have done my best", then you are a success.

3 The true measure of a human is how he or she treats his fellow man. Integrity and compassion cannot be learned in college, nor are these qualities inherited in the genes.

4 Every event that may appear to be catastrophic or tragic at the moment, you can turn around and make it work for you.

5 I cannot imagine life without work. It need not be a professional career or a factory job. Staying home and raising a family can be hard work too. This mad scramble for leisure time says something about our values. Somewhere along the line, work has picked up a bad name. I'd like to see it gain the respectability and prestige it once enjoyed. It's what made this country great.

6 Know yourself. Don't accept your dog's admiration as conclusive evidence that you are wonderful.

7 Anyone who does not change his ideas over a period of years is either pickled in alcohol or embedded in wood.

8 Common sense is better than any theory.

9 Never say, "It could not happen to us!"

10 If you have to err, err on the side of being too strict, not too permissive. The kid will be better off for it.

11 Hate, jealousy, envy eat you up. They are exhaustive and corrosive. They make you look old.

12 Sensual pleasures have the fleeting brilliance of a comet; a happy marriage has the tranquillity of a lovely sunset.

13 Trouble is the common denominator of living. It is the great equalizer.

14 Loved people are loving people.

15 Financial success, academic achievement and social or political status open no doors to peace of mind or inner security.

16 When I started writing the column at thirty-seven, I thought I was worldly and sophisticated. I knew what life was about. Let me tell you, I didn't know anything.

17 Expect trouble as an inevitable part of life and when it comes, hold your head high, look at it squarely in the eye and say, "I will be bigger than you. You cannot defeat me."

270

1 Very few publishing firms survive the death of their founder in recognizable form.

2 What happens after our time is beyond our control. As good gardeners or farmers we can only do our best to see that the soil is kept in good heart, free of weeds, and that the crops are not forced but allowed a natural growth in the knowledge that if these principles are followed our successors will continue to have the satisfaction from it that we have had ourselves.

3 The test that I applied to select a title was: "Is this a book which, had I not read it, and were I to see on sale for sixpence, would make me say, *This book I always wanted to read; I will get it now*".

271

1 I consider a director a kind of psychoanalyst. He has to sneak under the skin of his character.

2 Fate, with the Greeks and the Romans, was their God. Today it is something else; either a dictatorship or a fight against some aspect of society that holds down the individual, or tries to devour him.

3 In these days, when people no longer have religious beliefs, when we no longer believe in Hell, the only thing we fear is pain, and pain is the result of violence in some form or other.

4 Sometimes, maybe, with a strong will, you can change fate, but there is no guarantee. It won't happen if you just sit idle. At least you have to fight against it.

5 I respect the audience, which I believe to be moving towards better standards and higher truths on the screen as well as in life.

6 I am always suspicious of assumptions which discredit the audience, because they are used for lazy, unintelligent or inept productions.

7 I believe in artistic rebellion. I think new approaches, new forms are needed to reflect the changed world we are in. But I don't think the only alternative to sugar is poison.

8 A director must pay attention to detail, because out of detail is created atmosphere and atmosphere sets the mood and tempo which condition the whole action of the film.

9 Spontaneity is what every director tries to achieve. It comes from minute attention to detail and constant practice. That careless jerk of the thumb that halts the passing motorist, that flick of the wrist that empties the glass and sends the barman for another, these are the fruits of long endeavour. In film making too, spontaneity like atmosphere can only be created by piling detail on detail.

10 Censorship is an attempt to gloss over the sources of social ills, which, if they could be wiped out, would make censorship unnecessary. Failing to eradicate the real roots of crime - poverty, disease, unequal opportunity, inadequate education - we attempt with censorship to ignore and deny results of this failure.

11 I am not opposed to censorship because I wish to make sensational or sordid pictures. I hate bad taste and dirty jokes. But if stronger language or more outspoken description appear necessary to me in order to give a true characterization of a particular man or woman, I want to be in a position to use what is necessary, irrespective of rules designed to appease political censors.

12 The way of a real security or progress lies neither in the blind acceptance or rejection of new ideas; they should be scrutinized, tested and, if found of value, adopted. The censors deny us the very rights to examine what is new.

13 Films must draw strength from life, for only by modeling themselves on the ever-shifting patterns and conflict of society can they continue to interest, to stimulate, and by dramatizing society's problems, indicate the solutions.

14 Drama begins with emotion, strong emotion, and with conflicts of desire and temperament. Given a group of human beings, hemmed in by circumstances, driven by urges conscious or unconscious, their actions must march to a climax and from that climax to a resolution.

272

- Dorothea Lange
The Greatest Documentary-Photographer of America of Her Time
1895 - 1965

1 Photography is a gambler's game. Unless you work to a formula, the result is never a sure thing. You have to take chances. You must enjoy the process of making something. With your eyes, your hands, your heart, your imagination, you shape something and when you are finished, there it is, a real thing.

2 When I was seventeen years old and a poor child, I made up my mind to be a photographer. This came slowly. I had no camera. I had made no pictures. My mind made up itself, it was more like that.

3 There is a sharp difference in the role of a woman as an artist and the man. The woman's position is immeasurably more complicated. There are not very many first-class woman producers. They produce in other ways. Where they can do both, it's a conflict. I'd like to take one year, almost ask it of myself, "Could I have one year, just one, when I would not have to take into account anything but my own inner demands!"

4 That what people call art is a by-product - a plus something that happens when your work is done, if it's done well enough and intensely enough.

5 Photographs are everywhere. We see them unconsciously in passing, from the corner of our eyes, flashing at us. Because of this exploitation of photography our eyes have become *calloused*. The habit of many people is not to see; they look at things. The habit of most people is to talk; seeing is not a habit for them. So many fine visuals are buried under torrents of words.

6 Vision comes from the camera.

7 For better or worse, the destiny of the photographer is bound up with the destinies of a machine. His machine must prove that it can be endowed with the passion and humanity of the photographer. The photographer must prove that he has the passion and humanity with which to endow the machine.

273

- Niki Lauda
The Champion Autoracer Who Came Back from the Dead
Born in 1949

1 There isn't much time in life and you have to get on with enjoying it.

2 The real joy of winning is something to be savoured in silence at the precise moment of victory.

3 Once in your lifetime you have got to make the decision whether or not you want to practice this profession. Do you want it and all that involves? If you ask yourself that question and if you answer in all honesty with yes, then you can't be afraid any more because if you are then you must have answered that question with a lie.

4 You have got to develop a strong will and a stubborn head. You've got it already and you can cultivate it.

5 Some crashes are necessary for the career of any racing driver. What matters is whether you learn your lesson from them or not. There are people who were driving five years ago in Formula III and half killing themselves and they're still driving there and they're still going off the road.

6 I have no time for people who set examples. Nobody set me one and I don't think others should be set one either. I only know how to drive like a Lauda, I can't drive like a Rindt or a Stewart or anybody else. At most I could pick up a few tips but it would be a waste of time for me to say: I would like to be like this man or that.

7 In life you need certain amount of luck but the question is how much luck do you need. I think the luck is the minimum part of it. I think you can steer a lot of your life; you have the wheel and you can do much more for yourself than a lot of people think.

274

- Le Corbusier
One of World's Greatest Architects of All Time
1887 - 1965

1 Design should proceed from within to without; the exterior is the result of an interior.

2 A house is a machine for living. As to beauty, this is always present when you have proportions.

3 The birth of a project is for me like the birth of a little dog or a child. There is a long period of gestation; there is a lot of work in the subconscious before I make the first sketch. That lasts for months. Then one fine morning it takes a form

without my knowing it. Each problem provokes in me this interior meditation. I do not depend on my collaborators to solve it. I seek the solution myself, closed up in a room 3 meters by 3 meters.

4 Architecture is the conscious, correct and magnificent interplay of volumes assembled under light.

5 Each purely technological form is temporary. Man destroys it ruthlessly when it no longer serves his ends. But the art form is eternal and is not destroyed without detriment. With it a part of beauty disappears from the world. It comes from love, not from the calculating mind; its roots reach into the eternal, whereas the technologist must stand with both feet on ground and fit into the world.

6 Today I am accused of being a revolutionary. Yet I confess to having had only one master: the past; and only one discipline: the study of the past.

7 The course of a lifetime of work was born from a seed which was germinated since the beginning, proposing and imposing a course of conduct.

8 It is human to err.

9 People feel a greater sense of freedom when their surroundings preserve order.

10 The search for harmony is the noblest of human passions.

11 A problem must be correctly posed if it is to be correctly solved.

275

- Stephen Leacock
A Great Canadian Humorist of All Time
1869 - 1944

1 I am a great believer in luck, and I find that the harder I work, the more I have of it.

2 Advertising may be described as the science of arresting the human intelligence long enough to get money from it.

3 Literature as a profession is not very lucrative. Those who depend solely on their pen as their means of subsistence earn but a scanty recompense for their labour; and literary labour, whatever may be said to the contrary, is the severest of all toil.

4 The physiology of wrinkles can be very telling and accurate.

5 Humour goes upon its way, moving from lower to higher forms, from cruelty to horseplay. from horseplay to wit, from wit to the higher *humour of character*, and beyond that to its highest stage as humour of life itself. Here tears and laughter are joined, and our little life, incongruous and vain, is rounded with a smile.

6 In the wider sense, what I want to advocate is not to make education shorter, but to make it much longer, indeed make it last as long as life itself. What I find wrong is the stark division now existing between the years of formal education and entry into the world of life. All that is best in education can only be acquired by spontaneous interest; this gained, it lasts and goes on. Real education should mean a wonderful beginning, a marvelous initiation, a thorough smattering and life will carry it on.

7 Try to buy happiness, by the quart or by the yard, and you never find it. Motion it away from you while you turn to Duty, and you will find it waiting beside

your chair. So with Goodwill on Earth. Cannons frighten it. Treaties fetter it. The Spirit brings it.

8   There is for each of us a super-self, that comes out in emergency, in the effort of sacrifice, in the heroism of war, and in the creative ecstasy of the artist. There is no environment that can better develop it than a college. We can see it in the ideal professor.

276

- Louis B. Leakey
An Expert of Prehistoric Archeology and Paleontology
1903 - 1972

1   I see adversities as challenges and the more I have to exercise my ingenuity the happier I become.

2   Luck is largely a question of knowing where to look and then going on looking, again and again. It is the outcome of a touch of genius and persistence in the face of difficulties.

3   Sometimes I think of myself as a little bee. I go from one area of the studio to another and gather pollen and sort of stimulate everybody.

4   We should encourage more mixing of young people from different backgrounds, until they realize they are all one and the same. We should also teach them that faith and religion are two distinct subjects. Because of the destructive influence of dogmas and doctrines we are letting our young people lose faith. Having lost faith, because they confuse it with religion, they are not willing to abandon violence. You can't kill people if you feel that they also have a faith and are meaningful in this life.

277

- Antony van Leewenhoek
The Developer of the Microscope & Microscopic Studies
1632 - 1723

1   I don't see that much use would result from establishing a school for the training of young people to grind lenses. It's my conviction that for a thousand people there is not one capable of applying himself to such a study, for it requires much time and expenditure of money. Also, one's mind must ought constantly to be busy if one wants to accomplish anything. Moreover, most people are not of an inquiring mind, nay, some of whom one would never have expected it say, "What's the use whether we know or not?"

2   As the size of a small animalcule in the water is to that of a mite, so is the size of a honey bee to that of a horse.

278

1 If you get caught using drugs or stealing, you're going to go to prison, just like I did. But don't get the idea you'll be as lucky as I was. There won't be a major league baseball team waiting to sign you when you get out. Just because it happened to me, don't you expect a miracle, too.

2 Stealing and drug can only lead to trouble. I was lucky. If it hadn't been for baseball, I would still be in prison.

3 Trying to get revenge simply causes more problems.

4 I would never go back to crime. Even if I did not make it in baseball, I know I could find something to do. I look at myself differently.

279

1 While performing the role of Elsa of Brabant in *Lohengrin* I was so absorbed that I did not see the audience, I did not even see the face of the conductor; I forgot everything - where I was and what the evening meant for me. I was Elsa, that Elsa whom I understood for the first time.

2 My greatest opportunity came when I was asked to replace the indisposed Marie Gutheil-Schoder in the role of the composer. Overnight I became famous and doors opened for me abroad.

3 I cannot serve politics. I can only serve that which always has been and still is the mission of my life; I want to be an artist - nothing else. I want to sing the songs that I love, without questioning to what race the composer belonged.

4 God put music into my heart and a voice into my throat. I serve Him when I serve music. I no longer understand the land of my birth.

280

1 Without communication there can be no progress.

2 People should be concerned with those whose opinions they respect, rather than what the public in general thinks of them.

3 All my life I always wanted to be the best actor that I could be.

4 Acting is a tremendously healthy process. Its main appeal is that we'd all like to do it. We all do it as children, but as we grow up, we are taught that we're not supposed to do it.

5 What counts is being able to look back when you are washed up at sixty and taking pleasure in one or two things you have done.

6 I think we worry about failure too much. I don't think that failure very often can hurt anybody. It's fear of failure that will absolutely destroy you. Then when you walk down the middle of the street, you are never going to go down the little side streets that you look down and say, "Jeez, that looks interesting. But I don't know that. I know this street. I'll stay right here and just walk on this straight line."

7 When you become a star, you cannot act. You put a dime under your pillow and dream about great parts. You get them and then you suddenly find you are limited.

8 I want to accomplish more than merely winning popularity contests.

9 I don't believe that talent pops out suddenly, that if you have a painting talent, you will find yourself one day with a brush in your hand. It can happen, but I think what is more true is that you may stumble on to something that you have a talent for, and that if you are accepted doing it, you will continue, because you want the acceptance.

10 I have not wavered, really, in whatever my goals were, from the time before I could even get a job to, today. The basic goal, without really changing, has been to be as good an actor as I can be.

281
-Suzanne Lenglen
The Courageous Player Who Revolutionized Women's Tennis
1899 - 1938

1 I just throw dignity to the winds and think of nothing but the game.
2 Without confidence, without the will to win that allows no doubts, you cannot expect to be a consistent winner.

282
- Leonardo Da Vinci
A Legendary Artist and Scientist
1452 - 1519

1 Work is the seed from which grows all good things you hope for. A man who is afraid of hard work better be brave enough to accept poverty.

2 Iron rusts from disuse; stagnant water loses its purity and in cold weather becomes frozen; even so does inaction sap the vigor of the mind.

3 I prefer death to lassitude. I never tire of serving others.

4 The life that is well spent is a long life.

5 As a well-spent day brings happy sleep, so life well-used brings happy death.

6 Nature never breaks her own laws.

7 It is easier to resist at the beginning than at the end.

8 As every divided kingdom falls, so every mind divided between many studies confounds and saps itself.

9 Reprove a friend in secret, but praise him before others.

10 Every now and then go away, have a little relaxation, for when you come back to your work your judgment will be surer, since to remain constantly at work will cause you to lose your power of judgment. Go some distances away because then the work appears smaller, and more of it can be taken in at a glance, and a lack of harmony or proportion is more readily seen.

283

-R. G. LeTourneau
The Pioneer Manufacturer of Giant Earth-Movers
1888 - 1969

1 In my hour of greatest distress I have found my greatest asset in the revelation and discovery of a silent senior partner. I have since recognized this partner in my personal and business life. Everything that I have, everything I have done that has been worthwhile, I owe to Him.

2 I have spent all my life learning about the friction between materials but I wish I knew as much about the laws of friction between men as I do about the coefficient of friction between materials.

3 Mechanical friction is bad but human friction - the friction between man and man - is worse. The friction, the touchiness, the hate that is in this world today! Friction in the home probably is the bitterest of all friction in human relationships.

4 The most terrible, the most disastrous, the most tragic friction of all is between God and man. If I could eliminate that friction, I could eliminate friction between man and man.

5 You may set up for yourself a high standard of morals. You may resolve to be unselfish. You may work out for yourself an excellent code of ethics but the only way to solve the problems of this world is to let God work out His plan for each of our lives, and daily ask Him to lead us.

6 There is a danger in knowing too much, being certain something cannot be done because some theorist has proven to his satisfaction that it can't be done.

284

- Jerry Lewis
A Highly Acclaimed Clown of the American Show Business
Born in 1926

1 When I wake up in the morning, I think of *me* first and then my wife and then my children. I would like to meet a guy that can honestly admit he does differently.

2 If you are deprived of love when you are young, you can never have it given back to you.

3 An audience is nothing more than eight or nine hundred mamas and papas clapping their hands and saying, "Good Boy, baby". That's all. You will find that people who had enough "Good Boy, baby" from their actual parents rarely turn to comedy.

4 The man that doesn't advertise may know his business, but nobody else does.

5 Screen comedy is essentially a combination of situation, sadness and gracious humility.

6 Imitators never get anywhere.

285

- John Llewellyn Lewis
A Very Dynamic Leader of American Trade Unions
1880 - 1969

1 Ideals do not realize themselves, and must instead be worked out by human beings with frailties.

2 Life is a contest in which success does not go to the best sportsman or the man who follows rules but to the man who makes his own rules and plays the game according to current needs, not past rituals.

3 I am not concerned with history. I am concerned with the problems of today and tomorrow.

4 Those who seek to cheapen coal by cheapening men seek to reverse the evolution of American industry. It cannot be done.

5 Our whole economic system is man-made and will have to be judged by its fruits in human welfare and happiness.

6 In the days when people were besieged in a walled city and a soldier got upon the top of the wall and called to the enemy that the people were weak, they merely took his life and threw him off the wall to the dogs below. Today, in the modern days, we tolerate the lamentations of the timid and we even tolerate at times the words of a traitor.

7 You can't dig coal with bayonets.

286

- Abraham Lincoln
The American President Who Saved the Union and Freed the Slaves
1809 - 1865

1 You can fool some of the people all of the time, and all of the people some of the time, but you cannot fool all of the people all of the time.

2 Character is like a tree and reputation like its shadow. The shadow is what we think of it; the tree is the real thing.

3 My great concern is not whether you have failed, but whether you are content with your failure.

4 Most folks are about as happy as they make up their minds to be.

5 No man has a memory long enough to be a successful liar.

6 The Lord must love the common people - He made so many of them.

7 It has ever been my experience that folks who have no vices have very few virtues.

8 Prosperity is the fruit of labour. It begins with saving money.

9 A man watches his pear tree day after day, impatient for the ripening of the fruit. Let him attempt to force the process, and he may spoil both fruit and tree. But let him patiently wait, and the ripe fruit at length falls into his lap.

10 Die when I may, I want it said of me by those who knew me best, that I always plucked a thistle and planted a flower where I thought a flower would grow.

11 Do not worry. Eat three square meals a day, say your prayers, be courteous to your creditors, keep your digestion good, steer clear of biliousness, exercise, go slow, and go easy. May be there are other things, that your special case requires to make you happy, but, my friend, these I reckon will give you a good life.

12 Better give your path to a dog than be bitten by him in contesting for the right. Even killing the dog would not cure the bite.

13 It is difficult to make a man miserable while he feels he is worthy of himself and claims kindered to the great God who made him.

14 Too many of us become enraged because we have to bear the shortcomings of others. We should remember that not one of us is perfect, and that others see our defects as obviously as we see theirs. We forget too often to look at ourselves through the eyes of our friends. Let us, therefore, bear the shortcomings of each other for the ultimate benefit of everyone.

15 If I care to listen to every criticism, let alone act on them, then this shop may as well be closed for all other business. I have learned to do my best, and if the end result is good then I do not care for any criticism. But if the end result is not good, then even the praise of ten angels would not make the difference.

16 I desire so to conduct the affairs of this administration that if at the end, when I come to lay down the reins of power, if I have lost every other friend on earth, I shall at least have one friend left, and that friend shall be down inside of me.

17 Let us have faith that right makes might; and in that faith, let us, to the end, dare to do our duty as we understand it.

18 If you would win a man to your cause, first convince him that you are his sincere friend.

19 With the fearful strain that is on me night and day, if I did not laugh, I should die.

20 The sense of obligation to continue is present in all of us. A duty to strive is the duty of us all. I felt a call to that duty.

21 I will prepare and some day my chance will come.

22 Always bear in mind that your own resolution to succeed is more important than any other one thing.

23 If we could first know where we are, and whither we are tending, we could better judge what to do and how to do it.

24 Force is all-conquering, but its victories are short-lived.

25 If I have eight hours to chop down a tree, I'd spend six hours sharpening my ax.

26 A man devoid of religion is like a horse without a bridle.

27 The world will little note nor long remember what we say here, but it can never forget what they did here.. It is rather for us to be here dedicated to the great task remaining before us - that from these honoured dead we take increased devotion to that cause for which they gave the last full measure of devotion; that

we here highly resolve that these dead shall not have died in vain; that this nation, under God, shall have a new birth of freedom; and that government of the people, by the people, for the people, shall not perish from the earth.

287
- Charles Lindbergh
The First Person to Fly Non-stop New York to Paris
1902 - 1974

1 A great tradition can be inherited, but greatness itself must be won.

2 Life itself is more important than any material accomplishment life makes.

3 It's up to you to use nature wisely and to protect it.

4 Any coward can sit in his home and criticize a pilot for flying into a mountainside instead of lying in bed. I would rather, by far, die on a mountainside than in bed. What kind of a man would live where there is no daring? Is life so dear that we should blame men for dying in adventure? Is there a better way to die?

5 An over-emphasis of science weakens character and upsets life's essential balance.

6 There are but two measures of life's basic progress: heredity and environment, and these interweave generation after generation. The tyranny developed by human intellect has been seriously destructive to both. The genetic defects that affect each individual are obvious in our dependence on surgery and therapy and medication. And the planet's surface environment is breaking down.

7 Wildness created man, his intellect and his awareness together. The principles that created him have not changed. Man has simply turned his back on his birthright. The primary lesson taught by wildness is selection of individuals within the life stream. The wisdom of the wildness does not submerge the individual character, it brings it out. A sound individual is produced by a sound life stream.

288
- Art Linkletter
The Host of the Longest Running TV Program
Born in 1912

1 The first step toward a better self-image is to take your eyes off others and what they expect of you and to look deep inside yourself. You must become an inner directed person, rather than one whose life is controlled by the opinions of others.

2 Success in life comes to those who have confidence in themselves. If you believe you can do something, and if your faith never wavers as you keep trying to achieve your goals, chances are that you will succeed.

3 Ingesting any foreign substance for altering emotional attitudes is wrong.

4 The commercial process, like every other human behaviour, can be misused. But employed properly as a stimulant to and reward for our creative abilities, it results in a happier, easier and fuller life for us all.

5 One day, one month, one year, or ten years from its original ingestion, acid can strike with literally dizzying suddenness - in the time it takes to walk across kitchen floor - and turn a rational, composed individual into a raving lunatic.

6 I cannot sing or dance and I never was much of an actor. My art is getting other people to perform. If I had talent I'd probably be unbearable.

289

- Carl Linnaeus
The Classifier of Plants and Animals
1707 - 1778

1 Nature does not proceed by leaps.

2 A professor can never better distinguish himself in his work than by encouraging a clever pupil, for true discoverers are among them, as comets amongst the stars.

3 Live innocently. God is here.

4 Where religion is free, the land flourishes. Where theology reigns, there is nothing but wretchedness.

5 If you want to call Him Fate, you are not mistaken, for everything hangs by His finger; if you wish to call Him Nature, neither are you mistaken, for everything arises from Him.

6 There are no sharp boundaries in nature; the mineral kingdom merges almost imperceptibly into the plant kingdom; between plant and animals there are intermediate forms. The systematist has to know all this if he is to classify the multiplicity of creatures and reconstruct the plan of creation.

7 Harmony and balance are the central concepts in nature.

8 The closer we get to know the creatures around us, the clearer is the understanding we obtain of the chain of nature, and its harmony and system.

290

- David Livingstone
A Pioneer Explorer of Africa
1813 - 1873

1 If I live, I must succeed in what I have undertaken. Death alone will put a stop to my efforts.

2 Our mistakes even may be overruled for good, and when we are left to suffer their effects it is only for necessary discipline and chastisement.

3 I love peace as much as any mortal man. In fact I go quite beyond you, for I love it so much I would fight for it.

4 I shall not swerve a hair-breadth from my work while life is spared.

5 All I can add in my loneliness is, may Heaven's rich blessing come down on everyone - American, English or Turk - who will help heal the open sore of the world.

291

1 I firmly believe that any man's finest hour is that moment when he has worked his heart out in a good cause and lies exhausted on the field of battle, victorious.

2 A man must have goals established for himself. He must have dreams, desires, ambitions. These are the mechanisms for striving. But there is a price that must be paid for these. Nothing of value is free. You have to earn your own self-respect.

3 Fatigue makes coward of us all.

4 To play this game you must have that fire in you, and there is nothing that stokes a fire like hate. If they want to hate me, fine. I would prefer they hate the man across the line from them, but either way, I want to build that hate. It's not fear that motivates a football player, but hate. A hatred of losing, a hatred of being made to look foolish, a hatred of being second best. The will to excel and the will to win, they endure. They are far more important than any events that occasion them. They must be retained.

5 If I find a boy with talent, I feel that it is his moral obligation to fulfill it, and I will not relent on my own responsibility to him. Sometimes he won't even be aware of the talent he possesses, which serves only to make my job that much more difficult.

6 I wasn't born with much size or speed, and so everything I did in the field of athletics was a struggle. I had to try harder than anyone else because I did not want to fail again. I found that if I really wanted something badly enough, it was possible.

7 Winning isn't everything, but wanting to win is.

8 There are only three things that are important in your life: your God, your family and the Green Bay Packers.

9 Some people try to find things in this game that doesn't exist. Football is two things: blocking and tackling.

10 The harder you work, the harder it is to surrender.

11 It's not whether you get knocked down. It's whether you get up again.

12 Nobody ever attained greatness in anything who was not willing to continuously practice, drill and rehearse.

292

1 Publicity is a tiger - easy to jump on but very hard to ride. A loss of privacy is the price of the ride.

2 Success does not tolerate mistakes and journalists do not tolerate privacy of the successful.

3 Sometimes popularity can have frightening repercussions.

4 In solitude, I read and experience what I read. And in solitude I deal honestly with my feelings, and with myself. I test new ideas, I redress any missteps I have taken. Solitude for me is a house of undistorted mirrors. Solitude is guardian of my peace and contentment. When I am alone, I am never lonely. I have the company of what I am thinking and what I am reading.

5 In the beginning you welcome the glare of publicity because it leads to recognition and that leads to better and better roles and finally to the ultimate stardom, which means you can be choosy and even originate what you do. So, for the beginner in films, publicity has unique value although its origin is often unpredictable and its effect erratic.

6 Every woman I've known has experienced a certain fear at turning thirty. If she is not married, then on that birthday she is a self-ordained spinster. If she is childless, she fears that she will be forever barren.

7 Women who live for the next miracle cream do not realize that beauty comes from a secret happiness and equilibrium within themselves.

293
- Greg Louganis
One of the Finest Athletic-Divers of the World
Born in 1960

1 I don't want to be remembered as the greatest diver who ever lived. I want to be able to see the greatest diver.

294
- Joe Louis
The Longest-reigning World Heavyweight Boxing Champion
1914 - 1981

1 If I were a bullfighter I'd make the public think I was within inches of death, but I'd keep my margin of safety always. I did that in the ring. My God, against the men I beat when I was at my best, I was padding backwards round the ring for three rounds out of four. Defense always wins fights in the end, if it's good enough.

2 I just came along a time when the white people began to know that coloured people couldn't be terrorized no more, and the way I carried myself during that comin' up made some whites begin to look at coloured people differently.

3 If you dance, you got to pay the piper.

295
- Henry Luce
The Founder of Time, Life, Fortune and Sports Illustrated
1898 - 1967

1 A journalist's job is to find out the right side and to say so, emphatically.

2 The job of journalism is to foment and formulate. Facts should be married to imagination and passion.

3 One thing I was determined to do was to make *journalist* a good word.

4 When you put facts together to make stories of them, you endow them with values they did not have before. And that can raise hell with the truth. But since you also make them much more readable, you are successful in your field, which is communicating beyond your wildest dreams.

5 Give the public the truth we think it must have.

6 Give all the facts. First-rate writing means a base of facts. But predigest them and arrange them - or mis-arrange them- according to the *truth* you want to tell.

7 I always looked for writers who could see beyond the balance sheets and describe the lights and shadows of factories and the men who ruled them.

8 People aren't interested in mass; it's only individual who are exciting.

9 The business of business is to take part in the creation of The Great Society.

296

- Loretta Lynn
The Queen of Country Music of Her Time
Born in 1935

1 Be yourself. Always be honest with your audience. Don't try to imitate anybody else.

297

- Mary Lyon
The Founder of Mount Holyoke College
1797 - 1849

1 If anyone thinks he has no responsibilities, it is because he has not sought them out.

2 It is more solemn to live than to die.

3 What important consequences may depend on a single word, or on the most trifling deed! With how much care and deliberation should we regulate our conduct, and even our faculties; nay, more, we need constant instruction from heaven, and the daily guidance of the Holy Spirit.

4 It takes as much mind and character to descend as to rise with dignity.

5 It injures the character of a young person to receive gift after gift from a hand on which he has no natural claim. Such benefactions not only destroy the independence of a noble spirit, but also induces a habit of claiming as a right what is only a favour.

6 Gratitude is often a stranger in the hearts of young persons who are adopted into families and installed as children.

7 Those who receive their education as a boon from the purse of a stranger are apt to lose more in many self-dependence than they gain in mental culture.

298

1 When you have committed an action that you cannot bear to think about, that causes you to writhe in retrospect, do not seek to evade the memory; make yourself relive it, confront it repeatedly over and over till finally, you will discover through sheer repetition that it loses its power to pain you.

2 You start with something that's alive. And you don't question what that means. It's like a little germ culture you put on a glass, and then it starts developing. It's only after you have written a chapter that's sort of sprung out of it that you begin to know what it means. You *have* to know before you can get much further.

3 I think that it is natural that orphan children, rather looked down on in their family, and different from the little children they were growing among, would try to distinguish themselves. And instead of being distinguished unfavourably, would try to distinguish themselves favourably, on the whole.

4 The chief fallacy is to believe that Truth is a result which comes at the end of a thought-process. Truth, on the contrary, is always the beginning of thought; thinking is always resultless. That is the difference between *philosophy* and *science*; science has results, philosophy never. Thinking starts after an experience of truth has struck home, so to speak. The difference between philosophers and other people is that the former refuse to let go, but not that they are the only receptacles of truth.

5 What I do is take real plums and put them into imaginary cake.

299

1 We have not much choice in the mechanics of lives - the house we live in, the family or race we belong to, the colour of our eyes or skin - but in one respect we have liberty and that is in our attitude to life.

2 When we look back over our lives we can see most of our mistakes have come by not entering fully into the minds of other people. Sometimes this happened because of diffidence, sometimes from lack of interest, and sometimes it was plain, ordinary stupidity.

3 Children are great idealists, until the stupidity of their elders puts out the fires of their aspirations.

4 If I were young again - and I wish I could go back - I would spend my life as a teacher of young children, doing all in my power to give them a vision of the dignity and glory of being builders and planters, makers and menders.

5 Death is not the end. It is but the portal to a brighter, fairer world. Life is a circle. We see only a small jagged segment of it here, and even that small part, we see through a glass darkly. The part we see with our mortal eyes doesn't make sense; it is like the fragment of a story you read in a torn magazine - you know there must be more of it.

6 Those who sit in the wings see more than the players.

7 Words are the only things that live forever.

8 Writing is not like any other kind of work. There is a fervor in it that overcomes fatigue or even pain. It is a fire in the blood, a shot in the arm. It holds us when life begins to ravel, just as all the earth gathers itself into the brief brightness of Indian Summer before the stillness of winter falls.

9 Nothing is too good to be true,

10 *To bring about the even chance for everyone* is the plain and simple meaning of life. This is the war that never ends. It has been waged down the centuries by brave men and women whose hearts God has touched.

300
- Cyrus Hall McCormick
The Inventor of the Reaper
1809 - 1884

1 There was a greater than ever demand for a harvesting machine, but everyone knew that should it had been possible, someone must have invented it by then. That's why I decided to try it.

2 My father had already run many tests on a variety of harvesting machines. Unfortunately, none of them functioned properly. All I did is reworked on them and made the one that functioned properly.

301
- Willie McCovey
The Most Popular San Francisco Giants Baseball Player Ever
Born in 1938

1 I do what I think is right. I have experienced prejudice. I know something has got to be done, but I'm not knowledgeable as to what should be done. No matter what, I am a Negro. I am not going to put down the militant ones, but I don't condone violence on any side. I do not support anybody who believes in violence.

302
- Carson McCullers
At Age 23 Wrote The Heart Is A Lonely Hunter
1917 - 1967

1 Writing to me is a search for God.

2 I become the characters I write about.

3 Writing is a wandering, dreaming occupation.

4 If there is a funny scene or love scene in the face of sickness or ruin, it is offensive unless it is handled with the proper emotional progression.

5 Death is always the same, but each man dies his own way.

6 Death means only one billion zillion dead people who never return.

7 Anything a man can do, I can do better.

303

1 I have never been in doubt since I was old enough to think intelligently that I would someday be made President.

2 A system that provides a mutual exchange of commodities is manifestly essential to the continued and healthful growth of our export trade. We must not repose in fancied security that we can forever sell everything and buy nothing.

3 Be stern and summary where those qualities are necessary, but let moderation, kindness, leniency and adherence to the forms and rules that pertain to civil government be the characteristics of our rule while we continue to govern.

304

1 TV fame is ephemeral and lasts only as long as the show you are in.

2 I am not out to win any popularity stakes; I am out to get a job done.

3 If I had not been an actor, I would have been a criminal.

4 Nobody trusts anyone - or why do they put *tilt* on a pinball machine?

5 I'm half farmer and half street people. I've been in jail, in reform school. I get goose pimples every time I think I am going back to jail. I haven't done bad for a kid from an orphanage.

6 One little push and I coulda gone bad. I still don't know what kept me from it. I had no education, could hardly talk so people could understand me. I wanted to be an individual. I wanted recognition.

7 Success gave me a chance to find my place, to learn I didn't have to be a nut. I'm no longer a crazy kid. I've learned to read. The president of a company has to know what's going on.

8 Actors' kids get a bad handle. I worry about the mistakes I made, bringing them up; about what I tell them about what's right; about not giving them too much. And I worry about them being a target because of me.

305

1 One must be of one's time and paint what one sees.

2 The painter, the true painter to come, will be he who wrests from the contemporary scene its epic side and shows, through line and colour how great and poetic we are in our cravats and patent-leather boots.

3 Few men have the right to rule, for few men are moved by a great passion.

4 The ideal is not always preconceived. Often the meeting of a noble type,

gracious and rare, awakens the imagination and sustains works which, without this fortuitous event, would never have been born.

5 A great many painters and sculptors receive from the exterior their impression of beauty, and proceed from the material to the ideal. Instead of giving form to an ideal, they give an ideal to a form. It is no longer the soul which takes the body; it is the body which takes the soul. This last process seems to me the more simple.

6 Beauty is in the eyes, not in the brain; in the present, not in the past; in the truth, not in a dream; in life, not in death.

7 It's not that beauty changes completely; it evolves.

8 I painted what I saw.

9 Painting for painting's sake is the highest honour to the art.

306

- Horace Mann
A Crusader of Public Schools
1796 - 1859

1 Lost yesterday, somewhere between sunrise and sunset, two golden hours, each set with sixty diamond minutes. No reward is offered, for they are gone forever.

2 Habit is a cable; we weave a thread of it each day, and at last we cannot break it.

3 The power of concentration is one of the most valuable of intellectual attainments.

4 If any man seeks greatness, let him forget greatness and ask for truth, and he will find both.

5 Be ashamed to die until you have won some victory for humanity.

6 The scientific or literary well-being of a community is to be estimated not so much by its possessing of a few men of great knowledge, as its having many men of competent knowledge.

7 Unfaithfulness in the keeping of an appointment is an act of clear dishonesty. You may as well borrow a person's money as his time.

8 Genius may conceive, but patient labour must consummate.

9 Education is essential for democracy.

10 Work has always been to me what water is to a fish.

11 Keep one thing forever in view - Truth; and if you do this, though it may seem to lead you away from the opinion of men, it will assuredly conduct you to the throne of God.

12 Generosity during life is a very different thing from generosity in the hour of death. One proceeds from genuine liberality and benevolence, the other from pride or fear.

13 Jails and prisons are complement of schools; so many less as you have of the latter, so many more you must have of the former.

14 Resolve to edge in a little reading every day, if it is but a single sentence. If you gain fifteen minutes a day, it will make itself felt at the end of the year.

307

1 Hope is a wonder drug.

2 My first tour earned me about $100,000; today's players make that in one tournament. There's so much at stake. I wonder if it's still fun. It concerns me to see purses and endorsements becoming the measure of success, and young players aging faster than they should, under financial pressure.

3 Tennis is as mental as it is physical. Concentration and fighting spirit are as vital as the strokes.

308

1 Sometimes I don't understand the new breed. So many of them want an instant fame like instant coffee.

2 You have got to make boxing a kind of religion. You believe in yourself and you believe in the things you have to do. You never forget them for a minute. Then you get to the top and you think of what you had to go through and you ask yourself, "Was it worth it?" And it should have been. For me, it cost a lot, but it was worth everything.

3 If a champion spends his money foolishly, people ridicule him for that and if he doesn't spend it, they call him cheap.

4 Live fast, die hard.

309

1 Weak men wait for opportunities, strong men make them.

2 Men of mettle turn disappointments into helps, as the oyster turns into pearls the sand which annoys it.

3 No human being ever made a success trying to be somebody else, even if that person was a success.

4 If we could only rid ourselves of our imaginary troubles, our lives would be infinitely happier and healthier.

5 We tend to realize in the life what we persistently hold in the thought and vigorously struggle toward.

6 We starve ourselves in the midst of plenty because of our strangling thought.

7 Confidence is the father of achievement. It re-enforces ability, doubles energy, buttresses mental faculties, increases power.

8 Never allow yourself, or anyone else, to shake your confidence in yourself, to destroy your self-reliance, for this is the very foundation of all great achievement.

9 Count that man your enemy who shakes your faith in yourself, in your ability to do the thing you have set your heart upon doing, for when your confidence is gone, your power is gone. Your achievement will never rise higher than your self-faith.

10 Everyone is gravitating toward his aim just in proportion to the power and intensity of his desire, and his struggle to realize it.

11 The moment we cease to use our faculties, that moment they begin to deteriorate. Nature will let us have only what we use, and while we use it.

12 No matter how humble your work may seem, do it in the spirit of an artist, of a master.

13 Let every occasion be a great occasion for you cannot tell when fate may be taking your measure for a larger place.

14 The quality of your work will have a great deal to do with the quality of your life. If your work quality is down, your character will be down, your standards down, your ideals down.

15 Character is the cornerstone in building and maintaining success. The highest and best achievements are noble manhood and womanhood, and the achievement of true integrity and well-rounded character is in itself success.

16 The greatest thing a man can do in this world is to make the most possible out of the stuff that has been given him. This is success and there is no other.

17 Real happiness comes from the cultivation, the development, of the highest that is in us.

18 You can experience success if you only focus on possessing the virtues that you would like your children to have.

19 The man who succeeds has a programme.

20 The world always stands aside for the determined man. Will makes a way, even through seeming impossibilities.

21 The creator has bidden every man to look up, not down, has made him to climb, and not to grovel.

22 Labour is the parent of all the lasting monuments of this world, whether in verse or in stone, in poetry or in pyramids.

23 The intellect has little to do on the road to discovery. There comes a leap in consciousness, call it intuition or what you will, and the solution comes to you, and you know not how or why. All great discoveries are made this way.

24 It is the feeling of separateness from the great Power that makes us fear, just as the child's separation from its mother fills it with fear and terror.

25 No man can be truly rich who is selfish.

26 The world is always looking for men who are not for sale; men who are honest, sound from center to circumference, true to the heart's core; men whose consciences are as steady as the needle to the pole; men who will stand for the right if the heavens totter and the earth reels; men who can tell the truth, and look the world and the devil right in the eye; men that never brag nor run; men that neither flag nor flinch; men who have courage without shouting to it; men who know their own business and attend to it; men who will not lie, shirk nor dodge; men who are not afraid to say "No" with emphasis and who are not ashamed to say, "I can't afford it."

27 Association with good can only produce good; with the wicked, evil. No matter how sly, how secret, no matter if our associations have been in the dark, their images will sooner or later appear in our faces and conduct.

28 He is rich whose mind is rich, whose thought enriches the intellect of the world.

29 The man who has no money is poor, but one who has nothing but money is poorer. He only is rich who can enjoy without owning; he is poor who though he may have millions is covetous. There are riches of intellect, and no man with an intellectual taste can be called poor. He is rich as well as brave who can face compulsory poverty and misfortune with cheerfulness and courage.

30 It is easy to see the jewels and the flowers in other people's crosses but the thorns and heavy weight are known only to the bearers. How easy other people's burden seem to us compared with our own!

31 The strong willed, intelligent, persistent man will find or make a way where, in the nature of things, a way can be found or made.

32 The five basic rules of accomplishment are: (1)self-confidence; (2)positive, creative, thinking; (3)hard work; (4)concentrated effort; and (5)singleness of purpose and clean living.

33 Success is not measured by what a man accomplishes, but by the opposition he has encountered, and the courage with which he has maintained the struggle against overwhelming odds.

34 To know how to wring victory from defeat, and make stepping stones of our stumbling blocks, is the secret of success.

35 Every great man has become great, every successful man has succeeded, in proportion as he has confined his powers to one particular channel.

36 The greatest achievements are reserved for the men of single aim, in whom no rival powers divide the empire of the soul.

37 There can be no great courage where there is no confidence or assurance, and half the battle is in the conviction that we can do what we undertake.

38 Be larger than your task.

39 A great occasion is valuable to you just in proportion as you have educated yourself to make use of it.

40 No man can be ideally successful until he has found his place. Like a locomotive he is strong on the track, but weak anywhere else.

41 Your outlook upon life, your estimate of yourself, your estimate of your value are largely coloured by your environment. Your whole career will be modified, shaped, molded by your surroundings, by the character of the people with whom you come in contact every day.

42 A strong, successful man is not a victim of his environment. He creates favourable conditions. His own inherent force and energy compel things to turn out as he desires.

43 Make the uncommon effort into the common task; make it large by doing it in a great way.

44 It is not the straining for great things that is most effective; it is the doing the little things, the common duties, a little better and better.

45 Make it a life-rule to give your best to whatever passes through your hands. Stamp it with your manhood. Let superiority be your trademark.

46 Your expectation opens or closes the doors of your supply. If you expect grand things, and work honestly for them, they will come to you; your supply will correspond with your expectation.

47 No man is beaten until his hope is annihilated, his confidence gone. As long as a man faces life hopefully, confidently, triumphantly, he is not a failure; he is not beaten until he turns his back on life.

48 There can be no failure to a man who has not lost his courage, his character, his self-respect, or his self-confidence. He is still a king.

49 Most of our obstacle would melt away if, instead of cowering before them, we should make up our minds to walk boldly through them.

50 The beginning of a habit is like an invisible thread, but every time we repeat the act we strengthen the strand, add to it another filament, until it becomes a great cable and binds us irrevocably, thought and act.

51 Begin where you are; work where you are; the hour which you are now wasting, dreaming of some far off success, may be crowded with grand possibilities.

52 Opportunities are all around us, waiting for the observant eye to discover it.

53 Don't wait for extraordinary opportunities. Seize common occasions and make them great.

54 Power gravitates to the man who knows how.

55 Success is the child of drudgery and perseverance. It cannot be coaxed or bribed; pay the price and it is yours.

56 He is the richest man who enriches his country most; in whom the people feel richest and proudest; who gives himself with his money; who opens the doors of opportunity widest to those about him; who is ears to the deaf, eyes to the blind, and feet to the lame. Such a man makes every acre of land in his community worth more, and makes richer every man who lives near him.

57 Achievement is not always success, while repeated failure often is. It is honest endeavor, persistent effort to do the best possible under any and all circumstances.

58 All men who have achieved great things have been dreamers.

59 The hand cannot reach higher than does the heart.

310

1 No one can get anywhere in business by working only 40 hours a week.
2 Keep physically fit, mentally and spiritually strong.
3 Guard your habits - the bad ones will destroy you.
4 Pray about every difficult problem.
5 Men grow making decisions and assuming responsibility for them.
6 See the good in people and try to develop those qualities.
7 Think objectively and keep a sense of humour.
8 Ideas keep the business alive.
9 Good habits in general lengthen our lives and prepare us for death.

311
- Thurgood Marshall
The First Afro-American Justice of the U.S. Supreme Court
1908 - 1993

1 Everything has to come to an end sometime.
2 People are all people. Take the skin off, there is no difference.
3 In recognizing the humanity of our fellow beings, we pay ourselves the highest tribute.
4 Isn't it nice that nobody cares which twenty-three hours of the day I work!

312
- Dean Martin
The Man Who Rose from the Barber Shop to National Celebrity
1916 - 1995

1 Everybody loves somebody some day.
2 I can't stand an actor or actress who tells me acting is hard work. It's easy work. Anyone who says it isn't never had to stand on his feet all day dealing blackjack.
3 Nobody gets to know me.

313
- Harriet Martineau
A Highly Admired Writer of Her Day
1802 - 1876

1 The rich and the poor are necessary to each other and it is precisely the fable of the belly and the limbs; without the rich the poor starve, without the poor the rich would be compelled to labour for their subsistence.

314

1 I just love to compete. Just being out there and trying your hardest, that's what it's all about. If you win, you're all the more happy. But if you lose, you're satisfied as long as you gave it your best effort.

2 You have to be a pretty hard-nosed hermit to resist the spirit of goodwill.

315

1 I don't create a woman, I make a picture.

2 I have an interior scene to paint; I have before me a wardrobe that gives me a lively sensation of red, and I lay down a red that satisfies me. A relationship is set between this red and the whiteness of the canvas. If I add a green, if I represent the floor with a yellow, there will be a still satisfactory relationship between the green or the yellow and the whiteness of the canvas. But these different colours weaken each other. The various signs I use must be balanced so as not to destroy each other. I have to put some order in my ideas.

3 I want those who enter my chapel to feel purified and relieved of their burdens.

4 What I dream of is an art of balance, of purity and serenity .... a soothing, calming influence of the mind, something like a good arm chair.

5 He who loves flies, runs and rejoices; he is free and nothing holds him back.

6 In art, truth and reality begins when you no longer understand anything you do or know, and there remains in you an energy, that much the stronger for being balanced by opposition, white, pure, candid, your brain seeming empty in the spiritual state of a communicant approaching the Lord's table.

7 Once bitten by the demon of painting, I never wanted to give up.

316

1 No great project can succeed without some risk.

2 All knowledge is profitable.

3 No discoveries have conferred more honour and glory upon the age in which they were made, or been more beneficial to the world, than geographical discoveries.

- Dr. William Mayo
The Founder of the Mayo Clinic
1819 - 1911

1 No man is big enough to be independent of others.

2 The life of a doctor must be one of service; this profession demands of him a response to every call, whether there is pecuniary reward in it or not.

3 A man with unusual physical strength or with unusual intellectual capacity or opportunities owes something to the people.

4 A specialist is one who knows more and more about less and less.

5 I never felt the need of any religious faith, and therefore never had any. My own religion has been to do all the good I could to my fellow men, and as little harm as possible.

6 Throughout my life I kept scrupulous account of my reading time and maintained my desire to seek further training in the more practical aspects of my profession.

- Margaret Mead
One of America's Foremost Anthropologists
1901 - 1978

1 As the traveler who has once been from home is wiser than he who has never left his own doorstep, so a knowledge of one other culture should sharpen our ability to scrutinize more steadily, to appreciate more lovingly, our own.

2 If we are to achieve a richer culture, rich in contrasting values, we must recognize the whole gamut of human potentialities, and so weave a less arbitrary social fabric, one in which each diverse human gift will find a fitting place.

3 Life in the twentieth century is like a parachute jump: you have to get it right the first time.

4 Children not only have to learn what their parents learned in school, but also have to learn how to learn. This has to be recognized as a new problem which is only partly solved.

5 Today one can no longer save a society by dying for it; there won't be anything left to save. The big issue now is the survival of mankind.

6 Sooner or later I am going to die, but I am not going to retire.

7 It is very difficult to run an army if the general is in love with the sergeant.

8 Having two bathrooms ruins the capacity to cooperate.

319

1 The loss of one spoke in the gigantic wheel of the universe cannot prevent the wheel from turning and grinding in its endless orbit.

2 What is needed is a living example that, if given the opportunities, the blind can succeed. Such an example, from the outside, can do much more in creating opportunities for the blind.

3 No matter how fast I write, the writing of the life can never catch up with the crawl of my day-to-day life.

4 I sometimes feel I am leading two lives - the life I'm remembering and interpreting and my ordinary, day-to-day life.

5 The blind are a few persons living in a big sighted world. If they do not succeed in fitting into it, they will never amount to anything. They are like donkeys in a world of horses. They have to prove their worth - justify their very existence - to the horses. They have to show them that if, for instance, they don't have their gait and mane, can't run as fast as the horses can, they can lug more weight, work harder and put in longer hours.

320

1 One cannot and must not try to erase the past merely because it does not fit the present.

2 I am sorry I got the image of a tough woman. It's all wrong. Everybody thinks I spend my days planning, meeting, deciding. Nobody knows that what I like best is - to do nothing!

3 To be successful, a woman has to be much better at her job than a man.

4 Women's liberation is just a lot of foolishness. It's the men who are discriminated against. They can't bear children and no one is likely to do anything about that.

5 Old age is like a plane flying through a storm; once you are aboard, there is nothing you can do.

6 Don't be so humble; you are not that great.

321

1 The scientific incontrovertibility of physics leads directly to the ethical demand for veracity and honesty; and justice is inseparable from truth. Just as the laws of nature work consistently and without exception, on great things as in small, so too people cannot live together without justice for all.

2 Women have a greater responsibility and they are obliged to try, so far as they can, to prevent another war.

322

- Herman Melville
The Creator of Moby Dick
1819 - 1891

1 We cannot live only for ourselves. A thousand fibers connect us with our fellow men; and along those fibers, as sympathetic threads, our actions run as causes, and they come back to us as effects.

2 I am like one of those seeds taken out of the Egyptian Pyramids, which, after being three thousand years a seed and nothing but a seed, developed itself, grew to greatness and then fell to mould. Until I was twenty-five, I had no development at all. From my twenty-fifth year, I date my life.

323

- Gregor Mendel
The Father of the Science of Genetics
1822 - 1884

1 I am convinced that inheritance takes place according to definite laws or principles.

2 Without numbers there is little chance of one's hitting on something new and basic.

3 I have spent much time worrying about success or failure. There is too much to do. All I see before me is an interesting problem. The job of planning and thinking ahead should keep me busy during the next few years.

4 No one can think of science and research when his mind is weighed down by a thousand odds and ends of the practical world.

324

- Dmitri Mendeleyev
The Prophet of Chemical Elements
1834 - 1907

1 To be a successful scientist, one must experiment as well as theorize; one must know what has been done in the field already and one must have an intuitive feeling for where and how to look for evidence.

325

- Michelangelo
A Major Sculptor of All Time
1475 - 1564

1 If people knew how hard I had to work to gain my mastery, it wouldn't seem wonderful at all.

2 One cannot find peace except in the woods.

3 In every block of stone there lurks a perfect form.

4 The promises of this world are for the most part vain phantoms, and to confide on one's self, and become something of worth and value, is the best and safest course.

5 I am still learning.

6 Lord, grant me that I may always desire more than I can accomplish.

7 Trifles make perfection, but perfection is no trifle.

8 The more the marble wastes, the more the statue grows.

9 The true work of art is but a shadow of the divine perfection.

10 It is only well with me when I have a chisel on my hand.

326

- Arthur Miller
A Leading Modern American Dramatist
Born in 1915

1 You know you have reached a certain age when irony dominates whatever you see.

2 Memory keeps folding in upon itself like geologic layers of rock, the deeper strata sometimes appearing on top before they slope downward into the depths again.

3 Down deep in His heart God is a comedian who loves to make us laugh.

4 Glamour is a youth's form of blindness that lets in light, incoherent colour, but nothing defined. Like the rainbow, it is a once uplifting vision that moves away the closer you come to it.

5 The day will come when theater again will surmount everything for the simple reason that it is an irreducible simplicity. It's a man up there facing other men. Somehow or other this always has to be possible.

6 A good newspaper is a nation talking to itself.

327

- John Milton
A Major English Poet of All Time
1608 - 1674

1 He who reigns within himself and rules his passions, desires and fears is more than a king.

2 Truth is as impossible to be soiled by any outward touch as the sunbeam.

3 A good book is the precious life-blood of a master spirit, embalmed and treasured up on purpose to a Life beyond Life.

4 The pious and just honouring of ourselves may be thought the fountain-head from whence every laudable and worthy enterprise issues forth.

5 The child shows the man,
   As morning shows the day.

6 Give me the liberty to know, to think, to believe, and to utter freely according to conscience, above all other liberties.

7 The end of learning is to know God and, out of that knowledge, to love Him and to imitate Him, as we may the nearest, by possessing our souls of true virtue.

8 The mind is its own place, and in itself can make a Heaven of Hell, a Hell of Heaven.

9 The childhood shews a man, as morning shews the day.

328

- Jack Miner
The Pioneer Researcher of the Migration of Birds
1865 - 1944

1 It is the human race that is wild, not the birds. Birds are wild because they have to be, and we are wild because we prefer to be.

2 If I can get a child to build a birdhouse, he becomes a conservationist.

3 The more one studies these so-called wild creatures, the closer and closer will they bring him to God Who created them and gave man dominion over them.

4 Work consists of what you are compelled to, and don't want to do. Although I have moved hundreds of thousands of tons of clay with my own backbone and hands, I have never done any work. Yes, I am living because I want to... and am going to continue to live for another hundred years, or die in the attempt.

5 Men can go out together and live in bunches, have a good, clean, cheerful outing, and come home the better men for it, with greater love toward their fellow men. By taking such a month, away, far from the grind of life, it gives body, heart and nerves a rest and allows the soul to develop. We become better sons, husbands and fathers in our homes, and better citizens of the neighbourhood and the town, township, county and country in which we live.

6 There is one thing God gives us that He never takes away from us. That is our will. We can have a path of roses, or of broken glass or thorns. This He has left on us to decide.

329

- Comte de Mirabeau
A Major Leader of the French Revolution
1749 - 1791

1 Nothing is impossible to the man who can will, and then do; this is the only law of success.

2 *Impossible* - never let me hear that foolish word again.

3 The eternal truths which, based on the nature of man and society, see everything change about them and never change themselves, are the principle of every lasting regeneration.

330

- Joan Miró
A Foremost Exponent of Abstract and Surrealist Art
1893 - 1983

1 Rather than setting out to paint something, I begin painting, and as I paint the picture begins to assert itself, or suggest, itself under my brush. The form becomes the sign for a woman or a bird as I work. The first stage is free, unconscious.

2 If no one attacked my work, it would be a mediocre thing.

3 I have always felt like an insect equipped with antennae. I prowl and, mysteriously, along the way I come upon new discoveries.

4 More than the canvas itself, what counts is what emanates from it, what it gives off.

331

1 I never traveled with the mob.

2 I am not the kind of guy who thinks he knows it all. I can be talked into things.

3 I've still got the same attitude I had when I started. I haven't changed anything but my underwear.

4 I decided to play dead, I didn't have to be a hell of an actor.

5 I have two acting styles - with and without a horse.

6 Acting is strictly journeyman stuff.

7 I like the whole togetherness of movie making, the ambiance, the effort implicit in the manufacture of a film. I care about that; I really do.

332

1 If I had observed all the rules, I would never have got anywhere.

2 Fame is not really for a daily diet. That's not what fulfills you. It warms you a bit, but the warming is temporary. It's like caviare, but not when you have it every meal.

3 I have never quite understood this sex symbol business, but if I am going to be a symbol of something, I'd rather have it sex than some of the other things they've got symbols for.

333

1 Each of us has not always been a grown-up person. It was the child who instructed our personality.

2 When you try to point out something to your dog, it does not look in the direction that you are pointing but at your outstretched hand and finger. In the same way, you are paying so much attention to me. The highest honour and the deepest gratitude you can pay me is to turn your attention from me to the direction in which I am pointing - to the child.

3 Education is a natural process spontaneously carried out by the human individual and is acquired not by listening to words but by experiences in the environment.

4 The first essential for a child's development is concentration. They must find out how to concentrate and for this they need things to concentrate upon.

5 To influence society we must turn our attention to childhood. Out of this truth comes the importance of nursery schools, for it is the little ones who are building our future, and they can work only on the materials we give them.

6 The world of education is like an island where people, cut off from the world, are prepared for life by exclusion from it.

7 The prize and the punishment are incentives toward unnatural or forced effort. The jockey offers a piece of sugar to his horse before jumping into the saddle. The coachman beats his horse that he may respond to the signs given by the reins. And yet neither of these runs so superbly as the free horse of the plains.

334

- **Lucy Maud Montgomery**
The Creator of Anne of Green Gables
1874 - 1942

1 Writing is the best method of soul cultivation.

2 To write creatively, one has to be utterly alone in a silent room.

3 In the beginning, after receiving rejections after rejections, I felt dreadfully hurt. Tears of disappointment would come in spite of myself, as I crept away to hide the poor, crimpled manuscript in the depths of my trunk. But after a while I got hardened to it and did not mind. I only set my teeth and said, "I will succeed." I believed in myself and I struggled on alone, in secrecy and silence. I never told my ambitions and efforts and failures to any one. Down, deep down, under all discouragement and rebuff, I knew I would *arrive* some day.

4 When people tell me how they envy my gift of writing, I am inclined to wonder, with some inward amusement, how much they would have envied me on those dark, cold, winter mornings of my apprenticeship.

5 I have always hated beginning a story. When I get the first paragraph written I feel as though it were half done. The rest comes easily.

6 I had always kept a notebook in which I jotted down, as they occurred to me, ideas for plots, incidents, characters and descriptions.

7 I have never studied human nature; I have never met one human being who could, as a whole, be put into a book without injuring it. Any artist knows that to paint *exactly* from life is to give a false impression of the subject. *Study* from life he must, copying suitable heads or arms, approaching bits of character, personal or mental idiosyncrasies, making use of the real to perfect the ideal. But the ideal, his ideal, must be behind and beyond it all. The writer must *create* his characters, or they will not be life-like.

335

- **Henry Moore**
A Great Sculptor of 20th Century
1898 - 1986

1 The general public is very slow to accept new trends in art because it can't understand them.

2 The more you know about something, the more ambitious you become.

3 Happiness is to be fully engaged in the activity that you believe in and, if you are very good at it, well that's a bonus.

4 It is impossible to turn to a single influence in any work of art. It can only come by the development and experience of a lifetime combined with all these influences.

5 Just because throughout my sculpture I have been interested in the same subjects, mother and child, reclining figures, seated figures and so on does not mean I was obsessed with these themes. It just means I have not exhausted them and, if I were to live another hundred years, I would still find satisfaction in these subjects. I could never get tired of them. I can always discover new thoughts and new ideas based on the human figure. It is inexhaustible.

6 I would like my work to be thought of as a celebration of life and nature.

336

- Marianne Moore
A Major American Poet
1887 - 1972

1 Generosity is giving what you could use yourself.

2 One writes because one has a burning desire to objectify what it is indispensable to one's happiness to express.

3 For most defects, to delete is the instantaneous cure.

4 Writing is an expedient for making one's self understood.

5 Clarity depends on precision.

6 Straight writing is the one that is not mannered, overconscious or at war with common sense.

7 An author is a fashioner of words, stamps them with his own personality, and wears the raiment he has made, in his own way.

8 Genius is a combination of attributes, three of which are honesty, a sense of the really significant and the power of concentration.

337

- Akio Morita
The Inventor of the First All-Transistor Radio
Born in 1921

1 Marketing is really a form of communication.

2 No theory or plan or government policy will make a business a success; that can be done only by the people. Develop a healthy relationship with your employees, and create a family-like feeling within your company, a feeling that employees and managers share the same fate.

3 You should understand the difference between the school and a company. In school if you do well on an exam and score one hundred percent, that is fine, but if you don't write anything at all on your examination paper, you get a zero. In the world of business you face an examination each day and you can gain not one hundred points but thousands of points, or only fifty points. And if you make a mistake you do not get a simple zero; it is always minus something and

there is no limit to how far down you can go and therefore you can be a danger to the company.

4 It is important to use the technology to create products that people can use.

5 Having unique technology and being able to make unique products are not enough to keep a business going. You have to sell the products and to do that you have to show the potential buyer the real value of what you are selling.

6 To sell our recorders we had to identify the people and institutions that were likely to recognize value in our products.

7 A trademark is the life of an enterprise and it must be protected boldly. A trademark and a company name are not just clever gimmicks; they carry responsibility and guarantee the quality of the product.

338

- Grandma Moses
The Grand Old Lady of American Art
1860 - 1961

1 Life is what we make it; always has been, always will be.

2 As I finish each picture, I think I've done my last, but I go right on.

3 Let man be happy in adorning his home, in making his home the dwelling of happiness and comfort. Let him, as far as circumstances will permit, be industrious in surrounding it with pleasing objects, in decorating it within and without the things that tend to make it agreeable and attractive.

4 It's a good idea to build the sty before getting the pig; likewise with young men, get the home before the wedding.

5 A picture without a frame is like a woman without a dress.

6 What a strange thing is memory and hope; one looks backward, the other forward. The one is of today, the other is the tomorrow. Memory is history recorded in our brain; memory is a painter; it paints pictures of the past and of the day.

7 Work of any description adds to one's happiness.

339

- Daniel Patrick Moynihan
The Man Who Rose from Broken Families to Political Leadership
Born in 1927

1 Over-educated people in authority do not understand something that people from ordinary background know well - that awful things happen.

2 Not ever being frightened can be a formula for self-destruction.

3 To seek to do the impossible, with the passionate but misinformed conviction that it can be done, is to create the conditions for frustration and ruin.

1 The clearest way into the Universe is through a forest wilderness.

2 We have two ears and one mouth that we may hear more and speak less. Sometimes it seems as if I had only one ear and a dozen mouths.

3 We sometimes hear the Lord spoken of as if He were a little, cranky, old-fashioned being, fastened and sealed in by well-established rules, and that the parsons are on confidential terms with Him and know just what He intends.

4 Earth and heaven are the same - one and inseparable.

5 On a swift flood we are all borne forward and only when I am in wilderness is this current invisible, where one day is a thousand years and a thousand years one day.

6 Descriptive writing amounts to little more than *Hurrah, here's something! Come!* Nature's tables are spread and fires burning. You must go warm yourselves and eat.

7 Evolution! - a wonderful, mouth-filling word, isn't it? It covers a world of ignorance. Somewhere, before evolution was, was an Intelligence that laid out the plan, and evolution is the process, not the origin, of the harmony.

8 A jolly fellow is the grasshopper.

9 Any fool can destroy trees, which cannot defend themselves or run away.

10 Everybody needs beauty as well as bread.

11 People should have places where they could rest their bodies, lift their spirits, and be at peace with the world.

12 No dogma taught by the present civilization seems to form so insuperable an obstacle in the way of right understanding of the relations which culture sustains to wildness, as that which man declares that the world was made for the use of man. Every animal, plant and crystal controverts it in the plainest terms. Yet it is taught from century to century as something ever new and precious, and in the resulting darkness the enormous conceit is allowed to go unchallenged.

13 I have never yet happened upon a trace of evidence that seemed to show that one animal was ever made for another as much as it was made for itself.

14 Everything is governed by laws. But out here in the free unplanted fields there is not rectilinear sectioning of times and seasons. All things flow here in indivisible, measureless currents.

15 In the wilderness life seems neither long nor short, and we take no more heed to save time or make haste than do the trees and stars. This is true freedom, a good practical sort of immortality.

16 One of the most satisfying experiences in life is a deep appreciation of nature. Wealth, health, families, friends and fame can be taken from us but if we have a deep feeling for the beauty in nature, we can still be happy. Climb the mountains and get their tidings. Nature's peace will flow into you as sunshine flows into trees. The winds will blow their own freshness into you - and the storms their energy - while cares will drop off like autumn leaves.

341

- Emily Murphy
The First Female Magistrate in the British Empire
1868 - 1933

1 If we laughed more, there would be less need for medicine.

2 The commonest and cheapest of all pleasures is Conversation. It is the greatest pastime of life.

3 What is good enough for *company* is not good for your family; be it courtesy or the silver tea-pot.

4 The heart, like the body, hungers for food, and finds it in the heroic deeds and noble traits of those who have gone before.

5 Do not waste your powers by disclosing your plans to people of whose sympathies you are not certain. It will cripple your decisions.

6 Avoid like plague the company of despondent people; pessimism leads to weakness, as optimism leads to power.

7 Lean on no one. Find your own center and live in it, surrendering it to no person or thing.

8 It is quite possible that a plate of soup may be a comfort to the soul.

9 Everyone is a mixture of good and bad impulses, and the mark of a really fine woman is loyalty to her own sex. No woman can become or remain degraded without all women suffering.

10 If we only love enough, we may be successes in living.

11 There is a veritable life in death. The scene has all the suffering of tragedy with none of its dignity.

12 There is only one thing worse than a guilty custom and that is a guilty acquiescence.

13 One's best talents are required for the home.

14 There is a sense of isolation in the woods that you do not find to be loneliness. A large part of the pleasure is to discover that you can not only live without the modern conveniences and amusements of the city, but that you are really happier without them.

342

- Anne Murray
The Snowbird Queen
Born in 1945

1 I get tongue-tied when I visit backstage.

2 I have never been one to look into mirrors.

3 A working relationship is better when you stay removed from it.

4 Don't take yourself too seriously. Cultivate a sense of humour and an attitude - no matter what happens, it's not that important. You are just one little thing in the whole scheme of things.

5 When I choose records, I choose songs that are not only attractive to me but would be attractive to people who listen.

6 If you deal with the public, you have to try to get to them.

7 I have had a really good career, but quite frankly I'd rather be a well-rounded human being than a well-rounded performer. One thing I've always had is common sense, and a lot of people have found it boring. But it's kept me alive.

343

- Ralph Nader
The Consumers' Advocate
Born in 1934

1 How much has this nation lost because there are men walking around today with invisible chains?

2 I am an activist. If you are an activist you orchestrate, you do things that play back to strengthen one another.

3 The evils of bureaucracy do not afflict us.

4 Indians in the woods saw things that the white men never saw because the Indians were trained to see them. We can do the same in our technological society.

5 Once you begin to compromise, you erode yourself.

6 Information is the currency of democracy.

344

- Martina Navratilova
The Winner of 74 Professional Tennis Matches in a Row
Born in 1956

1 Sports are good for young women. It's good to compete, good to run, good to sweat, good to get dirty, good to feel tired and healthy and refreshed.

2 When I die, I don't want a lot of money in the bank. I'll be happy spending my money, but not on tanks or B-52's; all money wasted on warfare while millions of people starve to death. I would like to spend my money and my time working towards ending world hunger, helping preserve nature and wildlife, and cleaning up the environment that we have polluted so successfully.

345

- Willie Nelson
The King of Country Music of 1970s and 80s
Born in 1933

1 You can bring divine energy into your lungs by breathing. Feel the beat of your heart. It is holy light. When you become conscious of the Master in your heart, your whole life changes. Your aura goes out and influences everything around you. You have free will to recognize it or to blind yourself to it. Be quiet and ask your heart. I mean, really shut up and listen to your inner voice. It will tell you, this is the truth.

2 If the performer is not having a good time, chances are the audience won't enjoy it so much either. Musicians who grow tired and cynical and begin playing just for the money instead of for the love of music and for the crowds, find their audiences start slipping away.

3 Always let wisdom, strength and love be your guide.

4 I went to Nashville to make it as a singer and songwriter or die trying and I almost died before achieving my goal.

5 A long time ago when I walked onto a stage to do a show, I would search the room with my eyes. I was looking for somebody who was looking at me, who appeared interested in learning what I was doing. Once I found that friendly face, I would sing to that person all night long. I would zero in and make heavy contact with his spirit and it would grow. The flash of energy between me and one friendly face would reflect into others and it would keep growing, but it all had to start with one friendly face.

346
- Sir Isaac Newton
The Discoverer of the Earth's Gravity
1642 - 1727

1 Knowledge is an accumulation of vision, the vision of the present added to that of the past.

2 If I have ever made any valuable discoveries, it has been owing more to patient attention, than to any other talent.

3 If I have seen farther than others, it is by standing upon the shoulders of Giants.

4 I do not know what I may appear to the world, but to myself I seem to have been only like a boy playing on the seashore and diverting myself in now and then finding a smoother pebble or a prettier shell than ordinary, whilst the great ocean of truth lay undiscovered before me.

5 What I have done is due to past thought.

6 Errors are not in the art but in the artificers.

7 To every action there is always opposed an equal reaction.

8 Everybody continues in its state of rest, or of uniform motion in a right line, unless it is compelled to change that state by forces impressed upon it.

347
- Vaslav Nijinsky
A Towering Figure in the History of Ballet
1888 - 1950

1 I do not wish people to think that I am a great writer or that I am a great artist nor even that I am a great man. I am a simple man who has suffered a lot.

2 I was born a Russian; I can give thanks to my country, which made me an artist, and I will remain a Russian.

3 All movements by the human body can be notated by means of a notational system based on a segmented circle. Every part of the body makes a circular movement where the moving part is attached to another part - the arm to the shoulder, the leg to the hip, and so on.

4 The audience must be made to laugh, they must be made to laugh.

5 Grace comes from God; everything else can be acquired by study. The kind of grace that can be learnt stops short; the grace that is innate never ceases to grow.

348

- Alfred Nobel
The Founder of the Nobel Prizes
1833 - 1896

1 My homeland is wherever I am working and I work everywhere.

2 I wish all guns with their belongings and everything could be sent to hell, which is the proper place for their exhibition and use.

3 If I have a thousand ideas a year and only one turns out to be good, I am satisfied.

349

- Christopher Nolan
A Great Writer Despite Serious Physical Handicaps
Born in 1965

1 Sad thoughts destroy feasible mind's creation.

2 Teachers make or mar the confidence of their pupils.

3 Man is God hesitant and God is Man hesitantly trying to help.

350

- Rudolf Nureyev
A Highly Acclaimed Ballet-Dancer of 20th Century
1938 - 1993

1 My work is my only passport.

2 I don't miss Russia. I belong to the whole planet.

3 I believe there is something in me that is still waiting to be found.

4 It's quite difficult to dance. It needs commitment and passion; every time you dance it must be sprayed with your blood. So much effort for so little reward - not from the public or critics or the box office, but from yourself.

5 Since every dancer gives some performances when he is really in form, others when he cannot help being less than his best, the more you do altogether, the more good ones there will be among them.

6 I am not yet sure if I am a choreographer. It takes total involvement, more than I can have while I am still dancing. And it's very difficult to choreograph a ballet

for yourself to dance, because you go into your antics and there is nobody to tell you to stop.

7 You learn so much more about the structure of a ballet when you are actually in the middle of it, much more than by watching.

8 When a dancer's career begins, there's a bonus in the freshness of youth. Then comes a period when there is complete command. But after that, I don't think it is fair that a dancer should just be pushed aside when he still has something to offer. When someone has devoted his life to the stage, I think that as an artist, he should be given the right to die on stage, too.

351

- Diana Nyad
An Extraordinary Marathon Swimmer
Born in 1949

1 If you put your guts into something, you will do it.

2 If you want to touch the other shore badly enough, barring an impossible situation, you will. But if your desire is diluted for any reason, you will never make it.

3 The tricky part of success is having the good fortune to find a field in which you are genetically gifted.

4 Many of the champions in the world of sports were and are slightly deficient in some area of natural ability; but it is unheard of at the top to find an individual oozing with talent without a past history of ardent work. Most champions have put in thousands of extra hours in improving deficits or in strengthening their assets in order to overshadow their weaknesses. The endurance sports are the prime showcase for this theory; even minimal talent can couple with relentless drive to equal success.

5 The brain is much better equipped to store and recall information to which it is frequently exposed than information to which it is exposed only occasionally.

6 The overwhelming drive behind my success is that I am absolutely unafraid of pain. I am willing to put myself through anything; temporary pain or discomfort means nothing to me as long as I can see that the experience will take me to a new level. I am interested in the unknown, and the only path to the unknown is through breaking barriers, an often-painful process.

7 The body is a systematic machine, as is the mind. If you practice the clarinet once a week for three hours at a time, you will make one-tenth the progress than if you practiced thirty minutes a day six days a week for the same total three hours a week.

8 What interests me about marathon swimming is that it tests the human spirit. It is a sport of extremes.

352

1 Great acting parts are cannibals - they devour you.

2 I would prefer to be known as Larry. I won't use *Lord* on the theatre billboards, but it might help the British public to stop regarding actors as rogues and vagabonds.

3 Of all the things I have done in life, directing a motion picture is the most beautiful. It's the most exciting and the nearest that an interpretive craftsman, such as an actor, can possibly get to being a creator.

4 If I wasn't an actor, I think I'd have gone mad. You have to have some extra voltage, some extra temperament to reach certain heights. Art is a little bit larger than life - it's an exaltation of life - and I think you probably need a little touch of madness.

353

1 What artist, so noble... as he who ...sketches the outline, writes the colours, and directs the shadows of a picture so great that Nature shall be employed upon it for generations.

2 Men of literary taste or clerical habit are always apt to overlook the working-classes, and to confine the records they make of their own times, in a great degree, to the habits and fortunes of their own associates or to those of people of superior rank to themselves. The dumb masses have often been so lost in the shadow of egotism that, in later days, it has been impossible to discern the very real influence their character and condition has had on the fortune and the fate of nations.

3 You will find that it is what you have *been* and not what you have done that you care.

4 I never before had the question so clearly before me, how such a loitering, self-indulgent, dilettante sort of man as I was, could, at middle age, have turned into such a hard-worker and *doer* as I then suddenly became and have remained so ever since?

354

1 Being deaf is not a handicap. It is a challenge to conquer, similar to being called on to do a difficult stunt. Think positive. Never look back, and never give up.

355

1 You can save a lot of energy by being smart on the ice, by passing the puck more. Why crack through two defensemen yourself when you can pass the puck to a teammate, then sneak around behind the defensemen and get a return pass? Also, why go between a guy and the boards when the odds are that you won't make it?

2 I am lucky, I have been gifted but the world is full of people who have not been gifted. When I see one little girl that can't walk and yet keeps smiling at me, or someone who goes home with an iron lung every night and still gives me a kiss and a hug after every hockey game, I don't think I'm such a big hero any more. I think that compared to those people I'm a very small article! A very small, lucky article! It knocks me down pretty bloody fast. and cuts deep into me.

356

1 Know what has to be done, then do it.

2 The best way to prepare for tomorrow is to live today superbly well.

3 Live today as best as you can. By living today well, you do the most within your power to make tomorrow better.

4 We are here not to get all we can out of life for ourselves, but to try to make the lives of others happier.

5 The great physician cares more about the individual patient than for the special nature of the disease.

6 Success in the long run depends on endurance and perseverance. All things come to him who has learned to labour and wait, whose talents develop in the still and quiet years of unselfish work.

7 The philosophies of one age have become the absurdities of the next, and the foolishness of yesterday has become the wisdom of tomorrow.

8 In the life of a young man the most essential thing for happiness is the gift of friendship.

9 Nothing in life is more wonderful than faith - the one great moving force which we can neither weigh in the balance nor test in the crucible.

10 Throw away, in the first place, all ambition beyond that of doing the day's work well. Find your way into work in which there is an enjoyment of it and all shadows of annoyance seem to flee away. Let each day's work absorb your energy and satisfy your wildest ambition.

11 The greater the ignorance, the greater the dogmatism.

12 Things cannot always go your way. Learn to accept in silence the minor aggravations, cultivate the gift of taciturnity and consume your own smoke with an extra draft of hard work, so that those about you may not be annoyed with the dust and soot of your complaints.

13 In science the credit goes to the man who convinces the world, not to the man to whom the idea first occurs.

14 The desire to take medicine is perhaps the greatest feature which distinguishes man from animals.

15 No bubble is so iridescent or floats longer than that blown by the successful teacher.

16 Humanity has but three great enemies, fever, famine and war. Of these by far the greatest and most terrible is fever. As far back as history takes us, this noisome pestilence in some form or other has plagued mankind.

17 No other disease kills from one-quarter to one-third of all persons attacked, and so fatal is it that to die of pneumonia is the natural end of elderly people. Patients are divided into two classes, alcoholic and temperate. The majority of the former die in spite of all treatment; the majority of the latter get better with little or no treatment.

18 The Masterword in Medicine is Work, a little one, but fraught with momentous consequences; you can but write it on the tables of your heart, and bind it upon your forehead. The practice of medicine is an art, not a trade; a calling, not a business; a calling in which your heart will be exercised equally with your head. Often the best part of your work will have nothing to do with potions and powders, but with the exercise of an influence of the strong upon the weak, and of the shrewd upon the foolish. To you as the trusted family counselor the father will come with his anxieties, the mother with her hidden griefs, the daughter with her trials and the son with his follies. Courage and cheerfulness will not only carry you over the rough places of life, but will enable you to bring comfort and help to the weak-hearted, and will console you in the sad hours when you have to whistle that you may not weep.

19 Cultivate the habit of a life of day-tight compartments. Shut out the yesterdays, and shut off the future as tightly as the past. The life of the present lived earnestly, intently, without a forward-looking thought, is the only insurance for the future. Begin the day with Christ and His prayer. You need no other. Let no day pass without contact with the best literature of the world. Learn to know your Bible; though tough, it has still its ancient power. Life is a straight, plain business, and the way is clear, blazed for you by generations of strong men, into whose labours you enter and whose ideals must be your inspiration.

20 To have striven, to have made the effort, to have been true to certain ideals - this alone is worth the struggle.

21 When schemes are laid in advance, it is surprising how often the circumstances will fit in with them.

22 Work is the open sesame of every portal, the great equalizer in the world, the true philosopher's stone which transmutes all the base metal of humanity into gold.

23 No quality ranks with imperturbability. It is the essential bodily virtue. It means coolness and presence of mind under all circumstances, calmness amid storm, clearness of judgment in moments of grave peril. It is a blessing to you and a comfort to all who come in contact with you. With practice and experience you may expect to attain a fair measure. The first essential is extreme calmness, never to show or express anxiety or fear.

357

1 In long years of work and study, I have, it is true, attained great successes in the construction of gas engines, yet I believe there are others worthier than I to receive such an exalted distinction. I have always regretted, and do so now most especially, that in my youth I only went to high school and never had the advantage of academic education.

358

1 People's characters are formed by their environment and education.

2 It is the one great and universal interest of the human race to be cordially united, and to aid each other to the full extent of their capacities.

3 He who prays as he ought, will endeavour to live as he prays.

4 The greatest influence in forming man's character is found in his early environment.

359

1 When I came back after all the stories about Hitler and his snub, I came back to my native country and I could not ride in the front of the bus. I had to go to the back door. I could not live where I wanted. I wasn't invited to shake hands with Hitler, but I wasn't invited to the White House to shake hands with the President either.

2 After Berlin I came home as a temporary hero. But that died. They made me a lot of promises - movies, endorsements, things like that. The promises were never kept. They said the climate wasn't right for a black man to get so much attention.

3 My job here is not to complain but to try to make this a better world.

4 We should treat each other with kindness. We should treat each other as equals.

5 When you get to the point that you start hating a track suit, it's time to quit.

6 We all have dreams, but in order to make these dreams into reality it takes an awful lot of determination, self-discipline and effort. Sport teaches those things and others - respect of other people and how to live with your fellow man.

360

1 My experience was my armour and technical skills my weapons; so I approached London with confidence and a great hope.

2 To write the opera, which was a tremendous undertaking, I turned all my forces towards it and shut myself completely away from the world. The very thought of that project obliterated every other thought from my mind.

3 In a repertory which contains fifteen, eighteen, and sometimes twenty or more pieces, it is enough to have only a single piece, one little phrase, that you have not mastered, to completely unnerve you and beget the most dreadful fear.

4 Rhythm is the pulse of music. It marks the beginning of its heart, proves its vitality, attests its existence. It is order but this order in music cannot progress with the cosmic regularity of a planet, nor with the automatic uniformity of a clock. It reflects life, organic, human life, with all its attributes; therefore it is subject to moods and emotions, to rapture and depression. There is no absolute rhythm. In the course of the dramatic development of a musical composition, the initial themes change their character; it has to be energetic or languishing, crisp or elastic, steady or capricious.

5 Education and social position not give only rights but also place the obligation on intelligent people to excel in all virtues.

361

1 Don't look back. Something might be gaining on you.

2 I used to kill flying birds with rocks. Most people need shotguns to do what I did with rocks.

3 I threw my trouble ball, and they just wet their pants or cried. They thought of passing a law against me.

362

1 There comes a time in the life of a people suffering from an intolerable injustice when the only way to maintain one's self-respect is to revolt against that injustice.

2 Great suffering is endured by women because of the state of the law. We have presented petitions and we have held meetings greater than men have ever held for any reform. We have been misrepresented and we have been ridiculed. Contempt has been poured upon us. We have faced the violence of ignorant mobs. If you decided to bind us over, we shall not sign any undertaking. To

prison we must go. We are driven to this. We are determined to go on with the agitation. We are in honour bound to do so until we win. Just as it was the duty of your forefathers to do it for you, it is our duty to make this world a better place for women. If you had the power to send us to prison, not for six months but for six years, ten years, or for the whole of our lives, the government must not think they can stop this agitation.

3 War is not women's way. To the women of the Union human life is sacred.

4 If you convict me, gentlemen, whether the sentence be short or long, I shall not submit to it. I shall join the women already in Holloway on the hunger-strike.

5 I shall come out of prison, dead or alive, at the earliest possible moment and enter the fight again.

6 One thing we regard as sacred: human life. With that exception, we are justified in using all methods resorted to in time of war.

363
- Francis Parkman
A Great American Historian
1823 - 1893

1 My aim is to get at the truth. I have devoted my whole life to searching factual data and to creating a narrative both historically accurate and consistent with just historic proportion.

2 There is a universal law of growth.

3 The true aim of life is not happiness but achievement.

4 The first and fundamental requisites of women, as of men, are physical, moral and mental health. It is for man to rear the political superstructure; it is for women to lay its foundation.

5 God rules the world by fixed laws, moral and physical; and according as men and women observe or violate these laws will be the destinies of communities and individuals for this world and the next.

6 The higher education is necessary to the higher order of women to the end that they may discharge their function of civilizing agent; but it should be cautiously limited to the methods and degree that consist with the discharge of their functions of maternity. Health of body and mind is the one great essential.

7 Men are belittled and cramped by the competition of business, from which women are, or ought to be, free. Hence they have opportunities of moral and mental growth better in some respects than those of men.

364
- Gordon Parks
The First Black Director of a Major Movie Production
Born in 1912

1 Nothing is more noble than a good try.

2 It's a matter of giving more to this world than you take from it, so when you die, you don't owe it anything.

3 Success is filled with the agony of how and why - in the flesh, nerves and conscience. It takes you down a lonely road and you feel, at times, that you are traveling it alone. You can only keep walking. During the loneliness you get to know who you are. Then you face the choice - of holding on to everybody's friendship, or losing the one you have made with yourself.

4 You have to fight off fear. For that you need weapons. I don't mean guns and knives. The weapons I mean are things in your mind and your heart that help you overcome the fear. Years ago I found those weapons, one by one. They were half-hidden by the twistings and turnings of my early life and I chose them slowly, with pain and very great care.

365

- Rosa Parks
The Mother of the Civil Rights Movement in USA
Born in 1913

1 I have spent over half my life teaching love and brotherhood and I feel that it is better to continue to try to teach or live equality and love than it would be to have hatred or prejudice. Everyone living together in peace and harmony and love ... that's the goal that we seek, and I think that the more people there are who reach that state of mind, the better we will all live.

2 The only tired I was, was tired of giving in.

3 To this day, I am not an absolute supporter of non-violence in all situations. But I strongly believe that the civil-rights movement of the 1950s and 1960s could never have been so successful without Dr. King and his firm belief in non-violence.

4 When people made up their minds that they wanted to be free and took action, then there was a change. But they could not rest on just that change. It has to continue.

366

- Dolly Parton
A Country Music Star Despite Formidable Poverty
Born in 1946

1 If it weren't for laughter, I would have died years ago.

2 A true friend is one of the greatest gifts a person can ever have.

3 When I sit back in my rocking chair some day, I want to be able to say that I have done it all.

4 Poverty makes a person more creative.

5 Poverty is something you don't realize while you are in it - at least not if you are a kid with a head full of dreams and a house full of loving family.

6 Stick to your dreams. Stick to your guns. Have faith in yourself.

7 Believe in yourself. Work hard. Keep your sense of humour and your day job.

8 Get yourself three notebooks and sit down and tell God everything. In one, put

everything negative, all of your frustrations, your anger, who's ticking you off, what you are not getting that you feel you deserve. Be honest. Let it all out. In the second, write down all the good things in your life, even the little things. Try to find something good about all the people in your life. Try especially hard to find positive things about the people who are troubling you or disappointing you. Then, in your third book, write down your wishes, your dreams, your desires, all that you could or should have done. When you are done, hold your books up to the light. Ask God to consider all the things you have written down. Ask Him to clean up your life, past, present and future. Ask for forgiveness and direction. Then tear out just the pages of the books that you have used and burn them in a bucket or a fireplace or somewhere. As your thoughts burn, think of it as *holy smoke* - tiny, almost invisible particles that will go up to God for Him to put back together in the way they should be. Now look at the pages left in your books. Those are the clean, white pages on which you can write the rest of your life. You should feel cleansed, forgiven, rejuvenated, perfect.

367

- Louis Pasteur
The Founder of Bacteriology
1822 - 1895

1 Let me tell you the secret that has led me to my goal. My strength lies solely in my tenacity.

2 In the fields of observation, chance favours only the mind that is prepared.

3 Work, Will and Success fill human existence. Will opens the door to Success, both brilliant and happy. Work passes these doors, and at the end of the journey Success comes in to crown one's efforts.

368

- George Patton
An Extraordinary American Field Commander of World War II
1885 - 1945

1 Success is not how high and fast you reach the top, but how high and fast you bounce back when you hit the bottom.

2 If everybody is thinking alike, somebody isn't thinking.

3 An active mind cannot exist in an inactive body.

4 The right kind of fear can have a positive effect.

5 Take calculated risks. That is quite different from being rash.

6 Never tell people how to do things. Tell them what to do and they will surprise you with their ingenuity.

7 Any commander who fails to obtain his objective, and who is not dead or severely wounded, has not done his full duty.

8 Always go for the offensive; never dig in.

9 The leader must be an actor. He is unconvincing unless he lives the part.

10 Leadership is the thing that wins battles. It consists in knowing what you want

to do and doing it and getting mad if any one steps in the way. Self-confidence and leadership are twin brothers.

11 All the great leaders, good and bad, climbed to their positions of eminence by demonstrating a mastery of the circumstances. In order to wield influence on public events, a man has to be prominent. Not only must he excel in his career, but his excellence has to be recognized. Proficiency and character lead to advancement, but promotion alone is no guarantee of widespread approbation. One's superior qualifications have to be perceived and appreciated, even acclaimed. Only then can a leader perform on the stage of history.

12 You must be single-minded. Drive for the one thing on which you have decided.

13 For years I have been accused of making snap judgments. Honestly, this is not the case because I am a profound military student and the thoughts I express, perhaps too flippantly, are the result of years of thought and study.

14 Always do more than is required of you.

15 I do not fear failure. I only fear the slowing up of the engine inside of me which is pounding, saying, "Keep going, someone must be on top, why not you?"

369

- Dr. Norman Vincent Peale
A Crusader of Positive Thinking
1898 - 1993

1 The more difficult the obstacle, the stronger one becomes after hurdling it.

2 Think success, visualize success, and you will set in motion the power force of the realizable. When the mental is strongly enough held, it seems to control conditions and circumstances.

3 Successful people picturize, prayerize and actualize.

4 The whole trend and quality of anyone's life is determined, in the long run, by the choices that he makes.

5 The trouble with most of us is that we would rather be ruined by praise than saved by criticism.

6 The person who works the easiest does the most in the shortest time and his work shows the mark of skill.

7 Drop the idea that you are Atlas carrying the world on your shoulders. The world would go on even without you.

8 Tell yourself that you like your work. Change yourself and your work will seem different.

9 Plan your work for today and every day, then work your plan. Lack of system produces that "I'm swamped" feeling.

10 Say three times, "This one thing I do", emphasizing the word *one*. One step at a time will get you much more surely than haphazardly leaping and jumping. It is the steady pace, the consistent speed that leads most efficient start to destination.

11 Discipline yourself not to put off until tomorrow what you can do today.

12 I never let go of something that I desperately want to do or that I believe ought to be done. If I can't do it head-on, I look for a circuitous way to do it. The idea is to do it no matter what method you use.

13 I can write on planes, in airports, with thousands of people around. I can focus on what I am doing at the moment.

14 The word *worry* is derived from an old Anglo-Saxon word meaning to strangle or to choke. How well-named the emotion is, has been demonstrated again and again in persons who have lost their effectiveness due to the stultifying effect of anxiety and apprehension. A certain well-controlled carefreeness may well be an asset. Normal sensible concern is an important attribute of the mature person. But worry frustrates one's best functioning.

15 There is a basic law that like attracts like. That which you mentally project reproduces in kind, and negative thoughts definitely attract negative results. Conversely, if a person habitually thinks optimistically and hopefully, he activates life around him positively and thereby attracts to himself positive results. His positive thinking sets in motion creative forces, and success instead of eluding him, flows toward him.

16 A positive thinker does not refuse to recognize the negative; he refuses to dwell on it. Positive thinking is a form of thought which habitually looks for the best results from the worst conditions.

17 The secret of life isn't what happens to you, but what you DO with what happens to you.

18 Everyone has a God-given potential, in the essence, built into them. And if we are to live to its fullest, we must realize that potential.

19 Any fact facing us is not as important as our attitude toward it, for that determines our success or failure.

20 It is a fact that you project what you are.

21 Every problem has in it the seeds of its own solution. If you don't have any problems, you don't get any seeds.

22 When every physical and mental resource is focused, one's power to solve a problem multiplies tremendously.

23 We tend to get what we expect.

24 If you paint in your mind a picture of bright and happy expectations, you put yourself into a condition conductive to your goal.

25 Plan your work today and every day, then work your plan.

26 To achieve your goals of success, believe in yourself. Have faith in your abilities. Without a humble but reasonable confidence in your own powers you cannot be successful or happy. But with sound self-confidence you can succeed. A sense of inferiority and inadequacy interferes with the attainment of your hopes, but self-confidence leads to self-realization and successful achievement.

27 If you expect the best, you will be the best. Learn to use one of the most powerful laws in this world; change your mental habits to belief instead of disbelief. Learn to expect, not to doubt. In so doing you bring everything in the realm of possibility.

28 I certainly do not ignore or minimize the hardships and tragedies of the world, but neither do I allow them to dominate. You can permit obstacles to control your mind to the point where they are uppermost and thus become the dominating factors in your thought pattern. By learning to cast them from the mind, by refusing to become mentally subservient to them, and by channeling spiritual power through your thoughts, you can rise above obstacles which ordinarily might defeat you.

370

- Pelé
The Greatest Soccer Player of His Time
Born in 1940

1 Love is more important than what we take out of life.

2 I don't think about the goals I scored or the titles I won. I think about all the people I met around the world. I think about all the friends I met while playing soccer.

3 I just play and do the best I can do. I never make excuses for mistakes. If I play badly, I don't feel sorry for myself. I feel sorry for the fans. They paid money to see me play. I always want to give their money's worth.

4 I knew how to play soccer on the street, without shoes, without a professional ball, without a uniform. When I moved on to a very comfortable field covered with beautiful grass, why wouldn't I win?

5 I have an extra instinct for the game. Sometimes I can take the ball and no one can foresee any danger. And then, two or three seconds later, there is a goal. This does not make me proud, it makes me humble, because it is a talent that God gave me.

371

- Dr. Wilder Penfield
An Extraordinary Brain Specialist of All Time
1891 - 1976

1 All things work together for good for them that love God.

2 For most men there should be a time of shifting harness, of lightening the load one way and adjusting it for greater effectiveness in another. That is the time for the second career, time for the old dog to perform new tricks. The new career may bring in little money; it may be concerned only with good works. On the other hand, it may bring in much-needed support. It can be a delight to a man who comes at last to a well-earned job instead of a well-earned rest.

3 Every region of the earth has its charm. Before a writer can describe a desert, he must smell and hear and see and touch it. The blue of sky, the flaming movement of mirage, the unique beauty of a desert sunrise, the fragrance of acacia, a dust storm in the desert, the clattering sound of palm branches in the wind - these and a thousand other things must be experienced before they can be described.

4 By working together, each one contributing his own ideas and his own particular talent, it is amazing how much can be accomplished.

5 Good sportsmanship is one of the great needs of the world today. A good sport is one who gives something more than is required of him.

6 We must be satisfied with nothing less than the truth.

7 Compelling power is to be found not so much in the tradition of Hippocrates, of Virchow, or of Harvey, but in the memory of our seniors and predecessors.

8 Medicine is a guild for those who love their fellowmen - a trade, a science and a social mission.

372

- J. C. Penney
A Pioneer of Profit Sharing Retail Chain Business
1875 - 1971

---

1 Give me a stock clerk with a goal and I will give you a man who will make history. Give me a man without a goal, and I will give you a stock clerk.

2 Success in life does not depend on genius. Any young man of ordinary intelligence, who is morally sound and not afraid to work, should succeed in spite of handicaps and obstacles, if he plays the game and keeps everlastingly at it. The possibilities are measured by determination.

3 I am grateful for all my problems. As each of them was overcome I became stronger and more able to meet those yet to come. I grew on my difficulties.

4 Competition is no enemy; it is an ally, and when translated in service, it is a constant spur to betterment through more service and thus benefits all.

5 I never think of myself as retired. Retirement to me means inactivity. I do most certainly believe in a change of activity, when it becomes time for what is commonly called retirement.

6 The wisest decision I ever made was realizing I could not do everything by myself.

7 It is possible to possess material wealth and yet to be a failure.

8 When we cease to struggle, dry rot sets in.

9 There will always be a place for anyone with a good and practical idea, willing to work diligently to get it accepted and translated into terms of the service of practical use.

10 What I have done, anyone could have done. I haven't any special attainments.

11 Treat others as you would have them treat you.

12 Listening is not something that comes naturally; it is an acquired art. For most of us, listening, whether in a social conversation or around the table at a conference, is just a pause we feel obliged to grant a speaker until we again have a chance to air our own opinions. This is not real listening, in any sense of the word. Listening is not a passive activity during which we let our own thoughts intrude upon what someone else is saying. To actively listen to another person requires willpower, concentration, and great mental effort.

373

1 Every child is an artist. The problem is how to remain an artist once he grows up.

2 Art is a lie that enables us to realize the truth.

3 I am only a public entertainer who has understood the time.

4 When I was 14, I knew I could draw like Michelangelo and I spent the rest of my life learning to draw like a child.

5 For me a picture is neither an end nor an achievement but rather a lucky chance and art experience. I try to represent what I have found, not what I am seeking. I do not seek - I find.

6 The world today does not make sense, so why should I paint pictures that do?

7 Painting is my hobby. When I am finished painting, I paint again for relaxation.

8 Work is a necessity for man. Man invented the alarm clock.

9 In life you throw a ball. You hope it will reach a wall and bounce back so you can throw it again. You hope your friends will provide that wall.

10 Everybody wants to understand painting. Why is there no attempt to understand the song of the birds? Why does one love a night, a flower, everything that surrounds a man, without trying to understand it all?

11 I do not search; I find.

374

1 Ambition is a curse. It drives you and possesses you and keeps you from doing the things you want to do.

2 If you have made mistakes, there is always another chance for you. You may have a fresh start any moment you choose, for this thing we call failure is not the falling down, but the staying down.

3 When we desire to aid others, and to aid with love, that very moment puts us in tune with God and all good people everywhere.

4 Each one of us has at least one moment in his life that stands out with a burning sense of shame and self-guilt, a moment during which we committed a grave, though perhaps unintended, offense against a fellow human being. Some have the power to efface the pain of that moment from their minds; others find solace in appeasing their consciences by one means or another; still others have known how to distill a deeper understanding of themselves and others from their honest remorse.

1 I have been a governor now and then, but I am a forester all the time - have been, and shall be, to my dying day.

2 Forestry is tree farming. Forestry is handling trees so that one crop follows another. To grow trees as a crop is forestry.

3 A good forester must also be a good citizen.

4 The earth and its resources belong of right to its people. Without natural resources life itself is impossible. From birth to death, natural resources, transformed for human use, feed, clothe, shelter, and transport us. Upon them we depend for every material necessity, comfort, convenience and protection in our lives. Without abundant resources prosperity is out of reach.

5 The first duty of the human race on the material side is to control the use of the earth and all that therein is.

6 Conservation is the foresighted utilization, preservation, and/or renewal of forests, waters, lands, and minerals, for the greatest good of the greatest number for the longest time.

7 No nation is self-sufficient in all the resources it requires. Throughout human history one of the commonest causes of war has been the demand for land. Land (agricultural land, forest land, iron, oil, uranium and other mineral producing land) means natural resources.

8 Monopoly on the loose is a source of many of the economic, political and social evils which afflict the sons of men. Its abolition or regulation is an inseparable part of the conservation policy.

9 At each turning point in human history two great human forces have fought for control. One demanded a greater share of prosperity and freedom for the many. The other strove for the concentration of power, privilege and wealth in the hands of the few. One wanted to go forward to better things. The other strove to go back to what it called "the good old days".

1 If any action is to be taken, it cannot be left to Parliament. An appeal to public opinion is needed; the conscience of the nation must be aroused.

2 Working men, acting in combination and possessing a fund before hand, are better able to cope with a time of difficulty and to give their industry breathing time as it were, than men who stand alone and separate from each other. They can bring to each other comfort and courage in times of adversity.

377
- Jim Plunkett
An Extraordinary Quarterback Despite Many Adversities
Born in 1947

1 Sometimes I throw the ball out of my ear and sometimes it is not very pretty; but if it's caught, it gives us a first down and I take that chance.

2 I never wanted to be famous, just to be good. I was always dedicated and sincere.

3 I never felt sorry for myself; instead, I spent my time trying to improve.

4 The mind's eye is everything to the blind.

5 The blind do not require much sleep. People with normal vision grow tired when their eyes get tired. The blind need maybe four or five hours of sleep because their eyes do not get tired. Most blind people are keyed up, hyperactive.

378
- Edgar Allan Poe
A Great American Writer of All Time
1809 - 1849

1 Experience has shown, and a true philosophy will always show, that a vast, perhaps the larger, portion of the truth arises from the seeming irrelevant.

2 My habits are vigorously abstemious and I omit nothing of the natural regimen requisite for health; I rise early, eat moderately, drink nothing but water and take abundant and regular exercise in the open air. But this is my private life - my studious and literary life - and of course escapes the eye of the world. The desire of society comes upon me only when I have been excited by drink.

3 I love fame; I dote on it; I idolize it; I would drink to the very dregs of the glorious intoxication. I would have incense ascend in my honour from every hill and hamlet, from every town and city on this earth. Fame! Glory! - they are life-giving breath and living blood. No man lives unless he is famous.

4 The thirst for the beautiful belongs to the immortality of man. It is at once a consequence and an indication of his perennial existence. It is the desire of the moth for the star. It is no mere appreciation of the Beauty before us, but a wild effort to reach the Beauty above.

5 The demands of Truth are severe. She has no sympathy with the myrtles.

6 In the hands of the *true* artist the theme or "work" is but a mass of clay, of which anything may be fashioned at will or according to the skill of the workman. The clay is, in fact, the slave of the artist. It belongs to him.

- Sidney Poitier
The First Black Actor to Win an Oscar
Born in 1927

1 I have never worked with a good actor from whom I didn't learn something useful.

2 It's true that first-rate actors have exceptional gifts, but that, in and of itself, does not necessarily make a first-rate actor.

3 Many kids arrive in Hollywood and New York with the intention of becoming stars within a matter of weeks. They enroll in a class for a fast twelve weeks of drama study. They share a one-room efficiency apartment, sometimes three or four of them need to pull their resources in order to secure adequate housing. Generally, in less than three months their funds are gone - and so are they. It doesn't work that way. It requires hard work and patience.

4 We all suffer from the preoccupation that there exists, in the loved one, perfection.

- Alexander Pope
The Most Acclaimed Verse Satirist of English Literature
1688 - 1744

1 Fine sense, and exalted sense, are not half as useful as common sense. There are 40 men of wit to 1 man of sense. He that will carry nothing about him but gold, will be every day at a loss for readier change.

2 An excuse is worse and more terrible than a lie; for an excuse is a lie guarded.

3 A man should never be ashamed to own he has been wrong, which is but saying, in other words, that he is wiser than he was yesterday.

4 A little learning is a dangerous thing;
Drink deep, or taste not the Pierian spring.

5 The mouse that always trusts to one poor hole, can never be a mouse of any soul.

6 A brave man thinks no one is superior who does him an injury; for he has it then in his power to make himself superior to the other by forgiving it.

7 Blessed be he who expects nothing, for he shall never be disappointed.

8 Praise undeserved is scandal in disguise.

9 There is so much trouble in coming into the world and so much meanness in going out of it, that it's hardly worth while being here at all.

10 I am so certain of the soul's being immortal that I seem even to feel it within me, as it were my intuition.

11 Words are like leaves; and where they most abound,
Much fruit of sense beneath is rarely found.

12 Vice is a monster of so frightful mien,
As to be hated, needs but to be seen;
Yet seen too oft, familiar with her face,
We first endure, then pity, then embrace.

381
- Beatrix Potter
A Very Popular Author and Illustrator of Children's Books
1866 - 1943

1 I can't invent, I only copy.

2 I cannot rest, I must draw, however poor the result, and when I have a bad time come over me, it is a stronger desire than ever, and settles on the queerest things, worse than queer sometimes.

3 I have never cared tuppence either for popularity or for modern child; they are pampered and spoilt with too many toys and books. And when you infer that my originality is more precious than old Aesop's, you *do* put your foot in it!

4 The fewer the lines, the less error committed.

382
- John Wesley Powell
The Pioneer Explorer of the Colorado River
1834 - 1902

1 The association of a number of people prevents single individuals from having undue control of natural privileges.

2 I did not wish to trade, did not want any land. I simply wished to learn about the canyons and mountains, and about the people living there.

3 The wonders of the Grand Canyon cannot be adequately represented in symbols of speech, nor by speech itself. The resources of the graphic art are taxed beyond their powers in attempting to portray its features. Language and illustration combined must fail.

383
- William Prescott
A Great American Historian Despite Near Blindness
1796 - 1859

1 The man who writes a book which he is afraid to publish is a coward.

2 A man's style to be worth anything should be natural expression of his mental character. The best undoubtedly for every writer is the form of expression best suited to his peculiar turn of thinking, even at some hazard of violating the conventional tone of the most chaste and careful writers.

3 Originality - the originality of nature - compensates for a thousand minor blemishes.

4 One likes a noble character for his canvas.

5 To do well and act justly, to fear and to love God, and to love our neighbour as ourselves - in these is the essence of religion.

384

1 My moment of glory is being on the stage and singing and feeling all the love the audience sends to me. It's beyond any mortal high.

2 Don't forget, angels fly because they take themselves so lightly.

3 The world knows Elvis. They don't know me.

4 I long not to be regarded as a star, not as Elvis, but as a person.

385

1 Happiness is beneficial for the body, but it is grief that develops the powers of the mind.

2 The only real voyage of discovery consists not in seeking new landscapes but in having new eyes.

3 The life of everyday is supremely important, full of moral joy and beauty, which, though man may lose them through faults inherent in human nature, are indestructible and recoverable.

4 The time which we have at our disposal every day is elastic; the passions that we feel expand it, those that we inspire contract it; and habit fills up what remains.

5 We are healed of a suffering only by experiencing it to the full.

6 It is a mistake to speak of a bad choice in love, since as soon as a choice exists, it can only be bad.

7 One only loves that which one does not possess entirely.

8 If there were no such thing as Habit, Life would of necessity appear delicious to all those whom Death would threaten at every moment, that is to say, to all Mankind.

9 Of all human plants Habit requires the least fostering, and is the first to appear on the seeming desolation of the most barren rock.

10 We agree with those whose ideas are at the same degree of confusion as our own.

11 Man is the creature who cannot come forth from himself, who knows others only in himself, and who, if he asserts the contrary, lies.

12 An impression is for the writer what an experiment is for the scientist. In the case of the scientist the action of the intelligence precedes the event and in the case of the writer follows it.

386

1 Our Republic and its press will rise or fall together. An able, disinterested, public-spirited press, with trained intelligence to know the right and the courage to do it, can preserve the public virtue without which popular government is a sham and a mockery. A cynical, mercenary, demagogic, corrupt press will produce in time a people as base as itself.

2 I believe in self-made men.

3 There is only one way to get a democracy on its feet in the matters of its individual, its social, its municipal, its State, its National conduct, and that is by keeping the public informed about what's going on.

4 There is not a crime, there is not a dodge, there is not a trick, there is not a swindle, there is not a vice which does not live by secrecy.

5 If a newspaper is to be a real service to the public, it must have a big circulation, first because its news and its comment must reach the largest number of people, second because circulation means advertising, and advertising means money and money means independence.

6 Don't be content by making the best editorial page in town, because there is no other editorial page, and when you have made the best you are taking only a small part of your opportunity.

7 A life not largely dedicated to vigorous, serious, useful work cannot be happy and honourable.

8 Impartiality, entire dismissal of prejudice, or personal dislike, alone can discover the real truth.

387

1 Making music is an expression of joy in living. To me, that's what singing together is all about.

2 My music respects its audience. By understanding that children are whole people with important feelings and concerns, we give them the best chance of becoming healthy, loving adults.

3 I spend a lot of my free time reading. I can't do without it. Much of my reading is about how children grow and develop. My wife and my team members also read many books about children and we spend many hours discussing what we have read and deciding how to apply it to our work with children.

388

- Robert Redford
One of Hollywood's Most Popular Leading Men
Born in 1937

1 I went into acting predisposed against the life, and it took a long time to get down through all the muck and all the hang-ups.

2 You can only be as good as you dare to be bad.

3 I had a difficult time early in my career because I got angry easily.

4 If you want to get anything done in Hollywood, you've got to fight.

5 Acting requires that you live your character. It's like skiing. You can't be thinking too much. When you get on the hill, your skiis are doing the work. You would better hang on. Acting is a bit the same way. You have got to submit to what's going on around you and be able to do that fully. You have got to behave as the character. A lot of acting is *paying attention*.

6 I never learned as much in the classroom as I did staring out a window and imagining things.

7 Life doesn't reflect the Boy Scout code. It isn't about how you play the game. It's about winning the game. Winning is what we celebrate.

8 If you stay in Beverly Hills too long, you become a Mercedes.

389

- Pierre Renoir
One of the Founders of Impressionism
1841 - 1919

1 I keep painting despite those torturous pains because the pain passes but the beauty remains.

2 I don't think a day has passed without my painting.

3 I believe that I have done nothing but continue what others have done before me.

4 It is in the museum that one learns to paint.

5 One must do the painting of one's own time.

6 The taste for painting, which nature cannot give you, is gained in the museum.

7 You must protect the ends of your fingers; if you expose them, you may ruin your sense of touch, and deprive yourself of a good deal of pleasure in life.

8 What goes on inside my head doesn't interest me. I want touch, or at least to see.

9 How difficult it is to know just where the imitation of nature in a picture might stop. Painting need not stink of the model but it must have the perfume of life.

10 Each one sings his song if he has the voice.

11 When I look back at my life, I compare it to one of those corks thrown into the river. Off it goes, is caught by a grass, makes desperate efforts to get free and ends by losing itself, I do not know where.

12 When I look at the old masters, I feel like a simple, little man. Yet I believe that among my works there will be enough to assure me a place in the French School, that school that I love so much, which is so pretty, so clear, such good company, and with nothing rowdy about it.

390

1 Greatness is all around us. It's easy to be great because great people will help you.

2 Great people will share. Great people will tell you their secrets. Look for them, call them on the phone or buy their books. Go where they are; get around them; talk to them. It is easy to be great when you get around great people.

3 When science develops an 18- or 19- foot pole as easily handled as the 16-footers we now use, man may go as high as 20 feet.

4 I owe my success to determination and muscle-knotted strength and to the power of the Lord and the psychological influence He exerts over those who can search their souls and find strength to perform wonderful things.

391

1 Sweat is the greatest solvent for most players' problems. I know of no cure, no soluble way to get rid of a bad technique as quick as *sweat*. The same thing is true on the part of the coach or a teacher - infinite patience. Make a man do it over and over again.

2 A winner gets completely saturated with the desire to excel. He is on the high road to a personal championship. It makes men willing - indeed, anxious - to devote themselves with perhaps exclusive attention to their weaknesses.

3 Basic honesty allows a man to go to the mirror, look himself in the face, and not be ashamed ever.

4 If you are mentally apt, you can turn every supposed reversal into an *All Right*. What a blessing in disguise!

5 It is not the honour that you take with you, but the heritage you leave behind.

6 Don't be idle. Idleness is the most damnable thing.

7 First of all, a man, whether seeking achievement on the athletic field or in business, must want to win. He must feel the thing he is doing is worthwhile; so worthwhile that he is willing to pay the price of success to attain distinction.

8 Men can imitate. Men can learn. They do, but sometimes, and very often indeed, men who rely upon their own observations, initiatives or adaptations, do not improve very rapidly. Learning by imitation is a slow process.

9 Old man opportunity has long hair in front and he is bald behind. When he comes to you, you can snatch him and hold him tight, but when he is past, he could be gone forever.

10 Things don't happen without a cause. They just don't. There's a reason for pretty nearly everything that happens that I know about.

11 Intuition is our subconscious reaction in times of stress.

12 Never surrender opportunity for security.

392

1 It's too bad that society isn't to the point yet where the country could just send up a woman astronaut and nobody would think twice about it. There should be nothing at all remarkable about a woman in space.

2 It's important to me that people don't think I was picked for the flight because I am a woman and it's time for NASA (the National Aviation and Space Administration) to send one. I believe I was picked because I was the best person for the job at that time.

3 I did not particularly care that I was the role model, but I thought it was important that somebody be.

393

1 Let us wear out if we must, but never rust.

2 It is the accident of one's birth and the environment that a person grows up in, that produces criminal behaviour. Change those conditions through better health care, better education, better housing and the whole society will benefit.

3 Poor people need a chance, not a change; justice and not charity. Given a fair chance they will help themselves.

4 The people are all right, if we only give them half a chance. It is the prevention of poverty that society must concentrate, and not on its effects.

5 Some defeats are only installments to victory.

6 You cannot make a good citizen out of the lad whom you denied a chance to kick a ball across lots when that was his ambition and his right; it takes a whole boy to make a whole man.

7 A man cannot be expected to live like a pig and vote like a man.

8 The very enforcement of law has sometimes seemed a travesty; the boy who steals fifty cents is sent to the House of Correction; the man who steals a railroad goes free.

9 The bad environment becomes the heredity of the next generation, given the crowd, you have the slum ready-made.

10 The poor we shall have always with us, but the slum we need not have. These two do not rightfully belong together.

394

1 None may shirk his duty, for that would be to betray the ones who come after. Let no one in tomorrow's world be able to say that in the years of decision, when destiny was in our hands, we failed to measure up.

2 When I step on to a stage, I go on as a representative of the working class.

3 I must keep fighting until I am dying.

395

1 I had to fight hard against loneliness, abuse and the knowledge that any mistake I made would be magnified because I was the only black man out there. Many people resented my impatience and honesty, but I never cared about acceptance as much as I cared about respect.

2 I cannot accept the idea of a black supposedly fighting for the principles of freedom and democracy in Vietnam when so little has been accomplished in this country.

3 Life owes me nothing. Baseball owes me nothing. But I cannot, as an individual, rejoice in the good things I have been permitted to work for and learn while the humblest of my brothers is down in the deep hole hollering for help and not being heard.

4 There is one irrefutable fact of my life which has determined much of what happened to me: I was a black man in a white world. I never had it made.

5 The fans don't care to see the game. All they want is to be able to say that they were here.

396

1 Throughout my life, each setback has prepared me for a greater triumph. I never had a negative thought. It's merely a matter of time for that greater triumph to happen.

2 You will never amount to anything just banging around from one job to another. No matter what you want to do, tennis or music or what, you will be better at it if you get some education.

3 Every good fighter has got to be a cocky guy.

397

John D. Rockefeller
The First Billionaire in History
1839 - 1937

1 If you want to succeed you should strike out on new paths rather than travel the worn paths of accepted success.

2 The most important thing for a young man is to establish credit, a reputation, and character.

3 A friendship founded on business is better than a business founded on friendship.

4 The ability to deal with people is as purchasable a commodity as sugar or coffee. And I pay more for that ability than for any other under the sun.

398

- Jerome Rodale
A Pioneer of the Organic Farming Movement
1898 - 1971

1 Healthy living can overcome many ailments.

2 Years ago they heaped violence and poured ridicule on my head. I was called a cult and a crackpot. But no longer. Now even the chemical people have suddenly become respectful towards me and my manure philosophy. I am suddenly becoming a prophet here on earth and a prophet with profits.

399

- Washington Roebling
A Pioneer Designer of Steel Suspension Bridges
1837 - 1926

1 Nothing lasts forever. The most unforeseen circumstances will swamp you and baffle the wisest calculations. Only *vitality* and plenty of it helps you.

2 At first I thought I would succumb, but I had a strong tower to lean upon, my wife, a woman of infinite tact and wisest counsel.

3 It took Cheops twenty years to build his pyramid, but if he had a lot of trustees, contractors and newspaper reporters to worry him, he might not have finished it by that time. The advantages of modern engineering are in many ways over balanced by the disadvantages of modern civilization.

400

- Will Rogers
America's Foremost Political Humorist of His Time
1879 - 1935

1 Every human being has at least one good quality. I look for that when I meet a man and then try to compliment him on it.

2 Don't let yesterday use up too much of today.

3 Even when you are on the right track, you will get run over, if you just sit there.

4 We are just here for a spell and pass on. Believe in something for another World, but don't be too set on what it is, and you won't start out life with a disappointment. Live your life so that whenever you lose, you are ahead.

5 Lord, let me live until I die.

6 I never met a man I didn't like.

7 Everything is funny as long as it is happening to somebody else.

8 Get someone else to blow your horn and the sound will carry twice as far.

9 Half our life is spent trying to find something to do with the time we have rushed through life trying to save.

401 - Franklin Delano Roosevelt
The President Who Steered America out of the Great Depression
1882 - 1945

1 The only thing we have to fear is fear itself.

2 The only limit to our realization of tomorrow will be our doubts of today.

3 A radical is a man with both feet firmly planted in the air.

4 There is nothing I love as much as a good fight.

5 I am like a cat; I make a quick stroke and then relax.

6 Far better it is to dare mighty things, to win glorious triumphs, even though checkered by failure, than to rank with those poor spirits who neither enjoy much nor suffer much, because they live in the gray twilight that knows neither victory nor defeat.

7 Men are not prisoners of fate, but only prisoners of their own minds.

8 Happiness lies in the joy of achievement, in the thrill of creative effort.

9 To reach a port, we must sail - sail, not tie at anchor - sail, not drift.

10 The value of love will always be stronger than the value of hate. Any nation or group of nations which employs hatred eventually is torn to pieces by hatred.

11 Our true destiny is not to be ministered unto but to minister to ourselves and to our fellow men.

402 - Diana Ross
One of the Most Popular Pop Singers in History
Born in 1944

1 I may be down, but I ain't down.

2 I always wanted everybody to care about me. Love me, love me, love me, please.

3 One of my greatest accomplishments musically is to take the music of a specific community, put my own spin in it and take it out to the world.

4 I am a dreamer.

403

- Jean Jacques Rousseau
An Extraordinary European Thinker of 18th Century
1712 - 1778

1 Man is born free, but everywhere he is in chains.

2 A feeble body weakens the mind.

3 Patience is bitter, but its fruit is sweet.

4 Reason deceives us; conscience, never.

5 Nature never deceives us; it is always we who deceive ourselves.

6 He who is the most slow in making a promise is the most faithful in the performance of it.

7 Fame is but the breath of the people, and that often unwholesome.

8 People who know little are usually great talkers, while those who know much say little.

9 It is too difficult to think nobly when one only thinks to get a living.

10 One loses all the time which he might employ to better purpose.

11 Never exceed your rights, and they will soon become unlimited.

12 Remorse goes to sleep during a prosperous period and wakes up in adversity.

13 Provided a man is not mad, he can be cured of every folly but vanity.

14 It is not our wrong actions which it requires courage to confess, so much as those which are ridiculous and foolish.

15 There is a great difference between traveling to see countries and to see people.

404

- Helena Rubinstein
A Pioneer of International Beauty & Cosmetic Business
1870 - 1965

1 You have got to be lucky. Take advantage of the situation, every situation. Situations are produced by people. Learn how to use people, to drain them of their ideas. Develop the skill, the tenacity, the patience to turn those ideas into gold. And remember to remain faithful to everyone who contributes to your success.

2 If I had not done it, someone else would.

3 There are no ugly women, only lazy ones.

4 Diet is a way of eating for the kind of life you want.

5 You can achieve more by playing dumb than by acting too smart.

405 - Wilma Rudolph
The First American Woman to Win 3 Olympic Gold Medals
1940 - 1994

1 Just because I won three gold medals and am looked upon as a world-class athlete, does not make me a world-class person.
2 I would be very disappointed if I were only remembered as a runner because I feel that my contribution to the youth of America has far exceeded the woman who was the Olympic champion. The challenge is still there.

406 - Bayard Rustin
A Major Player in America's Civil Rights Movement
1910 - 1987

1 Vicious punishment does no good in reforming criminals. Such men return to the society not only uncured but with heightened resentment and a desire for revenge.
2 What can be loved, can be cured. It's only when we have rejected punishment and turned to the healing power of forgiveness and non-violence that we are able to change the lives of criminals and make them into productive citizens.
3 Love and non-violence are far superior to punishment.

407 - Babe Ruth
Baseball's Most Memorable Player
1895 - 1948

1 The only real game in the world, I think, is baseball.
2 It's hard to be on the outside of something you love. Just looking in doesn't help.
3 I was thinking about the same thing I always think about - the only thing I always think about. I was thinking about hitting a home run.
4 The best advice that I would give to young ball players is (1) to get out of smoking and drinking, (2) to get enough sleep and (3) to get the right things to eat.

408 - Jonas Salk
The Discoverer of the Vaccine for Polio
1914 - 1995

1 Our greatest responsibility is to be good ancestors.
2 I feel the greatest reward for doing is the opportunity to do more.
3 Many wise individuals have had no formal education. They possess a powerful intuitive faculty and are able to learn from experience, from what they observe.
4 Belief, knowledge and truth must not be confused - each must be used appropriately.

5 The wise will tend to give in the short run, to obtain gain in the long run. The unwise tend to take now but will likely lose later.

6 Is not wisdom a basis for selection among men, and is it not the ideal toward which some men have always aspired?

7 Even though Death eventually wins over Life so far as the individual is concerned, Life wins over Death in the perpetuation of the species.

8 The time has arrived in which we have to realize that we are all parts of a single organism and develop some new kinds of responses and relationships.

9 Life is an error-making and an error-correcting process, and nature in making man's papers will grade him for wisdom as measured by survival and by the quality of life of those who survive.

10 The scientist isn't a politician, and he isn't a propagandist. He observes and classifies facts, and then he reaches conclusions on the basis of the data at his disposal. He must avoid being influenced by the pressures on him, or even by the bias of his hypotheses.

11 To a scientist fame is neither an end nor a means to an end. I totally agree with Emerson who once said that the reward of a thing well done is to have done it.

409

- George Sand
The Most Successful Woman Writer of Her Century
1804 - 1876

1 There is only one happiness in life, to love and be loved.

2 There is but one virtue - the eternal sacrifice of self.

3 The whole secret of the study of nature lies in learning how to use one's eyes.

4 The beauty that addresses itself to the eyes is only the spell of the moment; the eye of the body is not always that of the soul.

5 Admiration and familiarity are strangers.

6 To be without responsibilities is its own sort of serfdom - something approaching the shame of a suspension of civil rights.

7 Work is not man's punishment. It is his reward and his strength and his pleasure.

410

- Carl Sandburg
An Extraordinary Historian and Biographer
1878 - 1967

1 I will be the word of the people. Mine will be the bleeding mouth from which the gag is snatched. I will say everything.

2 A baby is God's opinion that the world should go on.

3 Slang is a language that rolls up its sleeve, spits on its hands, and goes to work.

4 Life is like an onion; you peel it off one layer at a time, and sometimes you weep.

5 All men need solitude. Pascal was totally right when he said that the miseries of men come from not being able to sit alone in a quiet room.

6 Nothing happens unless first a dream.

7 Who could live without hope?

8 Time is the coin of your life. It is the only coin you have, and only you can determine how it will be spent. Be careful, lest you let other people spend it for you.

9 Our lives are like a candle in the wind.

411

- Harland Sanders
The Founder of Kentucky Fried Chicken
1890 - 1980

1 If you have something good, a certain number of people will beat a path to your doorstep; the rest you have to go and get.

2 There is no reason to be the richest man in the cemetery. You cannot do any business from there.

3 Every failure can be a stepping stone to something better.

4 You've got to like your work. You've got to like what you are doing. You've got to be doing something worthwhile so you can like it - because if it's worthwhile, that makes a difference.

412

- Margaret Sanger
The Pioneer of Birth Control Movement in America
1883 - 1966

1 The first right of every child is to be wanted, to be desired, to be planned for with an intensity of love that gives it its title to being.

2 To keep young and beautiful, one should acquire a great faith.

3 All the world of human beings is a passing show; they come and go. But the idea of human freedom grows ever closer around one's heart and comforts and consoles and delights.

4 Books are the compasses.

5 The world is much the same everywhere.

6 Sentiment has extolled the young love which promises to last through eternity. But love is a growth mingled with a succession of experiences. It is as foolish to promise to love forever as to promise to live forever.

7 If you present common sense people with the premise that birth control is common sense, they will react in a common sense way.

8 Birth control should be advocated for its own sake, on the general ground that the difference between planned birth control and voluntary, irrational, uncontrolled activity is similar to the difference between an amoeba and man. If we really believe that the more highly evolved creature is the better, we may as well act accordingly. As the amoeba doesn't understand birth control, it cannot

abuse it and therefore its state may be the more gracious; but it is also true that as the amoeba cannot write, it cannot commit forgery; yet we teach everybody to write unhesitantly, knowing that if we refuse to teach anything that could be abused, we should never teach anything at all.

413

- David Sarnoff
The Pioneer of Radio and TV for Entertainment
1891 - 1971

1 Nothing worthwhile has been attained except by overcoming obstacles.

2 Work is all important because that is the only visible and intelligible excuse for our existence. Man expresses the forces with which he is endowed. Work is the most satisfying experience of the day.

3 We cannot banish dangers, but we can banish fears. We must not demean life by standing in awe of death.

4 Competition brings out the best in products and the worst in people.

5 The great menace to the life of an industry is industrial self-complacency.

6 Science offers us wonderful tools for helping to create the Brotherhood of Man on earth. But the mortar of Brotherhood does not come from any laboratory. It must come from the heart and mind.

7 The final test of science is not whether its accomplishments add to our comfort, knowledge, and power, but whether it adds to our dignity as men, our sense of truth and beauty. It is a test that science cannot pass alone and unaided.

8 In every industry there are those who try to impede the progress of the pioneer.

9 Success, in generally accepted sense of the term, means the opportunity to experience and to realize to the maximum the forces that are within us.

10 I was lucky to have been born about the time the electron was discovered and that Marconi invented the wireless. I was lucky that at an early age I hitched my wagon to the electron.

414

- Robert Schuller
A Crusader of Possibility-Thinking
Born in 1926

1 Tough times never last, tough people do.

2 Don't ever give up. Always keep looking for another way.

3 Look at what you have left, not at what you have lost.

4 Courage isn't the absence of fear, it's facing horror in the eye.

5 Great people are ordinary people with extraordinary amounts of determination.

6 Failure is not failure to meet your goal. Real failure is failure to reach as high as you possibly can. No man will ever truly know that he has succeeded until he experiences an apparent failure.

7 Goals are not only absolutely necessary to motivate us, they are essential to really keep us alive.

8 Not having a goal is more to be feared than not reaching a goal.

9 Beginning is half won.

10 Winning starts with beginning.

11 Our greatest lack is not money for any undertaking, but rather ideas. If the ideas are good, cash will somehow flow to where it is needed.

12 You will suddenly realize that the reason you never changed before was because you didn't want to.

13 Never say never.

14 The deepest desire demanding fulfillment in the human heart provides a true sense of meaningfulness in living. This may create anxiety and tension but they can be the constructive motivating power in your life.

15 The goalless or goal-arrived human being suffers a far worse fate - boredom - which is a living death.

415

- Charles Schulz
The Creator of Charlie Brown & Peanuts Comic Strips
Born in 1922

1 I don't care what you do. You can be a circus tightrope walker; but never do anything you don't enjoy, and try to do it better than anyone else.

2 I was not an overnight success, even after I sold the strip. *Peanuts* did not take the world by storm immediately. It was a long grind. It took *Peanuts* about 4 years to attract nationwide attention, but it took 10 years to become really entrenched.

3 I have remained alive to everything that's going on about me. I am aware of new things that are happening in the world. I am always thinking about funny things, and getting ideas by listening to Talk Shows or just driving around or conversing with people.

4 I feel inferior in a lot of areas. I feel inferior that I can't draw better, that I don't have a wider, broader knowledge, which I would love to have. I feel that I don't have the extensive vocabulary I think it would be nice to have. I believe this is why I am able to function so well with Charlie Brown. I can caricature all these faults, realizing as I have grown older that these are common feelings, and you will meet almost no one who deep down doesn't really have feelings of inferiority.

5 My big worry has always been that my work would flatten out and cease to have any real spark to it.

6 No one would have been invited to dinner as often as Jesus was, unless he were interesting and had a sense of humour.

7 Success breeds success, but not always directly.

8 One of the most delightful aspects of life is conversation. Talking with a new friend, discovering new ideas and learning about each other can be one of the great experiences of life.

416

- Richard W. Sears
The Barnum of Merchandising
1863 - 1914

1 Your future will last largely on the goods and services that you give today.

2 Honesty is the best policy. I know. I've tried both ways.

3 The mail order pot can be kept boiling only with a red-hot fire.

4 The way to maintain corporate health is to keep selling more and more , to keep opening markets.

417

- Lord Shaftesbury
A Great Social Reformer and Philanthropist
1801 - 1885

1 I feel that my business lies in the gutter, and I have not the least intention to get out of it.

2 Search the records, examine the opening years of those who have been distinguished for their ability and virtue, and you will ascribe, with but few exceptions, the early culture of their minds, and, above all, the first discipline of the heart, to the intelligence and affection of the mother, or at least of some pious woman, who, with the self-denial and tenderness of her sex, has entered as a substitute on the sacred office.

418

- William Shakespeare
The Greatest Writer of All Time
1564 - 1616

1 Our doubts are traitors
And make us lose the good we oft might win
By fearing to attempt.

2 If to do were as easy as to know what were good to do, chapels had been churches and poor men's cottages princes' palaces.

3 It is the mind that makes the body rich.

4 Thoughts are but dreams until their effects be tried.

5 Lilies, that fester, smell far worse than weeds.

6 Our bodies are our gardens. Our wills are gardeners.

7 All that glitters is not gold.

8 Truth has a quiet breast.

9 A miser grows rich by seeming poor; an extravagant man grows poor by seeming rich.

10 The fault, dear Brutus, is not in our stars,
But in ourselves, that we are underlings.

11 There is nothing either good or bad, but thinking makes it so.

12 Sweet are the uses of adversity; which, like the toad, ugly and venomous, wears yet a precious jewel in his head.

13 Make not your thoughts your prisons.

14 There is a tide in the affairs of men which, taken at the flood, leads on to fortune.

15 My crown is in my heart, not on my head
Nor decked with diamonds and Indian stones,
Nor to be seen: My crown is called content;
A crown it is, that seldom kings enjoy.

16 The path is smooth that leadeth on to danger.

17 He is not great who is not greatly good.

18 No legacy is so rich as honesty.

19 We know what we are, but know not what we may be.

20 It is a wise father that knows his own child.

419

- Dmitri Shostakovich
A Foremost Russian Composer of 20th Century
1906 - 1975

1 I have never been a Formalist and never shall be. To malign a work as Formalist on the grounds that its form and meaning is not instantly apparent is to be inexcusably superficial.

2 We are all marionettes.

3 Music that doesn't stir up arguments could be soothing and charming, but it is more likely to be dreary.

4 Music illuminates a person through and through, and it is also his last hope and final refuge.

5 Nothing compares with the feeling you get orchestrating a revered composer. I think it's the ideal method for studying a work, and I would recommend that all young composers make their own versions of the works of those masters from whom they want to learn.

6 You don't enter by the front door in composition. You have to touch and feel everything with your own hand. Listening, enjoying, saying, "Ah, how wonderful!" isn't enough.

420

- Igor Sikorsky
The Builder of the First Practical Helicopter
1889 - 1972

1 I don't pretend to be a scientist, but I am still interested in volcanoes as a mighty and magnificent natural phenomenon. So I traveled to see them and I read what I could about them.

2 We must remain on the alert to eliminate any defects in our ship though neither the customer nor FAA (the Federal Aviation Administration) may require such modifications.

3 Man's moral personality, or soul, must advance in keeping with his rapid scientific progress.

4 No organized society can exist unless there is a certain amount of genuine high and noble impulses among its leaders and members.

5 Teamwork is an essential factor more than ever before, in science and perhaps in every other branch or technique.

6 The work of the individual still remains a very important factor; it still remains the spark that moves mankind ahead even more than teamwork. Teamwork comes into existence after the spark, the intuitive spark of a living man, starts something. Then later comes the teamwork to give a bigger body to the little soul which he created.

7 Nothing can replace the free work of free man; that's where real progress is started.

8 Science is strictly neutral to both good and evil. The same radio will transmit an excellent and elevating appeal, or the most dastardly lies promoting hate. Science is something of which mankind must be careful. A kid on a bicycle represents less danger to himself and others than the same kid placed in a high-powered car, or in a jet plane.

9 All the purely engineering predictions invariably tend to be optimistic over the short range but almost childishly pessimistic over the long range.

421 - Red Skelton
A Foremost Comedian Invited to Entertain the American President
Born in 1913

1 Comedy is fantasy to begin with. So, when you put in a dream, it's a dream within a dream and the audience gets confused.

2 The minute anybody hurts me or my family, I consider them dead and I never think of them again.

3 I would just like to be remembered as a nice guy.

4 Money is the last thing I think before falling asleep at night.

5 To be married to a comedian is no laughing matter.

6 A clown is a warrior who fights gloom.

7 I have always believed that God puts each one of us here for a purpose and mine is to try to make people happy. I was lucky to find it out so young.

422 - B. F. Skinner
The Pioneer of Experiments on Human Behaviour
1904 - 1990

1 I went on for about 15 years without making very much of a dent in the field. I think my pigeons were the things that reinforced me, not people's reactions.

2 The real problem is not whether machines think, but whether men do.

3 We should not teach great books; we should teach a love of reading.

4 Since all human beings are controlled, we should reinforce the kind of behaviour that benefits everyone.

5 If some Mephistopheles offered me a wholly new life on condition that all records and effects of my present life be destroyed, I should refuse.

6 Things go bad when you make a fetish out of individual freedom and dignity. If you insist that individual rights are the summum bonum, then the whole structure of society falls down. Actions are determined by environment; behaviour is shaped and maintained by its consequences.

7 We need to make vast changes in human behaviour and we cannot make them with the help of nothing more than physics and biology, no matter how hard we try.

8 What we need is technology of behaviour.

9 Give me a child and I will shape him into anything.

10 Education is what survives when what has been learnt has been forgotten.

423

- Benjamin Spock
The Most Loved Pediatrician in History
Born in 1903

1 The more people have studied different methods of bringing up children, the more they have come to the conclusion that what good mothers and fathers instinctively feel like doing for their babies is the best after all.

2 If there is something that the parents want to know, explain it without being bossy. With parents, as well as with readers, I try not to cram my ideas down their throats - just to present them with such knowledge as we have about what motivates children at different ages, and let them take over from there.

3 My aim has always been to avoid advocating a theory, but primarily to tell parents what children are like, including descriptions of their unconscious drives.

4 Parents should both respect their children and ask for respect for them.

5 I try to give readers confidence by reminding them that they already know a lot, and that the professionals do not know everything. I sympathize. I try not to be pompous and I bend over backwards to reassure parents, not to frighten or scold them.

6 I never thought of myself as changing society. I was not a sculptor, looking to make the ideal person of the future.

7 Men and women are quite different in temperament needs, and the feminists' efforts to deny this is increasing the rivalry between the sexes and impairing the pleasure of both.

8 Women are usually more patient in working at unexciting repetitive tasks.

9 Sports taught me to set goals for myself and then to go out and pursue them, but they aren't for everybody.

424

- Sylvester Stallone
A Movie Star Despite Serious Speech Handicaps
Born in 1946

1 I have run the entire course in this business. I haven't missed a bump or a pothole on the road to success.

2 I strip things down to the essentials. I always say, "Lead with your heart".

3 The champion represents the ultimate warrior - the nearest thing to being immortal while mortal. The champion lives on forever. The championship belongs to a single person who because of the nature of what he does, has the respect of everyone on the face of the earth.

4 I want to be remembered as a man of raging optimism, who believes in the American dream.

5 I knew when I came here that this town has a ninety-five percent guaranteed failure rate. Only the toughest usually endure. But if you hang around long enough, you will succeed.

6 Everything I am and everything I have boils down to Rocky Balboa. I did not create Rocky. He created me.

7 Life is very repetitious on a certain level. Without dependability and loyalty from a certain group of people that you can really feel safe with, every day looks the same.

425

- Henry Stanley
A Foremost Explorer of Africa
1841 - 1904

1 Only a thin barrier separates ferocity from amiability.

2 I have often been struck at the power of a quick decisive tone. It appears to have an electric effect, riding rough-shod over all fears, indecision and tremor.

3 The path to duty is the way to glory.

4 No African traveler is ought to be judged during the first year of his return. He is too full of his own reflection; he is too utterly natural; he must speak the truth, if he dies for it; his opinions are too much of his own.

5 The richest inheritance a father can give his children is an honoured name.

426

- Elizabeth Cady Stanton
An Initiator of the Women's Rights Movement in America
1815 - 1902

1 In all cases the highest good of one is the highest good of all and the highest good of all does not require sacrifice of one individual.

2 Womanhood is the great fact, wifehood and motherhood its incidents.

3 Just as the constituent elements of nitrogen and oxygen make the necessary atmosphere in which man can breathe and live, so are the male and female elements in their proportions necessary for our moral life.

4 As personal liberty in the true order comes before political freedom, woman must first be emancipated from the old bondage of a divinely ordained allegiance to man before her pride of sex can be so roused as to demand the rights of citizenship.

5 Each age has some word of momentous import with which to hound the lovers of truth and progress.

6 Progress is the law.

7 Society is based on fourfold bondage of woman - Church, State, Capital and Society - making liberty and equality for her antagonistic to every organized institution.

8 The radical reform must start in our homes, in our nurseries, in ourselves.

9 Lifting woman into her proper place is the mightiest revolution the world has yet known.

427

- Ellsworth Milton Statler
The Premier Hotelman of All Time
1863 - 1928

1 Life is service. The one who progresses is the one who gives his fellow human being a little more, a little better service.

2 If I can make it with my education and my handicaps then any American can make it, if he works as hard as I have.

3 Every complaint from a guest must be satisfied to his complete satisfaction. If you cannot solve the problem, take it to your superior. If he cannot solve it, he must take it to his superior. If necessary, the problem should come right on up to me. If it does, you may be sure I'll solve it.

4 Listen carefully to what is asked of you, and then go out of your way, if necessary, to be helpful. Try hard to give a patron the same attention that you would want to be shown if you were in his place.

5 A man may wear a red necktie, a green vest and tan shoes, and still be a gentleman. The unpretentious man with the soft voice may possess the wealth of Croesus. The stranger in cowhide boots, broadbrim and rusty black, may be president of a railroad or a senator from over the ridge. You cannot afford to be superior or sullen with any patron of this hotel.

6 Have everyone feel that for his money we want to give him more sincere service than he ever before received at any hotel.

7 Never be perky, pungent or fresh. The guest pays your salary as well as mine. He is your immediate benefactor.

428

1 I buy birthday presents three months ahead of time and I use the telephone whenever possible, especially when buying the kids' clothes from two shops that know what I like. I spend an hour a day planning up to six months in advance. I keep elaborate books that tell me when everybody needs their check ups and shots, when I'm taking business trips, and when I'm blocking out writing time. Everything is lists! Endlessly. On Monday, I publish a schedule outlining where I'll be every day of the week - and I carry a beeper so that I can be tracked at any time I'm needed.

2 I am still not great at delegating work and I have only come to do it as a matter of survival. I wish I could offer a tip for letting go, but I have not found it.

3 To be a writer it is important to write everyday and to write from experience.

4 Taking one day off in the middle of my writing may cost me five days of getting back in the mood. Going out to lunch can cost me anywhere from five hours to three days and for me it's not worth.

5 It takes me eight months to a year to think up the plot of a book. The actual writing takes me anywhere from ten to fourteen days. During that period I sit in my office in my nightgown and write. I still stop to see the kids. They come in and talk and bring their pictures and drawings. If they have a problem, I am there. The rewrite of a book takes me two to four days. The longest, hardest thing is the outline.

6 People assume I'm some kind of a dummy. It boggles my mind when they believe a tooth fairy arrived with an enormous suitcase of money one day. I have worked to have what I have, and it astounds me to be taken for granted.

7 I try to protect my children, maybe because nobody ever protected me.

429

1 Learning is somehow akin to personal inspiration.

2 No science has more fascination than that of astronomy, and there the strongest mathematical intellect finds full scope.

3 Spencer, Darwin and Hugo mean more to me than geometry or political economy.

4 'Tis glorious on a world-wide stage
To wear a hero's crown,
That shines with the gems of mighty deeds,
With the gold of a fair renown.
But every prize this world holds out,
Or has since the work began,
We renounce for the love of the woman we love,
And the life of a common man.

430

1 A thing is beautiful if it fulfills its purpose, if it functions. To my mind a modern ice box is a thing of beauty.

2 Women are the greatest undeveloped natural resource in the world today.

3 The artist in any medium, does not live in a vacuum. There is a relationship between everything that is being done and everything that has been done before. The modern artist is in step not only with the general cultural aspects of his time but also with the specific scientific aspects of research, invention and discovery. And the artist's understanding and appreciation is often far ahead of that part of the public which clings desperately to the things that have gone before.

4 A photograph of an object is, in a sense, a portrait. But the camera with its eye, the lens, and its memory, the film, can in itself produce little more than mirrored verisimilitudes. A good photograph requires more than that. When an artist of any kind looks at his subject, he looks with everything he is. Everything that he has lived, learned, observed , and experienced combines to enable him to identify himself with the subject and look with insight, perception, imagination and understanding. The technical process simply serves as a vehicle of transcription and not as the art.

5 Photography is a medium of formidable contradictions. It is both ridiculously easy and almost impossibly difficult. It is easy because of its technical rudiments which can readily be mastered by anyone with a few simple instructions. It is difficult because, while the artist working in any other medium begins with a blank surface and gradually brings his conception into being, the photographer is the only image maker who begins with the picture completed. His emotions, his knowledge, and his native talent are brought into focus and fixed beyond recall the moment the shutter of his camera has closed.

431

1 I cannot afford to be clear because if I was, I would risk destroying my own thought. Most people destroy their thought before they create it. That is why I often repeat a word again and again - because I am fighting to hold the thought.

2 What is sauce for the goose can be sauce for the gander but it is not necessarily sauce for the chicken, the duck, the turkey or the guinea hen.

3 Beauty, music, decoration, the result of emotion should never be the cause, even events should not be the cause of emotion nor should they be the material of poetry and prose. Nor should emotion itself be the cause of poetry or prose. They should consist of an exact reproduction of either an outer or an inner reality.

4 Writing should be the way of seeing what the writer chooses to see, and the relation between that vision and the way it gets down. When the vision is not complete the words are flat; it is very simple, there can be no mistake about it.

432

- Gloria Steinem
A Foremost Leader of Modern Feminist Movement
Born in 1934

1 I have wasted an enormous amount of time, and time is life. Time is all there is.

2 The revolutionary role of a writer is to make language that makes coalition possible; language that makes us see things in a new way.

3 Writing is much more efficient. You can travel six months and not reach as many people as you can if you write one thing. But you have to have the solitude and concentration to sit down and write something.

4 It is always hard to see yourself.

5 If a story is not brought to its own logical, or illogical conclusion, our imaginations are compelled to carry it on. That's why we hear more about James Dean than Gary Cooper, or about Jack Kennedy than Roosevelt. We are deprived of the natural end of a story, so our imaginations supply it.

6 Sometimes we need to exclude men from our organizations in order for women to learn to work together. We need our own psychic turf.

433

- Charles Steinmetz
One of the World's Foremost Electrical Engineers
1865 - 1923

1 Only men of little minds declare there is no God. The greater the mind, the greater the belief that each one of us is a part of a Supreme Mind.

2 The field that offers the greatest promise for future research is prayer.

3 No man really becomes a fool until he stops asking questions.

4 We have been a wasteful nation because of our great natural wealth. Nothing has been saved. We have lived in the today and never thought, nor prepared, for tomorrow. What have we done for years? We have been destroying our forests to get lumber in the most extravagant way. We have taken out crops year after year and never put anything back in the earth. There has been no such thing as conservation, It has been destruction.

5 All I want is good work; never sacrifice good work for speed.

434

- George Stephenson
The Inventor of the First Successful Locomotive
1781 - 1848

1 Never give up.

2 Of all the powers above and under the earth, there seems to me to be no power so great as the gift of the gab.

3 I have no great ambition to mix in fine company and feel out of place among such high folks.

1 A child should always say what's true
And speak when he is spoken to,
And behave mannerly at table;
At least as far as he is able.

2 The best things are nearest: breath in your nostrils, light in your eyes, flowers at your feet, duties at your hand, the path of Right just before you. Then do not grasp at the stars, but do life's plain, common work as it comes, certain that daily duties and daily bread are the sweetest things of life.

3 To believe in immortality is one thing; but it is first needful to believe in life.

4 You cannot run away from a weakness; you must some time fight it out or perish; and if that be so, why not now, and where you stand?

5 Childhood must pass away, and then youth, as surely as age approaches. The true wisdom is to be always reasonable, and to change with a good grace in changing circumstances.

6 A dash of enthusiasm is not a thing to be ashamed of in retrospect. If St. Paul had not been a very zealous Pharisee he would have been a colder Christian.

7 To be rich in admiration and free from envy, to rejoice greatly in the good of others, to love, these are the gifts of fortune which money cannot buy, and without which money can buy nothing.

8 To be truly happy is a question of how we begin, and not how we end, of what we want and not what we have.

9 Youth is the time to go flashing from one end of the world to the other both in mind and in body, to try the manners of different nations; to hear the chimes at midnight.

10 To be what we are and to become what we are capable of becoming, is the only end of life.

11 There is no duty we underrate so much as the duty of being happy.

12 So long as we love, we serve; so long as we are loved by others, I would almost say that we are indispensable; and no man is useless while he has a friend.

13 The habit of being happy enables one to be freed, or largely freed, from the domination of outward conditions.

14 Make the most of the best and the least of the worst.

15 An aim in life is the only fortune worth finding; and it is not to be found in foreign lands, but in the heart itself.

16 To travel hopefully is a better thing than to arrive.

1 There is a little difference in people, but that little difference makes a big difference. The little difference is attitude. The big difference is whether it is positive or negative.

2 Flash of inspiration comes from a burning desire.

3 Be generous! Give to whom you love; give to those who love you; give to the fortunate; give to the unfortunate; give specially to those whom you don't want to give.

4 Your most precious, valued possessions and your greatest powers are invisible. No one can take them. You, and you alone, can give them. You will receive abundance for your giving. The more you give, the more you will have.

5 Give a smile to everyone you meet. Smile with your eyes and you will smile and receive smiles.

6 Give a kind word, with a kindly thought behind the word. You will be kind and receive kind words.

7 Give appreciation, the warmth from the heart. You will appreciate and be appreciated.

8 Give honour, credit and applause, the victor's wreath. You will be honourable and receive credit and applause.

9 Give time for a worthy cause, with eagerness. You will be worthy and richly rewarded.

10 Give hope, the magic ingredient of success. You will have hope and be made hopeful.

11 Give happiness, the most treasured state of mind. You will be happy and be made happy.

12 Give encouragement, the incentive to action. You will have courage and be encouraged.

13 Give cheer, the verbal sunshine. You will be cheerful and cheered.

14 Give a pleasant response, the neutralizer of irritants. You will be pleasant and receive pleasant responses.

15 Give good thoughts, the nature's character builder. You will be good and the world will have good thoughts for you.

16 Give prayers, the instrument of miracles, for the godless and the godly. You will be reverent and receive blessings, more than you deserve!

17 The basic principles of success are (1) inspiration to action - self-motivation; (2) know-how; and (3) activity knowledge.

18 Action is a vital part of the power of persuasion for all human relations.

19 Love is the greatest motivator of all.

20 There is a miraculous power in prayer.

21 God is always a good God.

22 Truth will always be truth, regardless of lack of understanding, disbelief or ignorance.

23 Man is the product of his heredity, environment, physical body, conscious and subconscious mind, experience and particular position and direction in time and space. He also has the power to affect, use, control or harmonize with all of them.

24 Man was created in the image of God and he has the God-given ability to direct his thoughts, control his emotions and ordain his destiny.

25 Religious faith is a dynamic, living, growing experience. Its universal principles are simple and enduring.

26 One of the best ways to inspire another person to desirable action is to relate a true story that appeals to his emotions.

27 When you know what your specific objectives are concerning your distant, immediate and intermediate goals, you will be more apt to recognize that which will help you achieve them.

28 Try to be honest with yourself and recognize your strengths and weaknesses; engage in self-inspection with regularity and discover how to develop desirable habits and eliminate those you are convinced are undesirable.

29 If you want to know someone, get them to talk about themselves.

30 You always do what you want to do. This is true with every act. You may say that you had to do something, or that you were forced to, but actually, whatever you do, you do by choice. Only you have the power to choose.

31 You are a product of your environment. So choose the environment that will best develop you toward your objective. Analyze your life in terms of its environment. Are the things around you helping you toward success - or are they holding you back?

32 To solve a problem or to reach a goal, you don't need to know all the answers in advance. But you must have a clear idea of the problem or the goal you want to reach.

33 Try, try, try and keep trying is the rule that must be followed to become an expert in anything.

34 If you employed study, thinking and planning time daily, you could develop and use the power that can change the course of your destiny.

35 Self-suggestion makes you master of yourself.

437

- Harriet Beecher Stowe
The Author of Uncle Tom's Cabin
1811 - 1896

1 In all ranks of life the human heart yearns for the beautiful; and the beautiful things that God makes are His gift to all alike.

2 When you get into a tight place and everything goes against you, until it seems as though you could not hold on a minute longer, never give up then, for that is just the place and time that the tide will turn.

3 The heroic element was strong in me, having come down by ordinary generation

from a long line of Puritan ancestry, and it made me long to do something. I knew not what: to fight for my country, or to make some declaration on my own account.

4 Who can speak the blessedness of that first day of Freedom? ...To move, speak and breathe, go out and come in, unwatched and free from danger!

438 - Johan August Strindberg
The Greatest Swedish Playwright
1849 - 1912

1 My life has the peculiarity that it unfolds like novels, without my really being able to say why. I don't meddle in other people's destinies, since from my early youth I realized that this was criminal and brought its own punishment. But I have always been a kind of lime-twig; it attracts small birds, they finger my destiny, stick fast and then complain.

2 A question which can be decided by a vote is not a big question and does not carry the seeds of immortality; and men of talent should not rack themselves with small passing questions. Their field is literature, where they can speak for as long as they please without being interrupted or distracted by wrangling.

3 Alone, one withers.

4 I don't believe we leave this world until we had our measure of suffering. We seem to have a task to fulfill, and it is no use throwing oneself into the sea like Jonah to escape one's calling. We must stand forth and prophesy, and risk being disavowed like Jonah.

439 - Anne Sullivan
Helen Keller's Teacher
1866 - 1936

1 We are too much creatures of habit.

2 Every human being is a mystery, and you cannot, nor can any mortal, trace the endless windings of his mind.

3 If all people knew what was good for them and acted accordingly this world would be a very different world, though not nearly so interesting.

4 As long as there are those of us who refuse to accept as inevitable world turmoil, hatred, fraud and the clash of interests, there will be a chance for mankind to survive. We can look at history from above as well as from below and refresh our purposes with the music of the eternal spheres.

440

1 The fellow who says, "To heck with it, nobody is going to stop me", is the one who gets ahead. That's the way I felt when I was 21. Nothing could stop me. I've never stopped being grateful that I had that attitude. It was the most important single factor that helped me get ahead and I'm hanging on to it.

2 If you respect your audience, it respects you.

3 Every other variety show has always had a star as performer. I don't think you can ever get anybody but me content to just introduce an act and get off. The most difficult thing in the world is to shut up.

4 My experience as a newspaperman is the reason why we have lasted. I approach the show and put it together the way that a reporter handles a story. Because of my background I developed an instinct and a sensitivity to public trends.

5 On the TV I've been myself and it's the only thing that saved me. If I'd tried to whip up a phony smile, if I'd tried to be an actor or tell stories, the public would have tossed me the hell out.

6 A taped programme lacks a certain earthliness; a light will go out; something will be said wrong; that's okay. I'd rather have something go wrong and let the people know that the show was live than correct and polish the tape.

7 I think that my awkwardness on camera is the real reason I am still here today. I have aroused the mother instinct of America.

8 The secret of my success is that I'm an average American and the show reflects my taste.

9 I think people identify with me. I'm not a performer. I'm a host. Sort of like some ordinary guy from Iowa who somehow met someone famous and is throwing a party for his friends and says, "Hey, look who I got!"

441

1 There is no such thing as objective reality. We each select our experiences through the filters of our genes, values and belief systems.

442

1 I love excitement. I like to read about adventure. I also like to have my own adventures.

2 Women produce one-third of the material wealth necessary for humanity. They

are making a great contribution to the development of the world's culture and science. Economic incentives are not the only reasons that women participate in labour. They are coming to the conclusion that working in industry is the only way to attain equality, both in society and in the family.

443

- Nikola Tesla
A Pioneer of the Application of Electrical Power
1856 - 1943

1 A man has two reasons for the things he does - a good one and the real one.

2 We are but cogwheels in the medium of the universe.

3 I do not rush into the actual work. When I get a new idea, I start at once building it up in my imagination, and make improvements and operate the device in my mind. When I have gone so far as to embody everything in my invention, every possible improvement I can think of, and when I see no fault anywhere, I put into concrete form the final product of my brain.

444

- Margaret Thatcher
The First woman to Head a British Political Party
Born in 1925

1 We can't always have what we want. Sometimes we have to have what's good for us.

2 I am what I am, and will stay that way.

3 The nation is but an enlarged family.

4 You have to tell your children what's right and wrong and you must obviously have some rules, but you don't want rules for the sake of rules and you must explain them. They ask endless questions you need endless patience, but you have got to explain. You have got to try and give them answers. One of the big problems today is that some parents don't talk to their children enough.

5 It is possible, in my view, for a woman to run a home and continue with her career provided two conditions are fulfilled. First, her husband must be in sympathy with her wish to do another job. Secondly, where there is a young family, the joint incomes of husband and wife must be sufficient to employ a first-class nanny-housekeeper to look after things in the wife's absence. The second is the key to the whole plan.

6 Many women have the opportunities but do not use them; or are too easily contented with the job that they are doing and do not necessarily make the effort to climb the tree. Sometimes it is thought to be unfeminine. It isn't at all.

7 I don't notice that I am a woman. I regard myself as the Prime Minister.

8 I am absolutely satisfied that there is nothing more you can do by changing the law to do away with discrimination. After all, I don't think there's been a great deal of discrimination against women for years.

9 I don't think this country wants a weak government. I don't believe they want a

government to be so flexible that it becomes invertebrate. I think they want a government with a bit of spine. I don't want a government of flexi-toys.

10 We shall not be diverted from our course. To those waiting with bated breath for that favorite media catch-phrase, the U-turn, I have only one thing to say, "You turn if you want; the Lady's not for turning."

11 We don't change our tune to whoever we are talking.

12 Without the strong, who would provide for the weak? When you hold back the successful you penalize those who need help.

13 If you are to be a leader, you don't just sit back and mutter sweet nothings or listen and do nothing. That's not the essence of leadership.

14 I am not hard. I am frightfully soft. But I will not be hounded. I will not be driven anywhere without my will.

15 I am a tough boss and I drive people. I am not the great dictator. But I do know my own mind. I do know the direction in which I want to go and I do try to influence argument with argument.

16 Sometimes I cry. What human being with any sensitivity wouldn't? Men cry too. There's nothing wrong with crying at the appropriate time.

17 Power does create loneliness. Other people make the easy decisions so one is left with the difficult ones.

18 No one would have remembered the Good Samaritan if he'd only had good intentions. He had money as well.

19 You can't look after the hard-up people in society unless you are accruing enough wealth to do so. Good intentions are not enough. You do need hard cash.

445
- Isiah Thomas
A Star of Professional Basketball Despite His Limited Height
Born in 1961

1 It's great to be a hero and sink the game and sink the game winner, but more important to me is that I feel I am strong enough to take the heat when I miss the last shot. I do know that I'm the one who wants to take that shot, make or miss.

2 There is nothing to match the high you get from competing in game in front of a national television audience and 20,000 screaming fans.

446
- Lowell Thomas
An Extraordinary World Traveler, Reporter and Lecturer
1892 - 1981

1 Sleep when everyone else is sleeping at your destination, even its noon back home. Don't schedule important meetings or hectic sightseeing tours on your arrival date, but take a day or so to get in phase with local time. Eat and drink lightly.

2 When I was a boy in Colorado, a school year stretched into an eternity as we waited for summer. Now the years pass in a flash, and there is still so much to see and do.

3 Wherever I go, I encounter someone who has a great story to tell.

447
- Tom Thomson
An Extraordinary Landscape Painter
1877 - 1917

1 Painting is the only thing that compels me and gives me direction. Therefore, I will stick to painting as long as I can.

2 To paint the nature, lift it up and bring it out.

448
- Henry David Thoreau
A Pioneer of Civil Disobedience
1817 - 1862

1 If one advances confidently in the direction of his dreams, endeavors to live the life which he had imagined, he will meet with a success unexpected in common hours.

2 Dreams are the touchstones of our characters.

3 The eye may see for the hand but not for the mind.

4 In the long run men hit only what they aim at.

5 None are so old as those who have outlived their enthusiasm.

6 It matters not how small the beginning may seem to be, what is once well done is done forever.

7 Be resolutely and faithfully what you are; be humbly what you aspire to be. Man's noblest gift to man is his sincerity, for it embraces his integrity also.

8 Only that day dawns to which we are awake.

9 If you would convince a man that he does wrong, do right. Men will believe what they see. Let them see.

10 That man is the richest whose pleasures are the cheapest.

11 The man who goes alone can start today; but he who travels with another must wait till that other is ready.

12 The boy gathers materials for a temple, and then when he is 30, concludes to build a woodshed.

13 What people say you cannot do, you try and find that you can.

14 Read the best books first, or you may not have a chance to read them at all.

15 Books are the treasured wealth of the world and the fit inheritance of generations and nations. Their authors are a natural and irresistible aristocracy in every society, and more than kings or emperors, exert an influence on mankind.

16 The highest law gives a thing to him who can use it.

17 I know of no more encouraging fact than the unquestionable ability of man to elevate his life by a conscious endeavor.

18 To be awake is to be alive.

19 The mass of men lead lives of quiet desperation.

20 Nothing is so much to be feared as fear.

21 It is not enough to be busy. The question is, what are we busy about?

22 I would rather sit on a pumpkin, and have it all to myself, than be crowded on a velvet cushion.

23 When law and conscience are in conflict, it is conscience, rather than law, that should be obeyed. It is not desirable to cultivate a respect for the law, so much as for the right.

24 Water is the only drink of a wise man.

25 If you have built castles in the air, your work need not be lost; that is where they should be. Now put the foundations under them.

26 It is never too late to give up our prejudices.

27 To inherit property is not to be born - it is rather to be still-born.

28 To regret deeply is to live afresh.

29 There will never be a really and enlightened State until the State comes to recognize the individual as a higher and independent power, from which all its own power and authorities are derived and treats him accordingly.

30 Our life is frittered away by detail. ... Simplify, simplify. Let your affairs be as two or three, and not a hundred or a thousand; instead of a million, count half a dozen and keep your accounts on your thumbnail.

31 Do what you love. Know your own bone; gnaw at it, bury it, unearth it, and gnaw it still.

32 We shall see but a little way, if we require to understand what we see.

33 The only wealth is life.

34 However mean your life is, meet it and live it; do not shun it and call it hard names. It is not so bad as you are. It looks poorest when you are the richest.

35 If a man does not keep pace with his companions, perhaps because he hears a different drummer. Let him step to the music which he hears, however measured or far away.

449

- Jim Thorpe
The Greatest Athlete of the First Half of 20th Century
1888 - 1953

1 I have always liked sports, and I played and ran races only for fun. After my Olympic victories I received offers amounting to thousands of dollars, but I turned them down because I did not care to make money from my athletic skills.

2 Athletics gives you a fighting spirit to battle your problems of life. They build sportsmanship.

3 Sports will improve your health.

4 Sporting events keep young people out of trouble.

5 A good person is better than a great athlete.

6 I never realized until now what a big mistake I made by keeping secret my ball playing, and I am sorry that I did so. I did not know I was doing wrong because I was doing what several other college men had done, except that they did not use their names to play under, as I did.

450

- James Thurber
An Extraordinary Humorist
1894 - 1961

1 Do not look back in anger, or forward in fear, but around in awareness.

2 I do not have a psychiatrist and I do not want one, for the simple reason that if he listened to me long enough, he might become disturbed.

3 Don't count your boobies until they are hatched.

4 We all have flaws and mine is being wicked.

5 It is better to know some of the questions than all of the answers.

6 He who hesitates is sometimes saved.

7 Love is what you have been through with somebody.

8 Humour is emotional chaos remembered in tranquillity.

451

- John Tolkien
A Very Popular Writer of Fairy Tales
1892 - 1973

1 It is the message that is important in literature, not the messenger.

2 The investigation of an author's life reveals very little of the workings of his mind.

3 It does not do good to leave a live dragon out of your calculations, if you live near one.

4 The job that's never started takes the longest to finish.

452

- Leo Tolstoy
Russia's Greatest Novelist and Moral Philosopher
1828 - 1910

1 The only true pleasure is the pleasure of creative activity.

2 Blessedness lies only in progress towards perfection, and a halt at any stage is a cessation of this blessedness.

3 The strongest of all warriors are Time and Patience.

4 The vocation of every man and woman is to serve other people.

5 Faith is the force of life.

6 It is easier to write ten volumes of philosophy than to put one principle into practice.

7 Where love is, there is God also.

8 All happy families resemble one another; every unhappy family is unhappy in its own way.

9 Art is one of the ways of uniting people.

10 Science and art are as closely interconnected as the lungs and the heart so that if one organ becomes distorted, the other cannot function properly.

11 Pure and complete sorrow is as impossible as pure and complete joy.

453
- Lee Trevino
The Second Golfer to Reach $2 Million in Official Winnings
Born in 1939

1 There ain't nothing relaxed about me on a golf course. I'm very tightly wound. All that jabbering is a pressure valve. I could not do without it. The competitor inside you knows what has to be done. If the game doesn't eat you up inside, you can't possibly be a great player.

2 From 1960 to 1967, I did nothing but play golf fifteen hours a day and a thousand practice balls a day.

3 You want a life, you work for it.

4 Pride in what you do well is what makes a man.

454
- Edward Livingston Trudeau
A Pioneer of the Natural Healing of Tuberculosis
1848 - 1915

1 The conquest of fate is not by struggling against it, nor by trying to escape from it, but by acquiesce.

2 It is often through men that we come to know God.

3 I learned about courage, not from my own suffering but from my patients.

4 Spiritual courage is of a higher type than physical courage. It takes a higher type of courage to fight bravely a losing than a winning fight.

5 The success of a physician depends largely on his ability to deal skillfully and individually with the physical, psychological and sociological problems that arise with each patient.

455

1 Whenever you have an efficient government, you have a dictatorship.

2 It is a recession when your neighbour loses his job. It is a depression when you lose yours.

3 If you can't stand the heat, get out of the kitchen.

4 I believe in the brotherhood of man, not merely the brotherhood of white men but the brotherhood of all men before the law.

5 I have never deliberately given anybody hell. I tell the truth on the opposition - and they think it's hell.

6 The President hears a hundred voices telling him that he is the greatest man in the world. He must listen carefully indeed to hear the one voice that tells him he is not.

7 The best way to give advice to your children is to find out what they want and then advise them to do it.

8 It is understanding that gives us an ability to have peace. When we understand the other fellow's viewpoint, and he understands ours, then we can sit down and work out our differences.

9 Whenever a man does the best that he can, then that is all he can do.

10 We must have strong minds, ready to accept facts as they are.

456

1 The rich rob the poor and the poor rob one another.

2 The Lord gave me the name *Truth*, because I was to declare truth to the people.

3 It is better to have a coloured race a living force animated and strengthened by self-reliance and self-respect than a stagnant mass, degraded and self-condemned.

4 There is a great stir about coloured men getting their rights but not a word about coloured women and if coloured men get their rights and not coloured women theirs, the coloured men will be masters over the women and it will be just as bad as before.

5 Give power and significance to your life and in the great work of up-building; there is room for woman's work and woman's heart.

6 I know that it is hard for one who has held the reins for so long to give it up; it cuts like a knife. It will feel all the better when it closes up again.

457

1 Go free, or die.

2 I never ran my train off the track and I never lost a passenger.

3 I had reasoned this out in my mind; there was one of two things I had a right to, liberty or death; if I could not have one, I would have the other.

4 When I found I had crossed that line, I looked at my hands to see if I was the same person. There was such glory over everything; the sun came like gold through the trees, and over the fields. and I felt like I was in Heaven.

5 The moment I decided to escape, I was devoid of all personal fear. The idea of being captured by slave-hunters or slaveholders never entered my mind. I attribute my success of reaching Maryland only to my adventurous spirit and utter disregard of consequences.

458

1 Education is the most valuable capital an ambitious youth can have.

2 You cannot get advice from anyone when you are down on the floor. You are the loneliest man in the world.

3 I consider my association with George Bernard Shaw as one of the outstanding blessings of my life.

4 Simple and quiet living brings me most happiness.

5 Pugilistic genius is no more remarkable than respiration, or the bees building their hive.

6 A boxer's assets are his ability to judge and time the blows and to select almost instantaneously the right move at the right time.

7 The main characteristics of any specific ability are that it comes easy to those who possess it and is remarkable in proportion to the number of creatures who do not possess it.

459

1 Never forget who you are.

2 The chance of an accident is every time you sit on a horse.

3 The public doesn't realize this, but something dangerous happens in about 50 per cent of all races. If the horses do not finish in the money, there is no inquiry, but if you are around the jockeys' room, you know about it.

4 No matter how many times I look at my legs and tell them to walk, they ain't going to move. Some people have this and they can't face the world. That never bothered me. I never asked, "Why me?" I don't know why, but I know there has to be a force behind it. If God doesn't help me regain my legs, he's helping me in other ways - helping me cope it.

5 I do not believe in complaining. I just put up with the pain and do what I can do.

6 Whether I feel good or not, I just push myself to get going.

7 Having a role model - someone who can demonstrate that you can be whatever you want to be and that it's never too late - is very important.

460
- Ted Turner
The Founder of Cable News Network
Born in 1938

1 Your mind is similar to the muscles of your body. You can take just a skinny little guy and he can run 30 miles if he builds himself up to it. It is the same with your mind. The more you think, the more you use your mind to handle problems, the more you strengthen it.

2 I just love it when people say I can't do something. There's nothing that makes me feel better, because all my life people have said I wasn't going to make it.

3 The secret of my success is this: Every time, I tried to go as far as I could. When I climbed the hills, I saw the mountains. Then I started climbing the mountains.

4 You just have to be a step ahead of everybody else.

5 Don't pay too much for something if you see what the current owner of it doesn't see it. Every time something changes hands, every time there is a willing buyer and a willing seller, the guy that's selling thinks that he can do better by reinvesting his money in something else. The guy that's buying thinks that it's going to be worth more than it was to the previous buyer.

6 Human beings, when confronted with the information, will choose the intelligent course. If they don't, then there really was no hope for them in the beginning. With the right information we are hopefully going to make the right decisions.

461
- Mark Twain
The Most Widely Read Humorous Writer of All Time
1835 - 1910

1 When in doubt, tell the truth.

2 Let us endeavour to so live that when we die even the undertaker will be sorry.

3 A round man cannot be expected to fit in a square hole right away. He must have time to modify his shape.

4 The man who does not read good books has no advantage over the man who can't read them.

5 The man with a new idea is a crack until the idea succeeds.

6 The right word may be effective, but no word was ever as effective as a rightly timed pause.

7 One learns people through the heart, not the eyes or the intellect.

8 Thunder is good, thunder is impressive; but it is lightning that does the work.

9 Noise proves nothing. Often a hen, who has merely laid an egg, cackles as if she laid an asteroid.

10 Don't part with your illusions. When they are gone you may still exist, but you have ceased to live.

11 Training is everything. The peach was once a bitter almond; cauliflower is nothing but a cabbage with a college education.

12 Habit is habit, and not to be flung out of the window by any man, but coaxed downstairs a step at a time.

13 Everyone is a moon, and has a dark side which he never shows to anybody.

14 In his private heart no man much respects himself.

15 There are two times in a man's life when he should not speculate: when he can't afford it, and when he can.

16 I can live for two months on a good compliment.

17 When I was a boy of 14, my father was so ignorant I could hardly stand to have the old man around. But when I got to be 21, I was astounded at how much he had learned in 7 years.

18 Courage is resistance to fear, mastery of fear - not absence of fear.

19 Keep away from people who try to belittle your ambition. Small people always do that, but the really great make you feel that you, too, can become great.

20 It is better to deserve honors and not have them, than to have them and not deserve them.

21 The miracle, or the power, that elevates the few is to be found in their industry, application and perseverance under the promptings of a brave, determined spirit.

22 Always do right. This will gratify some people and astonish the rest.

23 It were not best that we should all think alike. It is the difference of opinion that makes horse races.

24 Work consists of whatever a body is obliged to do. Play consists of whatever a body is not obliged to do.

462

- Vincent van Gogh

A Forerunner of 20th Century Expressionism
1853 - 1890

1 The best way to know God is to love many things.

2 Happiness is not enough. Honesty is not enough. Man's aim must be the noble life devoted to the upraising of humanity.

3 The great things are not done only by impulse, but are a series of things brought

together. And great things are not something accidental but certainly must be willed.

4 Love is something eternal.

5 There is the same difference in a person before and after he is in love as there is in an unlighted lamp and one that is burning. The lamp was there, and it was a good lamp, but now it is shedding light too, and that is its real function.

463 - Cornelius Van Horne
The Builder of the Trans-Canada Railroad
1843 - 1915

1 Nothing is too small to know, and nothing too big to attempt.

2 Discipline is the foundation of character and the safeguard of liberty.

3 If you approach a big thing, make an extra effort and do the biggest thing.

4 The one best formula for success in any career is Interest - Work - Facility. The first induces and stimulates the second and practice of the second brings the third.

5 Give me a book for use. If the margins are too wide, cut them down. If the covers are too clumsy, tear them off. If you buy a book as a work of art, throw it in your cabinet and order a modern edition for reading.

464 - Cornelius Vanderbilt
The Great American Steamship and Railroad Builder
1794 - 1877

1 All you have to do is attend to your business and go ahead.

2 I never tell what I am going to do till I have done it.

3 Providence is as square as a brick.

465 - Giusseppe Verdi
Most Distinguished Italian Opera Composer of 19th Century
1813 - 1901

1 I am more of a bear than before. I have been wandering from country to country, and I have never said a word to a journalist, never begged a friend, never courted rich people to achieve success. Never, absolutely never! I shall always despise such methods. I do my operas as well as I can. For the rest, I let things take their course without ever influencing public opinion to the slightest degree.

2 I am what I am. There is no Italian music, nor German, nor Turkish. But there is music! I write as I please and as I feel. I detest all schools because they all lead to conventionalism. I love beautiful music when it is really beautiful, no matter who wrote it.

3 Art is a thing that moves by itself. If the author is a man of genius, he will make

art progress without seeking or wishing to do so.

4 Art devoid of spontaneity, naturalness and simplicity ceases to be art. The artist must know the technique that gives him the tools to develop his art. A composer must be able to write counterpoint and fugues.

5 To achieve success, a good ensemble is absolutely necessary. Consequently, the direction should be entrusted to only two men, who must be capable and energetic. One of them should direct all musical matters: singers, chorus, orchestra etc. The other should look after scenic matters: costumes, property, scenery, production etc. These two men must decide everything and assume all the responsibility. Only then will there be hope of a good performance and of success.

466

- Jules Verne
The Inventor of Science Fiction
1828 - 1905

1 Fortune smiles on the brave, on those who dare - but not on the reckless.

2 The true worth of man is measured not in terms of material success but in terms of the effort required to succeed.

3 We die but our acts do not die, because they are perpetuated in their consequences, which go on forever. We pass briefly here; yet our steps leave their imprints on the sands for all eternity. Nothing occurs without having been determined by what preceded it; and the future is composed of the unknown prolongations of the past.

467

- Voltaire
One of France's Most Famous Writers
1694 - 1778

1 Common sense is not so common.

2 Life is like a game of cards. Each player must accept the cards that life deals to him or her. With cards in hand, each person must decide how the hand will be played in order to win the game.

3 Work keeps us from three great evils - boredom, vice and need.

4 Use, do not abuse; neither abstinence nor excess renders man happy.

5 By appreciation we make excellence in others our own property.

6 The secret of being a bore is to tell everything.

7 Love truth, but pardon error.

8 Politeness is to the mind what is charm to the face.

9 I do not agree with a word that you say, but I will defend to the death your right to say it.

10 We never live; we are always in the expectation of living.

11 Providence has given us hope and sleep as a compensation for the many cares of life.

12 A good imitation is the most perfect originality.

13 If you wish to converse with me, define your terms.

14 It is better to risk saving a guilty person than to condemn an innocent one.

15 Whoever serves his country well has no need of ancestors.

16 Judge of a man by his questions rather than by his answers.

17 The discovery of what is true, and the practice of that which is good, are the two most important objects of philosophy.

18 Perfection is attained by slow degrees; she requires the hand of time.

19 I know of no great man except those who have rendered great services to the human race.

20 We cannot always oblige, but we can always speak obligingly.

21 If you do not want to commit suicide, always have something to do. A long life has time to combat time.

22 Books rule the world. Nothing enfranchises like education. When once a nation begins to think, it is impossible to stop.

23 God isn't on the side of the big battalions, but of the best marksmen.

468

- Richard Wagner
A Leading German Composer of 19th Century
1813 - 1883

1 Joy is not in things; it is in us.

2 He who gives joy to the world is raised higher among men than he who conquers the world.

3 Do not give alms, but acknowledge the right, the God-given human right; for, if you do not, you will live to see the day when nature, who has been so brutally despised, arms herself for a bitter conflict, whose savage cry of victory will be that of communism. Do you think these are idle threats? No! They are a warning to us all.

4 Whoever will not come to me for the honour and out of enthusiasm can stay where he is. I do not give a jot for a singer who will only come to me for one of those fantastic fees. A creature like that could never live up to my artistic requirements.

5 I am not in the slightest concerned whether people perform my works or not; I am only concerned that they perform them in the manner I intended. If they cannot, or will not, then let them desist altogether.

1 Everything that I have achieved has been possible only because I really love people.

2 No single activity can cure all the ills of society.

3 Reform can be accomplished only when attitudes are changed.

4 The commandment to honour one's parents has come down through the ages, but to honour thy daughter and thy son is a commandment no less imperative. Do not clip the wings of their idealism for the fear of the hardships that they may encounter.

1 For ten years the question of how changes of species could have been brought about was rarely out of my mind. Finally, in February 1858, during a severe attack of malaria at Gilolo, in the Moluccas, while thinking about human evolution, there suddenly flashed upon me the idea of the survival of the fittest. The theory was thought out, drafted in a single evening and written out in full in two succeeding evenings.

2 What at the time appeared to be the great misfortune of the loss of about half of my whole Amazonian collections by the burning of the ship in which I was coming home, was in all probability a blessing in disguise, since it led me to visit the comparatively unknown Malay Archipelago, and, perhaps, also supplied the conditions which led me to think out independently the theory of natural selection.

3 When I once begin any work in which I am interested, I can go steadily on with it till it is finished, but I need some definite impulse to set me going and require a good deal of time for reflection while the work is being done.

4 There are no absolutely bad men or women. There is no one who, by a rational and sympathetic training, and a social system which gives to all equality of opportunity, may not become useful, contented and happy members of society.

5 Distrust all first impressions.

6 We are, in every act and thought of our lives here, building up a character which will largely determine our happiness or misery hereafter.

7 We obtain the greatest happiness by doing all we can to make those around us happy.

471

- Andy Warhol
A Founder of Pop Art
1928 - 1987

1 The most exciting attractions are between two opposites that never meet.

2 I still care about people but it would be so much easier not to care. It's hard to care. I don't want to get involved in other people's lives. I don't want to get too close. I don't really believe in love. I don't like to touch things. That's why my work is so distant from myself.

472

- Booker T. Washington
The Builder of Tuskegee College
1856 - 1915

1 We measure a man's success in terms of the obstacles he had to overcome along the way.

2 You cannot hold a man down without staying down with him.

3 You must not judge a man by the heights to which he has risen, but by the depths from which he came.

4 I will let no man drag me down so low as to make me hate him.

5 I learned that assistance given to the weak makes the one who gives it strong; and that oppression of the unfortunate makes one weak.

6 All worry consumes, and to no purpose, just so much physical and mental strength that otherwise might be given to effective work.

7 No race can prosper till it learns that there is as much dignity in tilling a field as in writing a poem.

473

- George Washington
The First President of the United States
1732 - 1799

1 Associate yourself with men of good quality if you esteem your reputation; for it's better to be alone than in bad company.

2 Discipline is the soul of the army. It makes small numbers formidable; procures success to the weak, and esteem to all.

3 Undertake not what you cannot perform but be careful to keep your promise.

4 Few men have virtues to withstand the highest bidder.

5 Labour to keep alive in your heart that little spark of celestial fire called conscience.

6 To be prepared for war is one of the most effective means of preserving peace.

7 Be courteous to all, but intimate with few, and let those few be well tried before you give them your confidence. True friendship is a plant of slow growth, and must undergo and withstand the shocks of adversity before it is entitled to the appellation.

8 Liberty, when it begins to take root, is a plant of rapid growth.

474

- Tom Watson
The Founder of IBM
1874 - 1956

1 Everything starts with a sale. If there is no sale, there is no commerce in the whole of America.

2 Make things happen.

3 Beat your best.

4 Think.

5 Life is not as complex as many people would have you think and the older you grow, the more you will realize that success and happiness depend on a very few things. Vision, unselfishness, love, good character, good manners, real friendship and pride in record are your important assets. Reactionary ideas, love of money, unwholesome companions, lax character, lack of love for others and false friendship are your main liabilities.

6 Give full consideration to the individual employee; spend a lot of time making customers happy and go to the last mile to do a thing right.

7 Balance sheets reveal the past; they say nothing about the future.

8 Here is my formula of success: Double your rate of failure. You're thinking of failure as the enemy of success, but it isn't at all. You can be discouraged by failure - or you can learn from it. So go ahead and make mistakes. Make all you can. Because, remember that's where you will find success - on the far side of failure.

475

- James Watt
The Inventor of the Steam Engine
1736 - 1819

1 Today I enter the thirty-fifth year of my life, and I think I have hardly yet done thirty-five pence worth of good in the world.

2 My whole thoughts are bent on this machine. I can think of nothing else.

3 We must do the best we can and hope for quiet in Heaven, when our weary bones are laid to rest.

4 If I have excelled, I think now it has been by chance and by the neglects of others.

5 I conceived the idea of my steam engine in the Green in Glasgow. I had gone to take a walk on a fine Sabbath afternoon. I was thinking upon the engine at the time and suddenly the idea came to my mind that as steam is an elastic body it would rush into a vacuum, and if a communication was made between the cylinder and an exhausted vessel, it would rush into it, and might there be condensed without cooling the cylinder. Within a very short time the entire scheme was clear in my mind.

476

1 I'm just an ordinary goddamn American and I talk for all the ordinary goddamn Americans, the butchers and bakers and plumbers. I know these people; I know what they think.

2 If I had known what I know now, I would have put a patch on my eye 35 years ago.

3 I am in the third act of my life and six feet four inches tall. I have had three wives, seven children and lots of grandchildren and I still don't understand women and I don't think there is a man alive who does.

4 Tomorrow is the most important thing in life. It comes into us at midnight very clean. It's perfect when it arrives and it puts itself in our hands. It hopes we have learned something from yesterday.

477

1 Failure is more frequently from want of energy than want of capital.

2 Mind is the great lever of all things. Human thought is the process by which human ends are ultimately answered.

3 Opportunity is the time or occasion that is right for doing something.

4 If all my talents and powers were to be taken away from me by some inscrutable Providence, and I had my choice of keeping but one, I would unhesitantly ask to be allowed to keep the Power of Speaking, for through it I would quickly recover all the rest.

5 The most important thought I ever had was that of my individual responsibility to God.

6 There is nothing so powerful as truth - and often nothing so strange.

7 Keep cool; anger is not an argument.

8 Guilt cannot keep its own secret, suicide is confession.

9 Most good lawyers live well, work hard, and die poor.

10 I was born an American; I will live an American; I shall die an American.

11 There is always room at the top.

478

- Noah Webster
The Father of the American English Dictionary
1758 - 1843

1 Language as well as the faculty of speech, was the immediate gift of God.

2 We deserve all our public evils. We are a degenerate and wicked people.

3 All power is vested in the people. That this is their natural and inalienable right, is a position that will not be disputed.

4 Too much health is a disease. Too much liberty is the worst tyranny.

5 Let us never forget that the corner stone of all republican government is that the will of every citizen is controlled by the laws or supreme will of the state.

6 Popular errors proceeding from a misunderstanding of words are among the efficient causes of our political disorders.

7 I would, if necessary, become a troglodyte and live in a cage in winter, rather than be under the tyranny of our desperate rulers.

8 Nations, like animals, have their birth, grow to maturity and decay. Constitutions which began with freedom, end in tyranny, and those which are founded on the wisest maxims of justice and virtue, always crumble to pieces by the imperceptible influence of their own corruptions.

9 The essence of sovereignty consists in the general voice of the people.

10 A nation which is subject to the will of an individual is a nation of slaves, whether they be white or black.

11 Self-interest is the ruling principle of all mankind.

12 People in general are too ignorant to manage affairs which require great reading.

13 Nothing can be so fatal to morals and the peace of society as violent shock given to public opinion or fixed habits.

479

- Thurlow Weed
An Extraordinary Lobbyist
1797 - 1882

1 Old men live in the past.

2 Equal justice always excites fear, and therefore always gives offense; otherwise its way would be smooth and its sway universal. The abstractions of human rights are the only permanent foundations of society.

480

- Johnny Weissmuller
One of the Greatest Swimmers of All Time
Born in 1904

1 Concentrate on doing something the right way and you will get ahead.

481

- Lawrence Welk
The Liberace of the Accordion
1903 - 1992

1 My years of one-nighters taught me what the people really want.

2 The best answer to every single problem that plagues our young people today is simply to let them work.

3 Self-discipline gives you a handle to keep your life under control and to achieve far more joy and happiness than you could otherwise.

4 Don't be afraid to make mistakes. Look on failures as learning experiences and be grateful for them. Every businessperson, including me, has had a long, long list of failures.

5 Nothing builds character, nothing builds success, nothing builds personal happiness quite so much as *work*.

6 We learn and develop ourselves better by *doing* than in any other way.

7 There are no limits to dreams or achievements.

8 Whenever you share something, it increases.

9 It's a bad hurt when you are first brought face to face with the fact you are being held up to ridicule.

482

- George Westinghouse
The Inventor of the Air Brake
1846 - 1914

1 The more things we invent, the more things we need to invent.

2 Follow your own interests wherever they may lead you. Take your time to think things over and to explore possibilities - whether a month, a year or more - that's all right. But whatever you finally decide to do, pour your heart and your mind into it. Your decision will have to last a long time - for the rest of your life, in fact.

3 Man has succeeded in conquering Nature but he hasn't yet succeeded in harnessing his own wild and obdurate spirit. Perhaps man needs a chance to think things over, to learn how to control the marvelous new devices that have been placed at his disposal, to triumph over his own fears and misgivings.

4 Despite human shortcomings, man will never cease searching and groping into the physical unknown, they will quest and probe in their thirst to conquer new worlds.

5 Even in my advanced age, each morning, like clockwork, I arrived at the plant in time to greet the first shift and stayed on for the full working day and I devoted an hour or two each day at my drawing board working on some new invention.

6 Drafting is my method of relaxing. Besides, I knew no better way of discovering the kinks in a new idea than to try to work it out on the drafting board.

483

- James Whistler
One of the Leading Painters of His Time
1834 - 1903

1 An artist's career always begins tomorrow.

2 Art is a science - one step leading to another.

3 Distrust everything you have done without understanding it.

4 As the light fades and the shadows deepen all petty and exacting details vanish, everything trivial disappears, and I see things as they are in great strong masses: the buttons are lost, but the garment remains; the garment is lost, but the sitter remains; the shadow is lost, but the picture remains. And that *night* cannot efface from the painter's imagination.

484

- Gilbert White
The Clergyman Turned Extraordinary Naturalist
1720 - 1793

1 It is the hardest thing in the world to shake off superstitious prejudices; they are sucked in as it were with our mother's milk; and growing up with us at a time when they take the fastest hold and make the most lasting impressions, become so interwoven in our very constitutions, that the strongest good sense is required to disengage ourselves from them. No wonder therefore that the lower people retain them their whole lives, since their minds are not invigorated by a liberal education, and therefore not enabled to make any efforts adequate to the occasion.

485

- Walt Whitman
The Greatest of 19th Century American Poets
1819 - 1892

1 Behold, I do not give lectures or a little charity,
   When I give I give myself.

2 Why do folks dwell so fondly on the last words, advice, appearance, of the departing? Because those last words are not samples of the best but are valuable beyond measure to confirm and endorse the faith of the whole preceding life.

3 Comerado, this is no book,
   Who touches this, touches a man.

4 You must not know too much, or be too precise or scientific about birds and trees and flowers and watercraft; a certain free margin and even vagueness - perhaps ignorance, credulity - helps your enjoyment of these things.

5 I think I could turn and live with animals, they are so placid and self-contained. I stand and look at them long and long. They do not sweat and whine about their condition; they do not lie awake in the dark and weep for their sins, not one is dissatisfied, not one is demented with the mania of owning things.

6 Seeing, hearing, feeling, are miracles, and each part and tag of me is a miracle.

7 To me every hour of the light and dark is a miracle. Every cubic inch of space is a miracle.

8 I see that the elementary laws never apologize.

9 I believe a leaf of grass is no less than the journey-work of the stars.

486 - Eli Whitney
The Inventor of the Cotton Gin
1765 - 1825

1 A mechanical genius is a handyman who succeeds.

2 It is God that works within us both to will and to do of his own good pleasure.

3 Avoid the use of profane language. Such a habit is not only criminal but it will forever prevent your becoming interesting and respectable in conversation. If you contract the habit of using bad words, you will have no stock of good ones at hand.

4 Strive to render your voice harmonious and pleasant; but let it be natural. By all means avoid affectation. Nothing can render a person more unpleasant to others than drawling, muttering or an indistinct articulation and nothing is more painful than to be obliged to ask a person three or four times over what they have said.

5 Don't be over anxious to dive very largely into business at first. Take care to establish yourself on secure and solid foundations.

6 A small edifice founded on a rock is far preferable to a large building placed on sand.

487 - Emma Willard
A Pioneer of Women's Education
1787 - 1870

1 When a great man's heart is encouraged, he is strengthened.

2 Woman, having received from her Creator the same intellectual constitutions as man, has the same right as man to intellectual culture and development.

3 Whatever is to be done regularly requires a set time as well as a fixed place.

4 Fiction may mislead, even when it intends to do good; truth never. The mind that feeds on fiction becomes bloated and unsound and, already inebriated, still thirsts for more.

488 - Frances Willard
A Leader of the Temperance Movement
1839 - 1898

1 To believe is to act.

2 My strength is the strength of ten, because my heart is pure.

3 Though man's forehead be lifted toward the stars, his feet are firmly planted on the earth and a sound pure mind must have a pure sound body in which to dwell.

4 The sacred duty of every woman is to cultivate and utilize her highest gift; there is no more practical form of philanthropy than this.

5 Everyone who makes a place for himself *higher up*, leaves one lower down for some other woman.

6 Death is only a bend in the river of life that sets the current heavenward.

7 The deepest billows are many at sea; they never come in sight of shore. These waves are the years of God. Upon the shore-line of our earthly life come the waves of the swift years; they bound and break and are no more. But far out upon eternity's bosom are the great, wide, endless waves that make the years of God; they never strike the shore of time.

8 When an idea comes, I pull the string of the mental shower bath and take the consequences.

9 The first object of the teacher is to orient the pupil concerning heart within and God overhead, to teach him the divine truths upon which is based the physical well-being.

10 As words are the carriage in which thoughts ride, so the human body is the soul's chariot and the human soul will become a dethroned charioteer unless he understands his vehicle.

489

- Tennessee Williams
A Foremost American Playwright of Mid-20th Century
1911 - 1983

1 I have always been blocked as a writer, but I love writing so much that I always break through the block.

2 Once you fully apprehend the vacuity of a life without struggle, you are equipped with the basic means of salvation.

3 Having great wealth sometimes makes people lonely.

4 Physical beauty is passing, a transitory possession. But beauty of the mind and richness of the spirit and the tenderness of the heart aren't taken away, but grow!

490

- Kemmons Wilson
The Founder of the Holiday Inn Chain
Born in 1913

1 I believe that, to be successful, you have to work at least half a day. It doesn't make any difference which half, the first twelve hours or the last.

2 I would rather wear out than rust out.

3 Looking for land is like going on an Easter egg hunt, and sometimes you find the golden egg.

4 When you ain't got no education, you just got to use your brains.

491

1 You only have to believe you can succeed, that you can be whatever your heart desires, be willing to work for it, and you can have it.

2 You create your own blessings. You have to prepare yourself so that when the time comes, you are ready.

3 Success isn't as difficult as some people make it out to be. It boils down to setting goals and working toward them.

4 The more you praise and celebrate your life, the more there is in life to celebrate. The more you complain, the more you find fault, the more misery and fault you will have to find.

5 Knowledge is power. With knowledge you can soar and reach as high as your dreams will take you.

6 The more positive you are about your life, the more positive it will be. The more you complain, the more miserable you will be.

7 Don't let a bad childhood stand in your way.

8 Eat reasonably, diet privately and exercise regularly.

9 Don't be satisfied with just one success - and don't give up after failure.

10 Do what you want to do, when you want to do it and not a moment sooner.

11 You can't do it all by yourself. Don't be afraid to rely on others to help you accomplish your goals.

12 I try to move with the flow of life, and not to dictate what life should be for me, but let it flow.

13 There isn't any short cut to getting thin. You have to exercise and eat moderately and it takes time.

14 Think like a queen. A queen is not afraid to fail. Failure is another stepping stone to greatness.

15 I find exercise to be the best way for me to start the day. It helps me build energy for the many things I have to do.

16 I want my work to make people feel special.

17 If I can do it, so can you.

18 Excellence is the best deterrent to racism or sexism.

492

1 Being blind ain't no big problem with me. I don't like to speak of the unfortunate things I went through.

2 Music can measure how broad our horizons are. My mind wants to see to infinity.

3 When you are blind, you build up a lot of excess energy that other people get rid off through their eyes. You got to work it off some way and it's just an unconscious thing. This results in a behaviour, commonly known as blindism, which is unique for each blind person. Some rub their eyes without even realizing it.

493

- Grant Wood
A Founder of the American Scene Movement in Art
1891 - 1942

1 An artist must paint honestly and faithfully the things he knows best.

2 All I contend for is the sincere use of native materials by the artist who is in command of them.

3 It is the depth and intensity of the artist's experience that are of the first importance in art. More often than not, however, a preponderance of a man's significant experience is rooted to a certain region. In this way, a particular environment becomes important to his art.

4 Almost all of us have some dream power in our childhood but without encouragement it leaves us and then we become bored and tired and ordinary. In most of our studies we deal only with material things or in ideas that are materialistic. We are carefully coached in the most modern and efficient ways of making our bodies comfortable and we become so busy about getting ourselves all nicely placed that we are able to forget the dream spirit that is born in all of us. Then some day when we are physically comfortable we remember dimly a distant land we used to visit in our youth. We try to go again but we cannot find the way. Our imagination machinery is withered just as our legs or arms might whither if we forget for years and years to use them.

5 To avoid becoming heavy of body and hard-spirited, exercise your imaginations through travel, literature, music and art.

494

- F. W. Woolworth
A Pioneer of Retailing Methods
1852 - 1919

1 There is something to be learned even in a country store. We are apt to believe that sharp trades, especially dishonest tricks and unprincipled deceptions, are confined entirely to the city, and that the unsophisticated men and women of the country do everything on the square. I believe this to be measurably true, but know there are many exceptions to this rule. Many times I cut open bundles of rags brought to the store by country women in exchange for goods and declared to be all linen and cotton, that contained quantities of worthless trash in the interior, and sometimes stones, gravel, ashes etc.

2 People violate their own experience. Occasionally they do what they know they should not. I found myself often tempted to do things I had learned already not to do.

3 You can pull customers into your stores and they won't know it. Draw them in with attractive window displays and when you get them in, have a plentiful showing of the window goods on the counter. Let them look around to their heart's content. Don't try and press goods on them. Special sales are fine if the bargains are real. Be sure your ten cents specials cannot be bought elsewhere for less than 20 or 25 cents. Remember, your advertisements are in your show windows and on your counters.

4 Of all forms of tyranny, the least attractive and the most vulgar is the tyranny of mere wealth, the tyranny of plutocracy.

5 Nobody ever got on who was in bondage to the body. You can't build a business on thoughts of having a good time.

6 Thrift is the paramount virtue.

495

- Christopher Wren
The Architect of St. Paul's Cathedral in London
1632 - 1723

1 Architecture aims at Eternity, and therefore is the only thing incapable of modes and fashions in its principles.

2 There are two causes of beauty - natural and customary. Natural is from geometry consisting in uniformity, that is in equality and proportion. Customary beauty is begotten by the use, as familiarity breeds a love to things not in themselves lovely. Here lies the great occasion of errors, but always the true test is natural or geometrical beauty. Geometrical figures are naturally more beautiful than irregular ones; the square, the circle are the most beautiful; next are the parallelogram and the oval. There are only two beautiful positions of straight lines, perpendicular and horizontal; this is from Nature and consequently necessity, no other upright being firm.

3 A function of architecture is political - public buildings being the ornaments of a country; it establishes a nation, draws people and commerce; makes the people love their native country.

4 Since architecture aims at eternity, it must be based on the classical orders, that are incapable of modes and fashions.

5 Beauty and firmness depend upon geometrical reasons of optics and statics; convenience creates the variety.

496

- the Wright Brothers
The Pioneers of Aviation

- Orville Wright
1871 - 1948

1 If we all worked on the assumption that what is accepted as true is really true, there would be little hope of advance.

2   My life is my invention.

- the Wright Brothers

3   Faith in our calculations, and confidence in our system of control developed by three years of actual experience in balancing gliders in the air, had convinced us that the machine was capable of lifting and maintaining itself in the air, and that, with a little practice, it could be safely flown.

4   If the wheels of time were turned back, it is not at all probable that we would do again what we have done.

497

- Richard Wright
The Foremost Writer of Black American's Survival Struggles
1908 - 1960

1   I came across H. L. Mencken's *Book of Prefaces*, which served as a literary Bible for me for some years. Because I was not prepared to be anything else, I decided to become a writer.

2   The white South said that it knew *niggers*, and I was what the white South called a *nigger*. Well, the white south had never known me - never known what I thought, what I felt.

3   Religious belief or faith and superstition blinds man's insight into many human problems, because of dependency on God rather than on himself (and the god within himself).

4   False religion keeps man divided against himself by race, creed and class. But if man really wants to be healed and cured of hatred, racism, fascism and cruel imperialism, he can find a common ground of humanity through the use of his reason and will.

5   I have no race except that which is forced upon me. I have no country except that which I'm obliged to belong.

6   As long as I live in the United States, I can never change my profession, for I'm regarded totally as a Negro writer, that is, a writer whose ancestors were Negroes and therefore the Negro is my special field.

7   I am opposed to all racial definitions.

498

1 Death is the great enemy and robber in my profession, taking away so many friends over the years, all of them young; and facing death takes many kinds of courage.

2 When the going gets tough, just about all you can do is keep going forward, and press on.

3 There is no such thing as a natural-born pilot. Whatever my aptitudes or talents, becoming a proficient pilot was hard work, really a lifetime of learning experience. For the best pilots flying is an obsession, the one thing in life they must do continually. The best pilots fly more than the others; that's why they are the best. Experience is everything. The eagerness to learn how and why every piece of equipment works is everything. And luck is everything too.

4 I am always afraid of dying. Always. It was my fear that made me learn everything I could about my airplane and my emergency equipment, and kept me flying respectfully of my machine and being always alert in the cockpit.

499

1 Swinging an ax hardens the hands and builds up the shoulders and back.

2 I believe in putting the ball over the plate for hitting, trusting to the fielders, in this way saving your arm.

3 A pitcher amounts to but very little unless his pitching arm is strong.

500

1 A moment of happiness is a lifetime, and I have had a lot of happiness.

2 It's not enough for me just to play. I have to be able to try for championships.

Index

Note: In the following listing the number before the colon indicates the number of the main paragraph while the number after the colon indicates the number of the Word of Wisdom within the paragraph.

Aaron, Hank 1

Ability 8:3, 9:2, 17:4, 31:13, 42:1, 46:5, 51:6, 51:13, 51:17, 53:3, 56:1, 62:4, 86:4, 103:14, 129:2, 138:4, 145:9, 145:23, 145:27, 146:4, 163:11, 163:14, 167:2, 187:1, 214:3, 217:7, 232:3, 236:1, 250:2, 256:1, 267:10, 288:4, 309:7, 309:9, 318:1, 351:4, 369:26, 397:4, 417:2, 436:24, 448:17, 454:5, 455:8, 458:6, 458:7

Acceptance 65:2, 241:29, 254:5, 271:12, 280:9, 395:1

Accident 46:1, 145:5, 199:4, 231:3, 254:11, 393:2, 459:2, 462:3

Accomplish 46:6, 62:5, 75:37, 81:2, 83:3, 136:13, 137:1, 145:17, 160:3,163:19, 190:2, 200:4, 212:2, 226:1, 254:4, 254:13, 257:5, 277:1, 280:8, 281:8, 309:33, 325:6, 371:4, 395:2, 402:3, 413:7, 469:3, 491:11

Accomplishment 150:79, 163:4, 203:3, 267:4, 287:2, 309:32

Achieve 10:5, 23:1, 30:3, 51:1, 51:28, 59:5, 76:12, 80:3, 100:3, 109:6, 138:1, 145:4, 150:55, 152:8, 165:34, 167:10, 172:11, 196:1, 209:3, 209:4, 219:14, 219:19, 219:28, 236:3, 251:5, 257:7, 260:1, 271:9, 288:2, 309:58, 318:2, 369:26, 404:5, 436:27, 465:1, 465:5, 469:1, 481:3

Achievement 100:5, 104:1, 150:3, 157:3, 163:15, 218:1, 219:21, 219:38, 219:50, 244:2, 262:4, 269:1, 269:15, 309:7, 309:8, 309:9, 309:15, 309:36, 309:57, 363:3, 369:26, 373:5, 391:7, 401:8, 481:7

Acting 28:6, 49:4, 104:2, 168:1, 177:2, 232:3, 254:10, 280:4, 312:2, 331:5, 331:6, 352:1, 376:2, 388:1, 388:5, 404:5

Action 46:4, 85:1, 86:8, 86:8, 94:1, 112:1, 127:3, 127:4, 128:2, 136:13, 136:30, 150:28, 172:16, 219:31, 219:37, 221:4, 233:1, 234:5, 241:9, 264:5, 271:8, 271:14, 298:1, 322:1, 346:7, 365:4, 376:1, 385:12, 403:14, 422:6, 436:12, 436:17, 436:18, 436:26

Activity 25:1, 51:10, 51:12, 103:3, 202:5, 335:3, 372:5, 372:12, 412:8, 436:17, 452:1, 469:2

Actor 28:6, 33:2, 49:1, 67:2, 80:2, 109, 162:3, 225, 232:1, 254:10, 280, 280:3, 280:10, 280:6, 304:3, 312:2, 331, 331:4, 352:2, 352:3, 352:4, 368:9, 379, 379:1, 379:2, 440:5, 476

Actress 28:1, 202:8, 312:2

Adler, Alfred 2

Administration 100:5, 286:16, 392:2, 420:2

Adventure 12:3, 18:8, 217:3, 257:4, 287:4, 435, 442:1

Adversity 136:5, 160:1, 219:12, 276:1, 376:2, 377, 403:12, 418:12, 473:7

Advertising 275:2, 284:4, 386:5

Advice 69:6, 154:1, 186:6, 233:1, 236:16, 407:4, 455:7, 458:2, 485:2

Affirmation 110:3, 219:53, 219:54, 255:1

Afraid 31:15, 49:5, 53:3, 78:5, 163:17, 173:7, 241:21, 262:2, 273:3, 282:1, 309:26, 351:6, 372:2, 383:1, 481:4, 491:11, 491:14, 498:4

Agassiz, Louis 3

Age 8:2, 11:5, 25:4, 42:4, 62:4, 91:3, 101, 129:4, 163:6, 202:8, 229:5, 236:7, 302, 316:3, 320:5, 326:1, 353:4, 356:7, 413:10, 426:5, 435:5, 482:5

AIDS 17:2, 245:2

Aim 21:1, 25:4, 41:4, 79:2, 100:3, 105:4, 112:5, 167:9, 211:2, 309:10, 309:36, 363:1, 363:3, 423:3, 435:15, 448:4, 462:2

Air Brake 482

Alcott, Louisa May 4

Alexander, Grover 5

Ali, Muhammad 6

Alive 131:12, 148:10, 181:3, 196:6, 217:9, 298:2, 310:8, 342:7, 362:5, 414:7, 415:3, 448:18, 473:5, 476:3

Allen, Dick 7

Allen, Steve 8

Amateur 79:3, 150:16, 166:4, 254:6, 261:3

Education 2:4, 31:7, 41:7, 58:1, 68, 103:1, 123:3, 136:4, 149:8, 150:60, 150:71, 167:2, 203:4, 219:9, 236:1, 254:3, 262:26, 271:10, 275:6, 297:7, 304:6, 306:9, 333:3, 333:6, 357:1, 358:1, 360:5, 363:6, 393:2, 396:2, 408:3, 422:10, 427:2, 458:1, 461:11, 467:22, 484:1, 487, 490:4

Effort 66:6, 94:1, 103:3, 151:3, 157:1, 172:8, 172:11, 219:13, 219:32, 241:12, 252:3, 275:8, 309:32, 309:43, 309:57, 314:1, 331:7, 333:7, 350:4, 356:20, 359:6, 372:12, 378:4, 401:8, 444:6, 463:3, 466:2

Ego 121:4, 138:1, 172:2, 189:2, 262:11, 353:2

Eisenhower, Dwight 146

Elder, Lee 147

Eliot, George 148

Ellington, Duke 149

Emancipation 203:3, 426:4, 456

Emerson, Ralph Waldo 150

Emotion 30:4, 31:34, 47:3, 51:24, 179:6, 195:7, 205:3, 219:54, 241:8, 254:4, 271:14, 288:3, 302:4, 360:4, 369:14, 430:5, 431:3, 436:24, 436:26, 450:8

Encouragement 100:2, 276:4, 436:12, 487:1, 493:4

Endurance 75:5, 75:26, 351:4, 356:6

Endure 13:4, 31:25, 31:41, 53:4, 69:2, 83:4, 163:18, 253:4, 291:4, 380:12, 424:5

Enemy 31:23, 94:3, 128:8, 197:4, 232:1, 232:5, 285:6, 309:9, 372:4, 474:8, 498:1

Energy 51:25, 51:30, 126:1, 140:3, 158:3, 160:6, 163:4, 172:12, 188:2, 230:1, 309:7, 309:42, 315:6, 340:16, 345:1, 345:5, 355:1, 356:10, 477:1, 491:15, 492:3

Engineer 185, 262:18

Enjoy 18:1, 28:3, 51:24, 62:1, 62:5, 63:10, 81:6, 87:7, 114:1, 135:6, 177:2, 179:5, 219:4, 263:8, 272:1, 309:29, 345:2, 401:6, 415:1, 418:15

Enjoyment 31:13, 136:24, 219:24, 356:10, 485:4

Enlightenment 123:3, 244:2, 244:3

Entertainer 91, 121, 176, 373:3

Enthusiasm 42:5, 66:6, 98:3, 100:5, 136:4, 150:55, 150:81, 156:13, 163:4, 182:4, 236:7, 435:6, 448:5, 468:4

Environment 35:4, 78:4, 202:6, 210:3, 219:25, 275:8, 287:6, 309:41, 309:42, 333:3, 344:2, 358:1, 358:4, 393:2, 393:9, 422:6, 436:23, 436:31, 441, 493:3

Envy 185:4, 269:11, 334:4, 435:7

Err 171:2, 212:4, 269:10, 274:8

Erving, Julius 151

Ethic 283:5, 321:5

Evidence 81:12, 137:9, 269:6, 324:1, 340:13

Evil 92:3, 110:3, 168:2, 194:5, 241:6, 309:27, 343:3, 375:8, 420:8, 467:3, 478:2

Evolution 119, 149, 191:4, 285:4, 340:7, 470, 470:1

Excel 245:7, 291:4, 360:5, 368:11, 391:2

Excellence 82:2, 258:9, 368:11, 467:5, 491:18

Exercise 13:4, 118:4, 135:4, 135:10, 241:27, 276:1, 286:11, 356:18, 378:2, 491:8, 491:13, 491:15, 493:5

Existence 2:5, 9:2, 22:3, 35:4, 69:3, 78:1, 102:4, 119:4, 131:12, 136:33, 136:34, 150:71, 319:5, 360:4, 367:3, 378:4, 413:2, 420:6

Expect 7:2, 48:4, 64:6, 136:27, 159:4, 204:4, 269:17, 278:1, 281:2, 288:1, 309:46, 356:23, 369:23, 369:27

Expectation 309:46, 369:24, 467:10

Experience 16:11, 17:6, 68:3, 75:15, 97:1, 103:14, 113:3, 118:3, 120:3, 129:4, 139:6, 144:1, 144:2, 150:62, 163:14, 163:18, 172:12, 212:4, 217:9, 236:2, 256:3, 257:7, 257:12, 286:7, 292:4, 298:4, 309:18, 333:3, 335:4, 340:16, 351:6, 356:23, 360:1, 373:5, 378:1, 408:3, 412:6, 413:2, 413:9, 414:6, 415:8, 428:3, 436:23, 436:25, 440:4, 441:1, 481:4, 493:3, 494:2, 496:3, 498:3

Experiment 150:44, 150:90, 151:9, 152:7, 212:3, 212:6, 227:2, 324:1, 385:12